Understanding
RTI
in Mathematics

Understanding
RTI
in Mathematics
Proven Methods and Applications

edited by

Russell Gersten, Ph.D.

and

Rebecca Newman-Gonchar, Ph.D.

Instructional Research Group
Los Alamitos, California

·P A U L·H·
BROOKES
PUBLISHING Cº ®

Baltimore • London • Sydney

Paul H. Brookes Publishing Co.
Post Office Box 10624
Baltimore, Maryland 21285-0624
USA

www.brookespublishing.com

"Paul H. Brookes Publishing Co." is a registered trademark of
Paul H. Brookes Publishing Co., Inc.

Typeset by Spearhead Global, Inc., Bear, Delaware.
Manufactured in the United States of America by
Victor Graphics, Inc., Baltimore, Maryland.

The individuals described in this book are composites or real people whose situations are masked and are based on the authors' experiences. In all instances, names and identifying details have been changed to protect confidentiality.

Library of Congress Cataloging-in-Publication Data

Understanding RTI in mathematics: proven methods and applications/edited
by Russell Gersten and Rebecca Newman-Gonchar.
    p.   cm.
  Includes bibliographical references and index.
  ISBN-13: 978-1-59857-167-7
  ISBN-10: 1-59857-167-2
  1. Mathematics—Remedial teaching.   2. Response to intervention (Learning disabled children)
I. Gersten, Russell Monroe, 1947-   II. Newman-Gonchar, Rebecca.   III. Title.
QA20.I53U53 2011
371.9'0447—dc23   2011021242

British Library Cataloguing in Publication data are available from the British Library.

2021   2020   2019   2018   2017

10   9   8   7   6   5   4   3   2

Contents

About the Editors

Russell Gersten, Ph.D., Executive Director, Instructional Research Group, 4281 Katella Avenue, Suite 205, Los Alamitos, California 90720

In addition to his work at the Instructional Research Group, Dr. Gersten is also a professor emeritus in the College of Education at the University of Oregon. He is the director of the Math Strand for the Center on Instruction, the director of research for the Regional Educational Laboratory–South West, and the principal investigator for several What Works Clearinghouse projects. As Project Director of the Teacher Quality Distribution and Measurement Study, Dr. Gersten is currently working with a team of researchers from Harvard University to revise a mathematics observation measure that will be used to determine the effect of professional development on teachers' mathematics instruction. He is also a coauthor of a mathematics screening and progress monitoring measure for kindergarten and first-grade students that is in press.

His main areas of expertise include evaluation methodology and instructional research on students with learning disabilities, mathematics, and reading comprehension. Dr. Gersten has conducted numerous randomized trials, many of which have been published in major scientific journals in the field. He has either directed or codirected 42 applied research grants addressing a wide array of issues in education and has been a recipient of many federal and nonfederal grants (more than $20 million). He has advised on a variety of reading and mathematics projects using randomized trials in education settings and has written extensively about the importance of randomized trials in special education research.

In 2002, Dr. Gersten received the Distinguished Special Education Researcher Award from the American Educational Research Association's Special Education Research Division. He served as a member of the National Mathematics Advisory Panel, a Presidential committee to develop research-based policy in mathematics for American schools. Dr. Gersten also chaired the Panel that developed A Practice Guide on Response to Intervention in Mathematics for the U.S. Department of Education's Institute of Education Sciences (IES).

Rebecca Newman-Gonchar, Ph.D., Senior Research Associate, Instructional Research Group, 4281 Katella Avenue, Suite 205, Los Alamitos, California 90720

Dr. Newman-Gonchar manages the Math Strand for the Center on Instruction and serves as a co–principal investigator for a randomized field trial of professional development in vocabulary, funded by the U.S. Department of Education's Institute of Education Sciences (IES). She has worked extensively on developing observation systems to assess math and reading instruction for four major IES-funded studies and has contributed to several practice guides and intervention reports for the What Works Clearinghouse (WWC) in the areas of math, reading, response to intervention, and English language learners. She is also certified to complete experimental and single-case design reviews for the WWC. She has experience in project management, study design and implementation, and quantitative and qualitative analysis.

About the Contributors

Elaine Allensworth, Ph.D., Senior Director and Chief Research Officer, Consortium on Chicago School Research at the University of Chicago, 1313 East 60th Street, Chicago, Illinois 60637

Dr. Allensworth is known for her research on early indicators of high school graduation, college readiness, and the transition from middle to high school. She is one of the authors of the book *Organizing Schools for Improvement: Lessons from Chicago* (University of Chicago Press, 2010), which provides a detailed analysis of school practices and school and community conditions that promote school improvement.

Scott K. Baker, Ph.D., M.S., Associate Director of the Center on Teaching and Learning, University of Oregon; and Director, Pacific Institutes for Research, 1600 Millrace Drive, Suite 206, Eugene, Oregon 97403

Dr. Baker's education interests focus on teaching and learning in literacy and mathematics and the education needs of English language learners. He is particularly interested in the impact of instructional interventions in schools that use multiple tiers of instructional support (i.e., response to intervention frameworks). He is the principal investigator on a number of IES research grants to develop and test effective instructional approaches and interventions in early reading and mathematics.

Brian R. Bryant, Ph.D., Research Professor and Fellow, Department of Special Education and the Meadows Center for Preventing Educational Risk, The University of Texas, 1 University Station D4900, Austin, Texas 78712

Dr. Bryant has written more than 100 published works and has made more than 100 professional presentations in the United States and abroad. His research interests are in learning disabilities and intellectual disabilities, with an emphasis in reading, mathematics, support provision, and assistive technology applications.

Diane Pedrotty Bryant, Ph.D., Professor, Department of Special Education, The University of Texas at Austin, 1 University Station D4900, Austin, Texas 78712

Dr. Bryant is a fellow in the Cissy McDaniel Parker Fellow Fund and a member of the board of directors for the Meadows Center for Preventing Educational Risk at The University of Texas at Austin. She is the author of several textbooks and tests and has published numerous articles on instructional strategies for students with learning disabilities in refereed journals. Her research and writing focus on the development and validation of mathematics interventions for struggling students at the elementary and secondary levels.

Lauren Campsen, M.S., Principal, Ocean View Elementary School, 9501 Mason Creek Road, Norfolk, Virginia 23403

Ms. Campsen serves as a national mentor for the Response to Intervention Action Network and was recognized as a National Terrell Bell Principal for School Change in 2008.

Douglas Carnine, Ph.D., Professor, University of Oregon, Eugene, Oregon 97403

Dr. Carnine is a researcher and instructional designer specializing in Direct Instruction. He is an author or coauthor of more than 100 publications in refereed journals, 9 college texts, and dozens of texts for kindergarten through 12th grade. During the past decade he has focused on policies relating to the use of evidence-based practices.

Ben Clarke, Ph.D., Research Associate, University of Oregon, 1600 Millrace Drive, Suite 108, Eugene, Center on Teaching and Learning, 1600 Millrace Drive, Suite 108, Eugene, Oregon 97403

Dr. Clarke currently serves as a principal investigator on multiple Institute of Education Sciences grants to develop and evaluate early mathematics curricular programs. His interests include assessment and intervention work in the area of mathematics.

Leann DiAndreth-Elkins, Ed.D., Assistant Professor, Texas Tech University, at Lubbock, 2500 Broadway, Lubbock, Texas 79409

Dr. DiAndreth-Elkins has supported teachers in implementing response to intervention math programs, has worked with struggling learners and students with learning disabilities from kindergarten through college, and has developed a unique academic support program for college students with learning disabilities at Texas Tech University. She teaches undergraduate and graduate courses to prepare current and future teachers to meet the needs of struggling and diverse learners and has researched and presented nationally on the topics of inclusion, co-teaching, and transition.

Joseph A. Dimino, Ph.D., Senior Research Associate, Instructional Research Group, 4281 Katella Avenue, Suite 205, Los Alamitos, California 90720

Dr. Dimino's research interests include content area instruction, reading comprehension, early mathematics and literacy instruction, and translating research into classroom practice.

Christian T. Doabler, Ph.D., Research Associate, Center on Teaching and Learning, University of Oregon, 1600 Millrace Drive, Suite 108, Eugene, Oregon 97403

Dr. Doabler's interests include curriculum design, observation systems, and the prevention of learning difficulties.

Hank Fien, Ph.D., Research Associate, Center on Teaching and Learning, University of Oregon, 1600 Millrace Drive, Suite 108, Eugene, Oregon 97403

Dr. Fien currently serves as the coprincipal investigator on several Institute of Education Sciences–sponsored research and development grants, studying the feasibility and efficacy of early reading and early math curricula and interventions. His research interests also include the examination of systemic, tiered instructional approaches to ameliorate early reading and math problems.

Douglas Fuchs, Ph.D., Nicholas Hobbs Professor of Special Education and Human Development, 228 Peabody, Vanderbilt University, Nashville, Tennessee 37203

Dr. Fuchs's research focuses on instructional methods and classification issues concerning students with learning disabilities.

Lynn S. Fuchs, Ph.D., Nicholas Hobbs Professor of Special Education and Human Development, 228 Peabody, Vanderbilt University, Nashville, Tennessee 37203

Dr. Fuchs's research focuses on instruction and assessment for instructional planning in reading and mathematics, with a focus on low-achieving students and those with learning disabilities.

Alex Granzin, Ph.D., Educational Consultant, School Psychologist, and Special Education Services Coordinator, The Springfield School District, 525 Mill Street, Springfield, Oregon 97477

Dr. Granzin has been with the Springfield, Oregon, school district since the 1980s. He is the past president of the Oregon School Psychologists Association and is currently involved in the implementation of a middle school literacy study.

David D. Hampton, Ph.D., Assistant Professor of Special Education, Bowling Green State University, Bowling Green, Ohio 43403

Dr. Hampton is a doctoral candidate at the University of Missouri, Columbia. His research interests include validating formative assessment practices that teachers can use to make data-based instructional decisions for their students.

Kelly Haymond, M.A., Research Associate, Instructional Research Group, 4281 Katella Avenue, Suite 205, Los Alamitos, California 90720

Dr. Haymond has experience providing research support and conducting data analysis for various projects on topics related to cognitive psychology reading, mathematics, assessment, response to intervention, and professional development.

Elise Hendricker, Ph.D., School Psychologist, the Cypress-Fairbanks Independent School District, Cypress, Texas 77065

Dr. Hendricker's research interests include the prevention of academic and behavioral difficulties in young students and promoting systemic change within school settings.

Madhavi Jayanthi, Ed.D., Senior Research Associate, Instructional Research Group, 4281 Katella Avenue, Suite 205, Los Alamitos, California 90720

Dr. Jayanthi's research interests include effective instructional techniques for at-risk learners and students with disabilities.

Asha K. Jitendra, Ph.D., Rodney Wallace Professor for the Advancement of Teaching and Learning, University of Education, 245 Education Sciences Building, 56 East River Road, Minneapolis, Minnesota 55455

Dr. Jitendra's research focuses on evaluating the variables that have an impact on children's ability to succeed in school-related tasks, particularly word-problem solving. Dr. Jitendra has developed both mathematics and reading interventions and has tested their effectiveness with students with learning difficulties. In addition, she has scrutinized theoretical models that deal with the coherent organization and structure of information as the basis for her research on textbook analysis.

Kathleen Jungjohann, M.A., Senior Instructor and Research Assistant, University of Oregon, 5261 University of Oregon, Eugene, Oregon 97403

Ms. Jungjohann teaches coursework in special education math instruction at the University of Oregon and has extensive experience teaching math to struggling students in kindergarten through eighth grade. As part of a research team focusing on effective mathematics instruction, Ms. Jungjohann has coauthored *Early Learning in Mathematics* (Pacific Institute of Research, 2009), a core kindergarten math program, and math interventions for kindergarten and first-grade students.

Erica Lembke, Ph.D., Associate Professor, The University of Missouri, 311J Townsend Hall, Columbia, Missouri 65211

Dr. Lembke has been in the field of special education for more than 17 years as both a teacher and a researcher. Her primary interests are in response to intervention, curriculum-based measurement, and academic interventions for students who are struggling.

Debi Mink, Ph.D., Director of Student Academic Services, Winthrop University, 144 Withers, Rock Hill, South Carolina 29732

Dr. Mink has served as both an elementary teacher and administrator in the Miami-Dade County Public Schools, Miami, Florida, for 33 years before moving to Winthrop University. Her research interests are the integration of mathematics and literacy and the use of response to intervention in the classroom.

Takako Nomi, Ph.D., Senior Research Analyst, Consortium on Chicago School Research, 1313 East 60th Street, Chicago, Illinois 60637

Dr. Nomi's research areas include urban education, education policy, inequality in education, school and classroom organization, and research methodology. She is particularly interested in understanding strategies that lead to excellence and equity. Her recent studies examined the consequences of two major algebra policies in Chicago on students' academic outcomes.

Paul J. Riccomini, Ph.D., Associate Professor, Department of Educational Psychology, School Psychology, and Special Education, Pennsylvania State University, 214 CEDAR, University Park, Pennsylvania 16802

Dr. Riccomini's research focus is on effective instructional approaches, strategies, and assessments for students who are low achievers and/or students with learning disabilities in mathematics.

Greg Roberts, Ph.D., Director of the Vaughn Gross Center and Associate Director of the Meadows Center for Preventing Educational Risk, The University of Texas, Austin, Texas 78712

Dr. Roberts is trained as an educational psychologist, with experience in quantitative methodologies.

Robin Finelli Schumacher, Ph.D., Research Associate, Department of Special Education, Vanderbilt University, Nashville, Tennessee 37240

Dr. Schumacher earned her doctoral degree under the advisement of Dr. Lynn S. Fuchs. Currently, Dr. Schumacher is coordinating an intervention study to evaluate components of a tutoring program focusing on fractions. Her interests include mathematics interventions that focus on word-problem solving and fractions for students at risk for mathematics disabilities.

Gregory W. Smith, Ph.D., Assistant Professor, Department of Education, Hartwick College, Oneonta, New York 13820

Dr. Smith's research interests focus on the research and development of learning accommodations for students with learning disabilities and/or behavior disorders.

Jon R. Star, Ph.D., Nancy Pforzheimer Aronson Assistant Professor, Human Development and Education, Harvard Graduate School of Education, 442 Gutman Library, 6 Appian Way, Cambridge, Massachusetts 02138

Dr. Star is an educational psychologist who studies children's learning of mathematics in middle and high school, particularly algebra. In addition, Star is interested in the preservice preparation of middle and secondary mathematics teachers. Before his graduate studies, Star spent 6 years teaching middle and high school mathematics.

Mari Strand Cary, Ph.D., Research Associate, University of Oregon, Center on Teaching and Learning, 5292 University of Oregon, Eugene, Oregon 97405

Bringing a developmental perspective to her work in education, Dr. Strand Cary seeks to better understand and improve children's mathematical and scientific knowledge. She is particularly interested in the role that emerging technologies can play in mathematics classrooms.

Bradley S. Witzel, Ph.D., Associate Professor and Program Coordinator of Special Education, Department of Counseling, Leadership, and Educational Studies, Winthrop University, 700 Oakland Avenue, Rock Hill, South Carolina 29733

Dr. Witzel's research focus is on effective instruction and curriculum for students who struggle in mathematics.

John Woodward, Ph.D., Dean of the School of Education and Distinguished Professor, University of Puget Sound, 1500 North Warner #1051, Tacoma, Washington 98416

Dr. Woodward has conducted more than 20 years of research in the area of mathematics education for at-risk students. In addition to numerous professional articles on the subject, he is the senior author of *Transmath*, an intervention program for middle school students. He is also the lead developer for *NUMBERS*, a program of professional development for teachers in kindergarten through eighth grade.

Foreword

*"The essence of mathematics is not to make simple things com-
plicated, but to make complicated things simple."*

—S. Gudders

In this volume, Gersten and Newman-Gonchar provide an arsenal of information
about effective practices related to response to intervention (RTI) in math that
makes a complicated framework like RTI considerably simpler. RTI is an organizational framework for screening students to identify those with learning and
behavior problems, providing them with research-based classroom instruction
and, when necessary, successively more intensive interventions to meet their
educational needs. This much-needed book expands our understanding of RTI to
include research, largely conducted within the past decade, to improve core classroom mathematics instruction, as well as tools for screening students with math
difficulties and for providing effective interventions. This book assembles the
research-to-practice work of a core group of outstanding researchers who have
provided the best answers to date about research-based practices related to math
instruction within an RTI framework.

The chapters in this book are important reading not only for those who are
interested in RTI mathematics instruction but also for researchers and practitioners who are interested in education more broadly. What makes the contribu-
tions in this book so valuable, and in many ways, unique, is that many of the
findings are directly applicable both to solving important issues around implementing effective practices in mathematics within an RTI framework and to better understanding teaching and learning more broadly. For example, Woodward
and colleagues help us understand the importance of effort, motivation, and persistence in learning mathematics and how we can move away from a strict ability orientation in math. This focus may be highly important in math education,
but it is also essential to all learning.

There are also some surprises in this book. For example, it seems intuitive
that double-dosing students with mathematics difficulties in algebra will yield
positive outcomes, but in Chapter 10, Nomi and Allensworth reveal some unexpected findings from their important work.

The essential thread woven through every chapter in this book is the reliance on research findings from experimental studies to guide decision making about improving math instruction for all students, but notably for students with math difficulties. Gersten and colleagues summarize instructional practices from the research for providing secondary (Tier 2) and tertiary (Tier 3) interventions for students. Their chapter (Chapter 2) will be highly appealing to classroom teachers, administrators, and researchers. Noteworthy in this book are chapters on numeracy, problem solving, word problems, and algebra. This is not just RTI at the kindergarten and first-grade level—findings are presented that inform effective RTI across all grade levels.

This book is essential reading for educators, researchers, and educational leaders. This well-written, research-based, and highly informative book will be one that you will return to for many years for guidance on RTI, math instruction, and instructional practices.

Sharon Vaughn
University of Texas
Meadows Center for Preventing Educational Risk

Introduction

Issues and Themes in Mathematics Response to Intervention Research and Implementation

The field of special education seems to lurch forward into new initiatives, often with boundless enthusiasm, impassioned theoretical papers, and a dearth of empirical support. In that sense, the profession is much like many others—both inside and outside the field of education. During this initial surge of enthusiasm, supporters usually promise too much, and concerns raised by others in the field are treated as "resistance." Unfortunately, dicey issues are skirted or treated as trivial, and persistent problems are rarely studied and virtually never addressed.

Previous initiatives and innovations in special education, such as the enthusiastic embrace of the IQ–achievement discrepancy model in the 1960s and 1970s, the resource room in the 1970s, and prereferral interventions in the 1980s and 1990s, have taught us that we need rigorous research to inform this early enthusiasm for response to intervention (RTI). Ideally, this research should be conducted by using the What Works Clearinghouse standards developed by Institute of Education Sciences of the U.S. Department of Education in conjunction with national methodological experts from several different disciplines.[1] We need research that is *dispassionate*, that honestly addresses areas of strength and weakness of the various RTI approaches to help us avoid the waste seen with past initiatives and innovations.

Fortunately, there have been several research-based advances in the field of RTI in mathematics in the past decade. Our goal was to compile some of the best of this research into one volume. Rather than briefly (and, inevitably, superficially) try to summarize each chapter, we wish to raise a few issues that might help guide your thinking as you peruse this volume.

The most obvious issue is the relatively small amount of research on mathematics instruction in general, and on RTI in mathematics in particular. Although we are happy to report that, since we planned this volume, several

---

[1] http://ies.ed.gov/ncee/wwc/pdf/wwc_procedures_v2_standards_handbook.pdf

large-scale studies involving RTI in mathematics are likely to appear in the literature in the next year or so,[2] very little research has been published in this area to date. When the senior author examined the ratio of research on mathematics disabilities to reading disabilities several years ago (Gersten, Clarke, & Mazzocco, 2007), the ratio we found was 5:1 for the decade 1996–2005 and 16:1 in the previous decade. Thus, it is not surprising that there are huge swatches of RTI terrain that have been unexplored to date.

That said, we do possess a reasonable amount of knowledge of best practices, or at least promising practices, for several areas. In Chapter 1 of this volume, Riccomini and Smith provide a brief orientation to RTI in mathematics and vignettes that illuminate some of the rather abstract constructs.

One important area of RTI—really the foundational building block—is screening for at-risk status, particularly in the primary grades. Here, we can identify several constructs that invariably serve as moderately successful screening measures and that can be easily administered. These constructs and measures are discussed in Chapter 2 by Gersten, Dimino, and Haymond.

Progress monitoring and formative assessment measures have evolved more slowly and tentatively, and not as successfully as in the field of reading. Chapter 3, by Clarke, Lembke, Hampton, and Hendricker, comprehensively documents the progress to date. As Foegen, Jiban, and Deno (2007) noted, no one has discovered a quick and easy way to administer a means to capture a snapshot of a child's mathematics ability, similar to the way that oral reading fluency has proved to be a successful measure for overall reading ability for students in the elementary grades. Nor, we believe, are they likely to in mathematics given the complex web of topics, strands, concepts, and proficiencies.

A second major theme—one that has been underscored by a spate of research—is the importance of early intervention in mathematics. The devastating, long-term impact of entering first grade with weak knowledge of number concepts and operations has been a consistent finding in longitudinal research (Duncan et al., 2007; Morgan, Farkas, & Wu, 2009). Several chapters in this volume address best practices and evidence-based practices for successful early intervention. Chapter 4, by Clarke, Doabler, Baker, Fien, Jungjohann, and Strand Cary; and Chapter 5, by Bryant, Roberts, Bryant, and DiAndreth-Elkins, describe interventions for students in kindergarten and first grade. In Chapter 6, Fuchs, Fuchs, and Schumacher describe evidence-based practices for teaching elementary students to solve increasingly complex word problems. In Chapter 7, Jayanthi and Gersten discuss recurrent findings encountered in their research review of the entire body of instructional research on mathematics for teaching students with difficulties in mathematics. Their chapter highlights practical implications drawn from their recent meta-analysis (Gersten et al., 2009).

A similar theme involves the devastating effects of poor preparation for algebra, such as entering high school with weak knowledge of fractions,

---

[2] Here we refer to a study by Bryant et al. (in press) to appear in *Exceptional Children;* a report by Gersten et al. (2011) released by the Institute of Education Sciences (IES); and research of Fuchs et al. (in press) on a third-grade screening system to assess algebraic learning.

percentages, decimals, and proportion, which has been discussed in detail by the National Mathematics Advisory Panel (2008), or a limited ability to solve word problems. In Chapter 8, Jitendra, Woodward, and Star address a key component of algebra readiness—understanding of proportional reasoning. In Chapter 9, Witzel, Mink, and Riccomini amplify one of the key themes that emerged in the intervention research—effective use of concrete and visual representations to ensure understanding of mathematical concepts and ideas.

In Chapter 10, Nomi and Allensworth describe a common form of Tier 2 intervention at the high-school level—often called double-dose algebra. Based on their careful analysis of data from districtwide implementation of double-dose algebra, they describe the positive impacts for both students requiring Tier 2 intervention and those students who are on track. They also note the importance of targeted professional development for this type of program to succeed.

We have two themes that involve intervention research more broadly. In Chapter 11, Woodward discusses the critical, but often neglected, issue of motivation in the context of middle school. Finally, in Chapter 12, we offer a front-line view of mathematics RTI in action by Campsen, a principal; Granzin, a school psychologist; and Carnine, a brilliant thinker on issues of implementation and scaling up best practices. These authors provide some of the nitty-gritty details necessary for interpreting data, analyzing effectiveness of Tier 1 and Tier 2, and productively discussing and using data to raise mathematics proficiency of all students in a school.

REFERENCES

Bryant, D.P., Bryant, B.R., Roberts, G., Vaughn, S., Hughes, K., Porterfield, J., & Gersten, R. (in press). Effects of an early numeracy intervention on the performance of first-grade students with mathematics difficulties. *Exceptional Children.*

Duncan, G.J., Dowsett, C.J., Claessens, A., Magnuson, K., Huston, A.C., Klebanov, P., et al. (2007). School readiness and later achievement. *Developmental Psychology, 43,* 1428–1446.

Foegen, A., Jiban, C., & Deno, S. (2007). Progress monitoring measures in mathematics: A review of the literature. *Journal of Special Education, 41,* 121–139.

Fuchs, L.S., Compton, D.L., Fuchs, D., Hollenbeck, K., Hamlett, C.L., & Seethaler, P.M. (in press). Two-stage screening for math word-problem difficulty using dynamic assessment of algebraic learning. *Journal of Learning Disabilities.*

Gersten, R., Chard, D., Jayanthi, M., Baker, S., Morphy, P., & Flojo, J. (2009). *A meta-analysis of mathematics instructional interventions for students with learning disabilities: Technical Report.* Los Alamitos, CA: Instructional Research Group. Retrieved from http://www.inresg.org

Gersten, R., Clarke, B., Dimino, J., & Rolfhus, E. (2011). *Universal screening measures of number sense and number proficiency for K-1: Preliminary findings* (Report No. 2011-1). Los Alamitos, CA: Instructional Research Group.

Gersten, R., Clarke, B., & Mazzocco, M.M.M. (2007). Historical and contemporary perspectives on mathematical learning disabilities. In D.B. Berch & M.M.M. Mazzocco (Eds.), *Why is math so hard for some children? The nature and origins of mathematical learning difficulties and disabilities* (pp. 7–29). Baltimore: Paul H. Brookes Publishing Co.

Morgan, P.L., Farkas, G., & Wu, Q. (2009). Five-year growth trajectories of kindergarten children with learning difficulties in mathematics. *Journal of Learning Disabilities, 42,* 306–321.

National Mathematics Advisory Panel. (2008). *Foundations for success: The final report of the National Mathematics Advisory Panel.* Washington, DC: U.S. Department of Education.

1 Introduction of Response to Intervention in Mathematics

Paul J. Riccomini and Gregory W. Smith

 RESPONSE TO INTERVENTION CLASSROOM SCENARIO

Ms. Johnson has just finished her first month of teaching sixth-grade mathematics. She has utilized the instructional strategies that she was taught as an undergraduate mathematics education major: 1) Allow for independent inquiry and practice, 2) incorporate cooperative learning groups, 3) provide feedback in a timely manner, 4) scaffold instruction when necessary, and 5) provide multiple opportunities for student response and reflection. She recently began providing differentiated instruction by utilizing various methods to present instruction. It has been a very tiring, but also rewarding, first 4 weeks.

Two days ago during class, Ms. Johnson implemented the district's universal screening measures in the areas of computation, operations, concepts, and applications. Overall, she was pleased with the results; 17 of her 20 students were on track to meet end-of-year math benchmarks. But it is not the 17 students who drew her attention; it was the 3 students who were struggling with the material she was presenting.

As she contemplated the fact that three of her students were struggling in math, she remembered receiving a memo from her principal regarding something called *response to intervention*, or RTI for short. As she read the memo, Ms. Johnson remembered hearing very briefly about RTI in one of her undergraduate courses, but she could not quite remember what it was, whom it pertained to, or who was responsible for implementing it. She thought it had something to do with special education.

Later that night, she accessed the National Center on Response to Intervention's web site (http://www.rti4success.org). Within a few minutes, most of her questions were answered. According to the web site, RTI helps schools "identify students at risk for poor learning outcomes, monitor student progress, provide evidence-based interventions and adjust

1

the intensity and nature of those interventions depending on a student's responsiveness, and identify students with learning disabilities or other disabilities." All of these components sounded logical but very intimidating at the same time. After spending some more time browsing the web site, she was left with one lingering question: How was she, the classroom teacher, supposed to "adjust the intensity and nature of interventions depending on a student's responsiveness, and identify students with learning disabilities or other disabilities"? She thought to herself, *Isn't that something they do in special education?* For the first time this school year, she felt inadequate about her knowledge and skills.

The next morning, Ms. Johnson reread the memo regarding RTI. In it, her principal asked for teachers to submit the names of students who were not making adequate academic progress. The memo included a chart of scores arranged into three categories:

1. Low risk
2. Some risk
3. At risk

She was disappointed to have to submit the names of the three students who were in the categories of "some risk" or "at risk" according to the chart, but she was confident that she had done all she could do in the classroom. *Maybe they do have a learning disability—this would at least explain why they are not making progress like the rest of my students,* she thought. Ms. Johnson submitted the names of the three students, and then made the conscious decision to continue instructing the way she had been for the past 4 weeks; she was certain she was doing all that she could.

During sixth period, Ms. Johnson received a hand-written memo from her principal. This memo was again regarding RTI; her presence was being requested at a meeting that afternoon. As she entered the conference room, she was relieved to notice that her friend and colleague Mrs. Potter, a special education teacher, would also be in attendance along with the school psychologist. As Ms. Johnson sat at the small table and the meeting progressed, she became more and more at ease with her initial concerns regarding the RTI process, and she realized that this would be a team process.

The three students whom she had identified as not making adequate academic progress, as indicated on the district universal screening measures for math—Matthew, "some risk," and Jeremy and Tasha, both "at risk"—would continue receiving instruction in Ms. Johnson's class as they had for the past 4 weeks, along with receiving additional focused and more intensive instruction during class in small group settings (something Mrs. Potter would be helping Ms. Johnson plan and implement). Ms. Johnson, with the assistance of Mrs. Potter, would also monitor the progress of each of the three students once per week. After 5 weeks, Ms.

Johnson, Mrs. Potter, and the school psychologist would again meet to discuss the progress of the three students.

It has now been 5 weeks since their previous meeting, and the school psychologist, Ms. Johnson, and Mrs. Potter are beginning to review the strategies that were implemented in Ms. Johnson's class, along with the progress that each of the three students has made. They will use variety of performance data such as chapter tests and quizzes as well as the progress monitoring data on a valid and reliable measure collected weekly.

One of the students, Tasha, has excelled on her curriculum-embedded assessments as well as her progress-monitoring assessments. Last week, Tasha had the third-highest score on Friday's quiz. In addition, all five progress-monitoring data points indicated a trajectory that would meet or exceed the district benchmarks for math by the end of the year.

The other two students, Matthew and Jeremy, have not responded like Tasha to the additional instruction that was provided by Ms. Johnson in class during Tier 1 of the RTI process. Both students' progress-monitoring data showed little to no increase, and all five data points were below the students' goal line. The school psychologist explained that the students had not responded (increased learning) with the instruction they had received over the past 5 weeks and a more intensive intervention was warranted. A decision is made by the RTI team that both Matthew and Jeremy will receive an additional intervention in Tier 2. The more intensive intervention in Tier 2 will involve systematic and explicit instruction delivered in a small-group setting (fewer than five students). During Tier 2, Matthew and Jeremy will receive 30 minutes of additional needs-based small-group instruction 3 days a week (based on their individual requirements) in an intervention block delivered by a math interventionist. This 30 minutes is in addition to the general education math instruction Ms. Johnson will continue to deliver (Tier 1).

Mrs. Potter, the special education teacher, and the math interventionist will spend more time instructing and assessing the progress of both students. Matthew and Jeremy will continue to receive this focused instruction for the next 10 weeks. Following the conclusion of this 10-week Tier 2 instructional period, another meeting will take place to reevaluate the academic progress of both students.

Both Matthew and Jeremy have now spent a total of 15 weeks (i.e., 5 weeks in Tier 1 and 10 weeks in Tier 2) in the RTI process. During this meeting, and for each student, the RTI team has a decision to make on the basis of their student data: 1) to return the student to a Tier 1–only schedule (if he has met the mathematical goals established by the district), 2) to have the student continue Tier 1 with Tier 2 instruction (if he has made progress and is on track for his goal), or 3) to begin Tier 3 individual instruction (if he is not responding to Tier 1 plus Tier 2 instruction).

Over the past 10 weeks in Tier 2, Matthew has made significant progress. His progress-monitoring data have significantly increased; Matthew is now on track (i.e., low risk) to meet or exceed the district math benchmarks. Ms. Johnson and Mrs. Potter feel that Matthew can successfully learn in Tier 1 and no longer requires the additional Tier 2 supports. Even though Matthew's data have significantly improved, the RTI team decides to continue to monitor his progress for the next 6 weeks but will do so less frequently. Instead of monitoring weekly, Ms. Johnson will monitor his progress once a month to make sure he is still on track.

Jeremy, however, has not responded to the individualized instruction that he has received in Tier 2. The flat trend on his progress-monitoring data is alarming. Visual inspection of his progress-monitoring graph clearly shows that Jeremy has not made any progress. The school psychologist explains that Jeremy's trendline, which is flat and not on track to meet district benchmarks, shows that he is still in the at-risk category. Because of the lack of response to the instruction and intervention Jeremy has received in Tier 1 and Tier 2 of the RTI process, the RTI team decides to move him from Tier 2 to the most intense instructional component of the RTI process, Tier 3. The nature of instruction in Tier 3 is very intensive both in terms of instruction and time as well as being focused on specific student needs. Tier 3 is reserved for students with marked difficulties in mathematics who have not responded sufficiently to Tiers 1 and 2.

Recognizing the differences in Tier 3 options that were discussed by the team, they decide that during Tier 3, Jeremy will not only continue to receive math instruction from Ms. Johnson in the general education classroom but will also receive 60 minutes of an intensive and explicit mathematics intervention (once per day for 5 days a week) delivered by Mrs. Potter, the special education teacher. Jeremy, along with a few other students who have not responded to instruction in Tier 2 in other math classes, will receive an evidence-based instructional intervention program during the next 12 weeks. After this 12-week period, another meeting will take place between the school psychologist, Ms. Johnson, and Mrs. Potter to discuss Jeremy's progress.

It is now mid-April, and Jeremy has spent a total of 27 weeks in the RTI process. According to the weekly progress monitoring assessments given by both Ms. Johnson and Mrs. Potter, Jeremy has failed to respond to the intense intervention program provided to him during Tier 3 of the RTI process. It is determined that he has not made adequate academic progress. The RTI team was hoping to be able to make the decision to either 1) move him back to Tier 2 (if he had made sufficient progress, and was on-track to meet the district benchmarks) or 2) continue with Tier 3 instruction (if he had made gradual progress). However, because of his unresponsiveness to the instruction that he received not only in Tier 3 but also in Tiers 1 and 2, the RTI team decides to move forward with a more comprehensive evaluation for special education services.

Ms. Johnson is pleased with her participation in the RTI process; she has learned a great deal, especially regarding instructional strategies she will now use in her math classes for all students. She no longer feels inadequate about her knowledge and skills when it comes to instructing students who struggle and may have learning disabilities. Two of her three students (Tasha and Matthew) who were initially lacking progress in math are now succeeding in her classroom. The third student, Jeremy, is in the process of being evaluated for a learning disability. Because of her involvement in the RTI process, Ms. Johnson has become an advocate for the early screening and intense instruction of students who struggle to make adequate academic progress in the general education classroom.

INTRODUCTION

A leading concern among educators, policy makers, and parents is the number of students in the United States who demonstrate low achievement levels in mathematics. This is especially true for students with high-incidence disabilities and their low-achieving peers without disabilities in the elementary and middle grades (see Gersten et al., 2009; National Mathematics Advisory Panel, 2008). The 2007 National Assessment of Educational Progress report stated that 81% of fourth-grade students with disabilities and 92% of eighth-grade students with disabilities failed to achieve a basic level of proficiency in mathematics (Lee, Grigg, & Dion, 2007). The day-to-day impact of deficits in mathematical knowledge is unmistakably evident in the following statistics reported in the *Foundations for Success: Final Report of the National Mathematics Advisory Panel* (2008): 1) 78% of adults cannot explain how to compute interest on a monetary loan, 2) 71% of adults cannot calculate miles driven per gallon of gasoline used, and 3) 58% of adults cannot calculate a 10% gratuity tip when dining out.

In response to poor academic performance and possible negative societal consequences, schools are aggressively implementing a variety of early and preventive interventions:

- Accentuating number sense and critical foundations of algebra
- Emphasizing the importance of mathematics instruction and learning to teachers
- Providing before- and after-school programs that provide additional mathematics instruction
- Increasing parental involvement
- Refocusing professional development efforts for teachers and staff in the area of effective mathematics instruction

These efforts by educators are described in the context of additional targeted interventions to supplement the mathematics program for struggling students through an instructional tiered approach often referred to as *response to intervention* (RTI; Hughes & Dexter, 2008a; Hughes & Dexter, 2008b; Riccomini & Witzel, 2010) and *response to instruction and intervention* (RTII; California Department of

Education, 2009; Pennsylvania Department of Education, 2009; Pennsylvania Training & Technical Assistance Network, 2008).

The purpose of this chapter is to present a context for which the remaining chapters of this book are to be viewed when one is developing, implementing, and refining RTI in mathematics. The chapter begins with a general overview. We discuss the core components of RTI and essential roles of school staff. In the course of reading this and subsequent chapters, one should refer to the RTI vignette presented at the beginning of the chapter; the vignette will help the reader to make better sense of the information discussed in this chapter as it illustrates the practical implementation of the RTI process.

OVERVIEW OF RESPONSE TO INTERVENTION

Before 2004, the only recognized method of identifying students with specific learning disabilities (SLDs) was through a discrepancy model in which the main criteria used for determining eligibility was a discrepancy between a student's IQ score and his or her academic achievement levels. Over the years, this approach was criticized for at least four reasons:

1. A lack of consistency across states in how to measure the discrepancy
2. Ineffective early preventative efforts
3. Absence of instructionally relevant information for educators
4. Possible overidentification or misidentification of students with SLDs (Berkeley, Bender, Peaster, & Saunders, 2009)

When Congress reauthorized the Individuals with Disabilities Education Improvement Act (IDEA) of 2004 (PL 108-446), states were allowed and encouraged to explore RTI as an alternative option to identifying students with SLDs.

The historical roots of RTI are found in special education research dating back more than three decades, as well as in more recent public policy. The work of Deno and Bergan in the 1970s is often referenced as the initial pedigree of current RTI elements (National Association of State Directors of Special Education [NASDSE], 2006). Although aspects of RTI appear in many academic areas, most of the research was concentrated in the area of reading. This, however, should not come as a surprise. Reading is often a focus of special education research because many students who are at risk for SLDs experience difficulties in learning how to read. As more and more research on RTI demonstrated that improvements in reading outcomes for struggling students was both practical and possible, momentum and acceptance of this tiered instructional practice increased and thus resulted in the inclusion of RTI in the reauthorization of IDEA in 2004.

RTI DEFINED

In the years following the reauthorization of IDEA, RTI has taken many forms. For example, one school's RTI process may include procedures for identifying struggling students through a computer-based assessment system and then providing those at-risk students 15 minutes of pull-out computer time. In another school's RTI process, at-risk students may be identified through a series of universal screening measures, and those students who are at or below the 50th percentile receive a double dose of an algebra program specifically designed for struggling students. Clearly, the RTI models in both schools would fall into the broad definition of RTI; however, the implementation processes, including the identification of those who are eligible for additional instruction and the actual interventions, are very different.

Next, we briefly examine a few common definitions of RTI, which identify some of the universally implemented core components of this practice and areas open to different interpretations. Regardless of the source and/or definition, common elements emerge across each definition that include assessment, instruction, interventions, and decision making. All of these core components are expanded upon in the forthcoming chapters of this book.

The NASDSE provided the following definition:

> Response to Intervention (RtI) is the practice of providing high-quality instruction and interventions matched to student need, monitoring progress frequently to make decisions about changes in instruction or goals and applying child response data to important education decisions. (2005, p. 3)

The National Research Center on Learning Disabilities (NRCLD) provided the following definition:

> RTI is an assessment and intervention process *for systematically monitoring student progress and making decisions about the need for instructional modifications or increasingly intensified services using progress monitoring data* [emphasis added]. (Johnson, Mellard, Fuchs, & McKnight, 2006, p. 2)

These definitions, like most others, stress regular monitoring of student progress and providing extra help to students who are failing to make progress in mathematics, reading, or other academic areas. It is intentionally broad as to precisely how a school or district or state puts it into operation, realizing that, as a field, we are only beginning to develop models for successful RTI implementation. At its most basic level, RTI is about informed instructional decisions aimed at improving learning outcomes.

CORE ELEMENTS OF RTI FOR MATHEMATICS

In the past few years, RTI has exploded into the discipline of mathematics instruction, which is refocusing educators on the importance of effective instruction by highlighting the fact that many students with and without disabilities struggle to learn mathematical computations, applications, and concepts. The following section provides a brief description of each of the core elements of RTI.

Assessment

The use of appropriate assessments is crucial to the RTI process. There are two main purposes of implementing assessments in the RTI process:

1. To identify students at risk for learning problems (screening)
2. To monitor the progress of students who have been identified as at risk (progress monitoring)

Universal screening measures are evaluations that are generally administered to all students three or four times per year. The results are used to identify students who are at risk for learning difficulties in math as well as to establish local norms. Typical universal screening measures are relatively brief and simple to administer and score, and remain technically adequate in terms of reliability and validity—especially predictive validity. After these screening measures are analyzed, students who are deemed to be at risk for learning problems are then monitored more frequently to determine the progress they are making.

Progress monitoring is the frequent academic assessment of students to determine whether the students are benefiting (i.e., learning) from their instructional program at an acceptable rate. Often the measures used for progress monitoring are similar (and in some cases the same) to the universal screening measures. Progress monitoring can occur biweekly or as little as one time per month. Because progress monitoring is intended to assess learning across the academic year, the results can also be used to make decisions regarding the effectiveness of curriculum, instruction, and interventions utilized.

Instructional Tiers

The organization of the process of RTI is founded on a tiered system of instruction and interventions that are based on student needs. The RTI models are commonly represented by a triangle with three or four tiers. Some schools utilize more tiers when implementing RTI than others (e.g., four tiers of instruction, as opposed to three); however, regardless of the number of tiers in a specific RTI model, the instructional supports, interventions, and assessments become more intensive as students move through the tiers (see Berkeley, Bender, Peaster, & Saunders, 2009; Burns & Gibbons, 2008).

Tier 1 is the instructional program that all students receive, or core instruction, which sometimes includes differentiated instruction for struggling students. Most models suggest that the core instructional program should appropriately address the learning needs of 80% of the student population (Burns, Deno, & Jimerson, 2007; Johnson et al., 2006; NASDSE, 2006). Tier 2 instruction is more intensive than the instruction in Tier 1 and almost always includes an increase in instructional time (Vaughn, 2003). Instead of replacing core instruction as in a pull-out model (Riccomini & Witzel, 2010), Tier 2 involves the addition of extra instructional opportunities that serve to supplement, enhance, and support the instruction in Tier 1.

Typically, but not always, Tier 1 and Tier 2 instruction take place within the general classroom. Most models (Bender & Shores, 2007; NASDSE, 2006) suggest that 15% of a student population may require Tier 2 instruction. Tier 3 is the most intensive of the three tiers, and is reserved for students who have received evidence-based instruction at various levels of intensity in both Tier 1 and 2 and have yet to achieve adequate academic progress. If the effectiveness of Tiers 1 and 2 has been maximized, no more than 5% of a student population should require Tier 3 (Johnson et al., 2006; NASDSE, 2006).

Figure 1.1 contains a representation of Pennsylvania's three-tiered RTII model. It is important to note that some states (e.g., California's "RtI²" and Pennsylvania's "RTII") call the RTI process *response to instruction and intervention;* although the names are slightly different (an added *I*), the processes involved in each model are essentially identical to those of states who call the process *response to intervention.* Even though instruction is an important aspect of all RTI models, adding the additional *I* for *instruction* emphasizes the importance of the general education instruction, or Tier 1.

Figure 1.2 contains a representation of the Berkeley County School District's four-tiered RTI model. The purpose of a system of tiers is to provide instructional supports that can be implemented at the onset of a student's identified academic struggle, while also offering a realistic means of monitoring and maintaining such supports throughout the academic calendar year.

Content Emphasis

The discussion regarding what to teach in mathematics is often a contentious point of debate among educators, parents, researchers, and policy makers. A definition of mathematical proficiency is pertinent to any discussion of RTI.

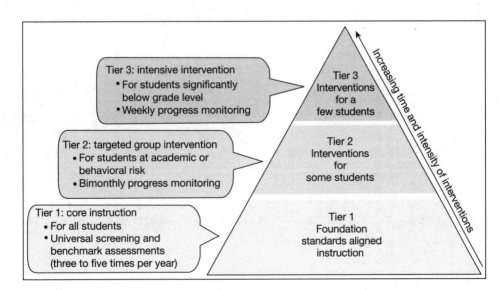

Figure 1.1. Pennsylvania's three-tiered response to instruction and intervention model. (From Pennsylvania Training & Technical Assistance Network [2008]. *Response to instruction and intervention implementation guide.* Retrieved from http://www.pattan.net/teachlead/responsetointervention.aspx.)

RTI

Response to instruction

- Interventions prescribed on basis of student needs supported by data.
- Student movement throughout Tiers is fluid in nature.
- Identified special education students' Tiers placement is prescribed by their individualized education program.

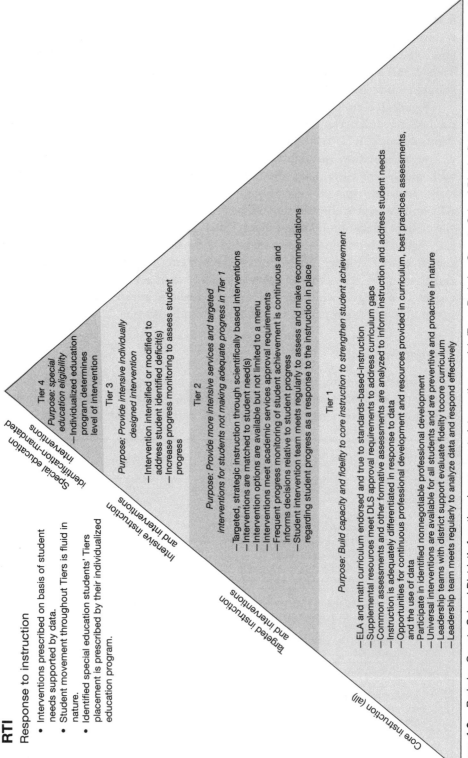

Special education identification-mandated interventions

Intensive instruction and interventions

Targeted instruction and interventions

Core instruction (all)

Tier 4
Purpose: special education eligibility
—Individualized education program determines level of intervention

Tier 3
Purpose: Provide intensive individually designed intervention
—Intervention intensified or modified to address student identified deficit(s)
—Increase progress monitoring to assess student progress

Tier 2
Purpose: Provide more intensive services and targeted interventions for students not making adequate progress in Tier 1
—Targeted, strategic instruction through scientifically based interventions
—Interventions are matched to student need(s)
—Intervention options are available but not limited to a menu
—Interventions meet academic services approval requirements
—Frequent progress monitoring of student achievement is continuous and informs decisions relative to student progress
—Student intervention team meets regularly to assess and make recommendations regarding student progress as a response to the instruction in place

Tier 1
Purpose: Build capacity and fidelity to core instruction to strengthen student achievement
—ELA and math curriculum endorsed and true to standards-based-instruction
—Supplemental resources meet DLS approval requirements to address curriculum gaps
—Common assessments and other formative assessments are analyzed to inform instruction and address student needs
—Instruction is adequately differentiated in response to data
—Opportunities for continuous professional development and resources provided in curriculum, best practices, assessments, and the use of data
—Participate in identified nonnegotiable professional development
—Universal interventions are available for all students and are preventive and proactive in nature
—Leadership teams with district support evaluate fidelity to core curriculum
—Leadership team meets regularly to analyze data and respond effectively

Figure 1.2. Berkeley County School District's four-tiered response to intervention model. (From Berkeley County School District [http://www.berkeley.k12.sc.us]; reprinted by permission.)

Therefore, educators operating within an RTI model must make decisions regarding what content to teach when students struggle (Gersten et al., 2009).

The National Mathematics Advisory Panel (NMAP, 2008) recommended that an effective mathematics program should adequately develop the following subcontent areas of mathematics: 1) conceptual understanding, 2) computational fluency, 3) factual knowledge, and 4) problem-solving skills. Any program that addresses each of these areas is likely to result in fewer students requiring additional tiers of instruction. To achieve proficiency when problem solving, students demonstrate a mastery of the following competencies: 1) understand key concepts, 2) achieve automaticity in addition and subtraction facts, and 3) develop flexible, accurate, and automatic execution of the standard algorithms (NMAP, 2008). Students must have a working knowledge of concepts, procedures, facts, and problem solving (see NMAP, 2008; Riccomini & Witzel, 2010; Siegler et al., 2010).

Essentially, math proficiency is not an either–or scenario; rather, it is the combination and interaction of mathematical knowledge that facilitates mathematical proficiency. Thus, the importance of selecting a core mathematics program that addresses and promotes student learning in each of these areas is imperative.

Instructional Approach

Much debate regarding how to teach mathematics to children has taken place over the past century; it is often contentious and frequently results in confusion on behalf of the teachers. This debate regularly revolves around how much instruction and guidance students should be provided. Either the instruction is *student centered* or *teacher directed*. The two approaches differ in when and how much instruction and guidance students are given during the learning of mathematical topics. Although both approaches can differ significantly, they both share the same goal: effective student learning.

Within any RTI model, it is imperative that the instructional approaches applied have a solid research base for support. The NMAP (2008) report attempted to address this ongoing debate by reviewing all available high-quality research on effective instructional approaches for mathematics for students performing well below average. The recommendation put forth by the NMAP is that all students should be exposed to a balance of student-centered and teacher-directed approaches. Furthermore, the panel clearly states that use of either approach exclusively is not supported in the research. The NMAP (2008) recommends that students who are low achieving, at risk for mathematical difficulties, and/or have disabilities should receive access to explicit methods of instruction on a regular basis. As students (with and without a documented disability) who are struggling with the material move through the tiers of an RTI model, instruction should become more systematic and explicit. Therefore, students moving into Tier 2 should receive more systematic and explicit instructional opportunities than they received in Tier 1. The degree of explicitness should vary depending on content and student learning characteristics. This concept of

Table 1.1.   Research recommendations on effective mathematics instruction and interventions for struggling students

Themes from RTI math research[a]	NMAP (2008) recommendations	RTI in mathematics IES practice guide[b]
Increase instructional time	Explicit instructional methods	Screen and provide interventions
Small group	Development foundation needed for algebra	Focus on whole numbers
Explicit instruction	Focus on conceptual development with use of concrete models	Explicit and systematic instruction
Use of concrete representations	Development of fluency with operations and computation skills as well teaching a problem-solving strategy	Instruction on solving word problems that focus on underlying structure
Strategy instruction for problem solving		Use of pictorial representations
Focus on computation		At least 10 minutes of computational fluency practice
Alignment with Tier 1		Progress monitoring
Progress monitoring		Motivational strategies

Key: RTI, response to intervention; NMAP, National Mathematics Advisory Panel; IES, Institute of Education Sciences.
[a]Riccomini, P.J., & Witzel, B.S. (2010). *Response to intervention in math.* Thousand Oaks, CA: Corwin Press.
[b]Gersten, R., Beckmann, S., Clarke, B., Foegen, A., Marsh, L., Star, J. R., et al. (2009). *Assisting students struggling with mathematics: Response to Intervention (RtI) for elementary and middle schools* (NCEE 2009-4060). Washington, DC: National Center for Education Evaluation and Regional Assistance, Institute of Education Sciences, U.S. Department of Education. Retrieved from http://ies.ed.gov/ncee/wwc/publications/

providing explicit instruction to students who struggle or have learning disabilities is thoroughly supported by current research (see Gersten et al., 2009; Jayanthi, Gersten, & Baker, 2008; Newman-Gonchar, Clarke, & Gersten, 2009; NMAP, 2008; Riccomini & Witzel, 2010).

Explicit instruction generally involves teachers providing students with clear explanations and multiple demonstrations of specific and inconspicuous strategies for the targeted mathematics content. In addition, students are provided numerous opportunities for questions as well as time to contemplate the process of problem solving (NMAP, 2008). The key elements of explicit instruction generally include teacher modeling followed by guided and independent practice opportunities using carefully developed and sequenced examples. Furthermore, teacher corrective feedback occurs routinely during all aspects of the instructional episode as needed, and maintenance and generalization opportunities are numerous (see Table 1.1).

Reliance on Evidence-Based Instruction

The RTI process requires educators to use effective instructional programs. If students are not making adequate progress, instructional changes are considered. These instructional changes can include many different approaches and strategies. Until recently, these approaches were based on educators' experiences and current fads. Now, the No Child Left Behind Act of 2001 (107-110) and IDEA 2004 require that evidence-based strategies be used in all academic interventions. This is a problem given the paucity of research on the topic.

It is crucial for school districts to be mindful of the fact that the implementation of evidence-based approaches by teachers is imperative for the success of any RTI model. If the best-available research findings are not used to guide the instructional approaches used within the RTI process, far too many students will require Tier 2 and Tier 3 instructional supports. It is important to keep in mind that RTI is not a teaching *strategy*, but a model of *how* evidence-based educational practices should be utilized in the classroom to facilitate instruction.

Decision Making

Educational decisions are a major part of the RTI process and can serve several purposes. In the RTI classroom vignette presented at the beginning of this chapter, four educational decisions were made. First, students were identified (based on a universal screening assessment) to receive additional targeted instructional assistance. Second, the effectiveness of the intervention was determined on the basis of the progress monitoring data. Third, decisions were made as to which students return to or advance through the instructional tiers. Finally, the RTI team concluded that a decision of eligibility for special education services was warranted.

Because the RTI process is based on the collection of scientific data, school districts are afforded the opportunity to make decisions pertaining to additional educational procedures, including

- Effectiveness of instructional program curriculum and instruction
- Effectiveness of interventions
- Determination of when an intervention is required
- Progress toward end-of-year learning goals
- Eligibility for special education

Regardless of the number of steps in the RTI process, educational decisions (periodically required throughout the implementation phase) are an integral part of the model. Ultimately, the success of RTI relies upon the effectiveness of the decision-making process by the RTI team.

ESSENTIAL ROLES IN RTI PROCESSES IN MATH

The importance of active participation of classroom teachers in an effective RTI process cannot be overstated. The importance of carefully aligning Tiers 1 and 2 to supplement each other is well documented (Fuchs, Fuchs, & Hollenbeck, 2007; Newman-Gonchar et al., 2009; Vaughn, 2003). Careful alignment of Tier 1 and Tier 2 is likely only if classroom teachers are involved in the process from the beginning. In addition, as described previously, the RTI process is founded on assessment, instruction, and decision making—*all* of which occur in the first instructional tier in the general education classroom.

The classroom teacher should be involved with 1) all of the facets of the universal screening measures and 2) the progress monitoring of each student identified as at risk for academic failure. Assessment results are used by the classroom teacher to identify students in need of additional instructional supports. It is the combination of progress monitoring and instructional strategies delivered by the general education classroom teachers that allows for early and appropriate decision making regarding the implementation of additional interventions. A fundamental premise of RTI is that additional instruction is provided early and quickly when students struggle. Often, this is done in consultation with school psychologists, RTI coordinators, interventionists, math coaches, or special education teachers.

School psychologists have specialized training and knowledge of assessment administration, data collection, and analysis. Often, school psychologists are asked to provide support in collecting and interpreting data results in the decisions to move students through the tiers, and in some cases, assist in the selection of interventions.

Interventionists are teachers or paraprofessionals whose primary responsibility is to deliver specific intervention programs that are not delivered within the general education classroom. These interventions often 1) require specialized training, 2) involve small groups of students, and 3) require specific time allotments beyond that of the core instruction. Interventionists, school psychologists, and special education teachers work closely in the decision-making process for students who do not exhibit adequate academic progress.

A relatively new role in the RTI process is that of the math coach or RTI coordinator. The responsibilities of these professionals vary widely but generally include managing data, providing classroom teachers with instructional support, and making recommendations for students who are struggling according to progress monitoring data. In addition, coaches and coordinators are often in a position to offer insight into the professional development needs, as well as other types of needed support, for members of the RTI team.

Because of their expertise in identifying effective instructional practices for students who are struggling with the curriculum, special educators also serve a vital role on the RTI team. As illustrated in the RTI classroom scenario, special education teachers are involved with many aspects of the RTI model. They have specialized training in data collection, analysis, and interventions for struggling students and often collaborate with classroom teachers to help provide specialized instruction for struggling students as well as students with disabilities included in Tier 1. The role of the special educator will likely, but not always, include *supplementing* the core program, or delivering an additional mathematics program.

The success of RTI hinges on the involvement of professionals in the educational system working together as a team. Once the classroom teacher provides a student with the necessary additional instructional supports and no meaningful progress is documented, efforts are then focused on instructional supports at Tiers 2 and 3. Regardless of the tier level, collaboration between the classroom teacher and the rest of the RTI team is essential for successful implementation of the RTI process.

REFERENCES

Bender, W.N., & Shores, C. (2007). *Response to intervention: A practical guide for every teacher.* Thousand Oaks, CA: Corwin Press.

Berkeley, S., Bender, W.N., Peaster, L.G., & Saunders, L. (2009). Implementation of response to intervention: A snapshot of progress. *Journal of Learning Disabilities, 42*(1), 85–95.

Burns, M.K., Deno, S.L., & Jimerson, S.R. (2007). Toward a unified response-to-intervention model. In S.R. Jimerson, M.K. Burns, & A.M. VanDerHeyden (Eds.), *Handbook of response to intervention* (pp. 428–440). New York: Springer.

Burns, M.K., & Gibbons, K.A. (2008). *Implementing response-to-intervention in elementary and secondary schools: Procedures to assure scientific-based practices.* New York: Routledge.

California Department of Education. (2009). *Core components-RtI²: Core components to a strong response to instruction and intervention.* Retrieved from http://www.cde.ca.gov/ci/cr/ri/rticorecomponents.asp

Fuchs, L.S., Fuchs, D., & Hollenbeck, K.H. (2007). Extending responsiveness to intervention to mathematics at first and third grades. *Learning Disabilities Research & Practice, 22*(1), 13–24.

Gersten, R., Beckmann, S., Clarke, B., Foegen, A., Marsh, L., Star, J.R., et al. (2009). *Assisting students struggling with mathematics: Response to Intervention (RtI) for elementary and middle schools* (NCEE 2009-4060). Washington, DC: National Center for Education Evaluation and Regional Assistance, Institute of Education Sciences, U.S. Department of Education. Retrieved from http://ies.ed.gov/ncee/wwc/publications/

Hughes, C., & Dexter, D.D. (2008a). Selecting a scientifically based core curriculum for Tier 1. Retrieved from RTI Action Network Web, National Center for Learning Disabilities web site: htttp://www.rtinetwork.org/learn/research/ar/researchreview

Hughes, C., & Dexter, D.D. (2008b). *Universal screening in the context of RTI.* Retrieved from RTI Action Network Web, National Center for Learning Disabilities web site: http://www.rtinetwork.org/learn/research/universal-screening-within-a-rti-model

Individuals with Disabilities Education Improvement Act (IDEA) of 2004, PL 108-446, 20 U.S.C. §§ 1400 *et seq.*

Jayanthi, M., Gersten, R., & Baker, S. (2008). *Mathematics instruction for students with learning disabilities or difficulty learning mathematics: A guide for teachers.* Portsmouth, NH: RMC Research Corporation, Center on Instruction.

Johnson, E., Mellard, D.F., Fuchs, D., & McKnight, M.A. (2006). *Responsiveness to intervention: How to do it.* Lawrence, KS: National Research Center on Learning Disabilities.

Lee, J., Grigg, W., and Dion, G. (2007). *The nation's report card: Mathematics 2007* (NCES 2007-494). National Center for Education Statistics, Institute of Education Sciences, U.S. Department of Education, Washington, D.C.

National Association of State Directors of Special Education (NASDSE). (2006). *Response to intervention: Policy considerations and implementation.* Alexandria, VA: Author. Retrieved from http://www.5.nasdse.org

National Mathematics Advisory Panel NMAP. (2008). *Foundations for Success: The Final Report of the National Mathematics Advisory Panel.* Washington, DC: U.S. Department of Education. Retrieved from http://www.ed.gov/mathpanel

Newman-Gonchar, R., Clarke, B., & Gersten, R. (2009). *A summary of nine key studies: Multi tier intervention and response to interventions for students struggling in mathematics.* Portsmouth, NH: RMC Research Corporation, Center on Instruction. Retrieved from http://centeroninstruction.org/files/Summary%20of%209%20studies%20on%20RTI%20math%20and%20struggling%20math%20students.pdf

No Child Left Behind Act of 2001, PL 107-110, 115 Stat. 1425, 20 U.S.C. §§ 6301 *et seq.*

Pennsylvania Training & Technical Assistance Network. (2008). *Response to instruction and intervention implementation guide.* Retrieved from http://www.pattan.net/teachlead/responsetointervention.aspx

Riccomini, P.J., & Witzel, B.S. (2010). *Response to intervention in math.* Thousand Oaks, CA: Corwin Press.

Siegler, R., Carpenter, T., Fennell, F., Geary, D., Lewis, J., Okamoto, Y., et al. (2010). *Developing effective fractions instruction for kindergarten through 8th grade: A practice guide* (NCEE #20010-4039). Washington, DC: National Center for Education Evaluation and Regional Assistance, Institute of Education Sciences, U.S. Department of Education. Retrieved from http://whatworks.ed.gov/publications/practiceguides

Vaughn, S. (2003, December). How many tiers are needed for response to intervention to achieve acceptable prevention outcomes? Paper presented at the NRCLD Responsiveness-to-Intervention Symposium, Kansas City, MO. Retrieved from http://www.nrcld.org/symposium 2003/vaughn/index.html

2

Universal Screening for Students in Mathematics for the Primary Grades

The Emerging Research Base

Russell Gersten, Joseph A. Dimino, and Kelly Haymond

Response to intervention (RTI) begins with universal screening on some brief, but reliable and valid measure. It is important that the screener be brief and relatively easy to administer. It is also important that the screener be performance-based and have standardized, objective administration and scoring procedures.

Without universal screening, there is no RTI. Recently, we conducted a systematic review of the research literature on early screening in mathematics (Gersten et al., under review). In this chapter, using a question–answer format, we summarize the highlights of current research on screening measures in mathematics for students in the primary grades. We provide information on the characteristics of both new and commonly used measures and draw attention to the uncertainties and complexities faced by schools or school districts in selecting the right screening measures or in using them appropriately. We also list resources, including those currently available at no cost to the public on web sites. These include appraisals of the technical merits of screening measures on the web site of the National Center on Response to Intervention and a practice guide developed by Institute for Education Sciences (Gersten et al., 2009), available at http://www.rti4success.org/tools_charts/screening.php and http://ies.ed.gov/ncee/wwc/publications/practiceguides, respectively.

The goal of this chapter is to answer eight critical questions about screening in mathematics. These questions reflect concerns expressed by educators to the senior author, who has presented on this topic at seminars and conferences around the country over the past several years:

Why is there so much interest in screening measures in mathematics for students in the primary grades?

This chapter was supported in part by grant S283B050034A from the Office of Elementary and Secondary Education. The authors wish to thank Sara Woodruff for her work in examining and compiling the contemporary research on early screening.

What are the differences between screening measures, progress monitoring measures, and diagnostic measures?

Have there been any serious advances in the development of valid and reliable screening measures in mathematics for students in kindergarten and first grade? If so, what have we learned?

What do the single proficiency measures look like?

What do the multiple proficiency measures look like?

What is the nature of the evidence base?

What things should we consider when selecting measures and interpreting scores?

Have we been successful in early mathematics screening measures?

WHY IS THERE SO MUCH INTEREST IN SCREENING MEASURES IN MATHEMATICS FOR STUDENTS IN THE PRIMARY GRADES?

Probably the most important reason for the interest is that after a decade of reasonably successful implementation of early screening measures in reading and their use in identifying students who need extra help to learn how to read, many educators have wondered if the same type of procedure might work for mathematics. As recently as a decade ago, little was known about the trajectory of mathematics disabilities and difficulties (Gersten, Clarke, & Mazzocco, 2007). Also, little was known about how to detect those students who were likely to require intensive interventions to succeed in mathematics.

A major advance in the 1990s was the research of Okamato and Case (1996), which indicated that students entered kindergarten and first grade with drastic differences in their knowledge of number concepts, counting, and addition. Many low-income students entered school with very limited knowledge of numbers and basic mathematical principles. At that point in time, however, few researchers had studied whether these problems in kindergarten led to enduring problems in mathematics.

That situation has changed dramatically in the past decade. A host of studies (Duncan et al., 2007; Jordan, Kaplan, Ramineni, & Locuniak, 2009; Morgan, Farkas, & Wu, 2009) demonstrates that students who complete kindergarten with weak knowledge of mathematics tend to experience consistent difficulties with mathematics. Screening measures in mathematics are available to identify at-risk students and provide them with the necessary instructional supports to help them succeed in mathematics.

WHAT ARE THE DIFFERENCES BETWEEN SCREENING MEASURES, PROGRESS MONITORING MEASURES, AND DIAGNOSTIC MEASURES?

Response to intervention has brought the terms *screening* and *progress monitoring* into educators' vernacular. At times, researchers have used the terms *screening* and *progress monitoring* almost interchangeably. A major reason for this confusion is that many progress monitoring measures can also serve as screening measures (e.g., Seethaler & Fuchs, 2010). Nevertheless, it is important for education professionals to know the difference between the two, especially as the field moves to more sophisticated technology-based means of assessment.

So, what is the difference between screening and progress monitoring? Screening is the first step in a prevention and intervention model such as RTI. Screening or benchmarking assessments are brief, efficient, and inexpensive measures administered to all students three times each year: fall, winter, and spring. Typically, screening measures address reading, mathematics, and behavior. The purpose of these measures is to identify students who do not achieve a predetermined score and who are likely to be at risk in the area targeted by the assessment. Students identified as at risk may receive in-depth diagnostic assessment to pinpoint their areas of strength and weakness, leading to the development of an intervention plan. At times, screening results alone provide the starting point for a student's intervention plan.

Like screening measures, progress monitoring assessments are quick, efficient, and low cost. They are administered regularly throughout the school year to students whose performance on the screening measures has deemed them to be at risk in one or more areas. The purpose of this system of formative assessment is to provide information regarding the effectiveness of the intervention students currently receive. In other words, the purpose is to determine whether the intervention is working or not, and, if the data indicate that the intervention is not working, to either switch interventions or somehow adjust instruction so that the student is making demonstrable progress. Students receiving Tier 2 intervention should be progress monitored at least twice per month. Typically, a student's response to Tier 3 interventions is assessed weekly.

HAVE THERE BEEN ANY SERIOUS ADVANCES IN THE DEVELOPMENT OF VALID AND RELIABLE SCREENING MEASURES IN MATHEMATICS FOR STUDENTS IN KINDERGARTEN AND FIRST GRADE? IF SO, WHAT HAVE WE LEARNED?

The short answer to this question is yes. The past decade has witnessed a virtual revolution in research on valid and reliable screening tools in mathematics. These measures display reasonable predictive validity, as shown in the tables throughout this chapter.

There are two types of measures—those that encompass a single proficiency and the somewhat longer multiple proficiency measures that address a wide array of operations and procedures involving whole numbers. The single proficiency measures derive from important constructs in developmental and cognitive psychology. Some multiple proficiency measures derive from cognitive or developmental psychology, and others derive from analysis of state standards or other curricula frameworks.

WHAT DO THE SINGLE PROFICIENCY MEASURES LOOK LIKE?

We present examples from our recent research (Clarke et al., 2011) which consists of three 1- to 2-minute timed measures administered to students in four school districts in two states from 2009 to 2011. This reliability and validity study involved 323 kindergartners and 348 first graders.

These measures, as with many other current screening measures for children in kindergarten or first grade, evolved from current cognitive psychology research, which addresses the development of mathematics proficiency in young students. Specifically, it focuses on numeral identification, strategic counting, magnitude comparison, and solving base-10 addition and subtraction math facts. Researchers (e.g., Geary, 2004; Kalchman, Moss, & Case, 2001) have identified two essential aspects in the development of proficiency in mathematics: the students' sense of the relative magnitude of numbers (i.e., the ability to determine the greatest number in a set) and their capacity to execute approaches to count efficiently and strategically. Students who have a sense of the relative magnitude of numbers know that 14 is a little bigger than 12 but much bigger than 6. Counting strategically and efficiently involves students' sense of the commutative property, in which 14 + 3 will yield the same sum as 3 + 14. Therefore, it is more efficient to begin with 14, and count up 3 to calculate the sum, 17.

Kindergarten and first-grade students are usually administered the Magnitude Comparison and Missing Number subtests (Clarke et al., 2011). Number identification and basic addition and subtraction facts are added to the kindergarten and first-grade batteries, respectively, to cover other important areas of mathematics appropriate for that age range (see Figure 2.1). Students' ability to learn any type of formal mathematics requires them to be able to quickly and accurately identify Arabic numerals. By the middle of first grade, students' ability to quickly and automatically retrieve arithmetic facts becomes critical for success in mathematics, as decades of research has indicated (e.g., Geary, 2004; Goldman, Pellegrino, & Mertz, 1988).

Magnitude Comparison

In this measure, students are able to make increasingly complex judgments about magnitude as their understanding of number and quantity grows and becomes more sophisticated. The Magnitude Comparison measure requires an understanding of place value and calls for students to perform mental calculations. Because screening measures are not meant to be comprehensive, an efficient screener is composed of subtests, such as Magnitude Comparison, that tap more than one critical component of number sense.

The student probe consists of a sheet of paper containing a series of individual boxes each containing two randomly selected numerals, 0–20 for kindergarten students and 0–99 for first graders (see Figure 2.2). Students are directed

8	3	10	20	2	5	14	17

Figure 2.1.   Sample items from Number Identification subtest. (From Clarke, B., Gersten, R., Dimino, J., & Rolfhus, E. [in press]. *Assessing Student Proficiency in Early Number Sense* [working title]. Longmont, CO: Cambium Learning Sopris.)

Kindergarten

3	0	12	4	16	10	12	17

Grade 1

38	16	43	57	4	12	37	48

Figure 2.2.   Sample items from the Magnitude Comparison subtest. (From Clarke, B., Gersten, R., Dimino, J., & Rolfhus, E. [in press]. *Assessing Student Proficiency in Early Number Sense* [working title]. Longmont, CO: Cambium Learning Sopris.)

to tell the assessor which number is bigger. The student's score is the number of correct responses in 1 minute.

Note that the format of this measure is virtually identical to that administered in the research conducted by Clarke and Shinn (2004), who developed this format; Stock, Desoete, and Roeyers (2010), who used the Clarke and Shinn measure in their research; and Lembke and Foegen (2009). However, although the format is the same, the measures sometimes use a different range of numbers. For example, the kindergarten measure developed by Baglici, Codding, and Tryon (2010) and Gersten et al. (2011) includes numbers from 0 to 20, whereas the measures developed by Clarke, Baker, Smolkowski, and Chard (2008) and Seethaler and Fuchs (2010) include only numbers up to 10. Some first-grade measures go through 99; others stop at 20.

The different researchers also used different outcome measures (sometimes called *criterion measures*). Baglici et al. (2010) used a quick-timed mathematics computation test for kindergartners, whereas most other researchers used far broader measures of mathematical proficiency.

Strategic Counting

Students' ability to understand how to count efficiently appears to be a cornerstone of mathematics proficiency at this age (Siegler & Robinson, 1982). Geary (2004) found that implementing inefficient or inaccurate counting strategies is a clear indicator of a learning disability in mathematics. Thus, a timed measure of counting that asks students to quickly begin a count sequence from numbers other than 1 and then quickly count backward from a given number appears to be an excellent possible screener for this age range.

The Gersten et al. (2011) measure taps students' proficiency in this area by asking them to name the missing numeral from a series of numerals between 0 and 20 for kindergarten and between 0 and 99 for first grade. The student's probe includes a sheet with boxes containing a sequence of three numerals where the first, middle, or last numeral of the sequence is missing (see Figure 2.3). Students are instructed to tell the assessor the number that goes in the

Kindergarten

1	2	___	___	12	13	17	18	___

Grade 1

28	29	___	76	___	78	14	15	___

Figure 2.3. Sample items from the Missing Number subtest. (From Clarke, B., Gersten, R., Dimino, J., & Rolfhus, E. [in press]. *Assessing Student Proficiency in Early Number Sense* [working title]. Longmont, CO: Cambium Learning Sopris.)

blank for each box. The student's score is the number of correct responses in 1 minute.

Number Identification

Accurate number identification is a goal in kindergarten mathematics instruction and appears to be a nice addition to the other measures in kindergarten. This is especially true for students who enter kindergarten with low mathematics knowledge and may flounder. For this reason, many researchers (Chard et al., 2005; Clarke et al., 2008; Clarke & Shinn, 2004; Lembke & Foegen, 2009) have included this subtest in their screening batteries. Although the Number Identification subtest appears to be essential for lower performing students, this skill is required to solve the problems in the screeners listed earlier.

With this measure, kindergartners are asked to name numerals as quickly as possible. The student probe consists of two sheets of paper containing a grid of individual boxes each containing a randomly chosen numeral from 0 to 20 (see Figure 2.1). The score is the number of correct numerals that the student has named in 1 minute.

Basic Arithmetic Facts and Base 10

The research addressing mathematics difficulties has consistently found that students who were identified as having a mathematics disability in the upper grades were unable to automatically and rapidly respond to addition and subtraction number facts (Goldman, Pellegrino, & Mertz, 1988; Hasselbring et al., 1988). In 2004, Geary reported that many students who have trouble in mathematics do not readily make the transition from counting on their fingers or using manipulatives to mentally solving problems. In short, fluency and automaticity with basic math facts is critical for understanding mathematical concepts.

This subtest requires students to solve basic fact problems that contain elements that can be composed or decomposed in the base-10 system (e.g., 5 + 9 becomes 4 + 10). Students are presented a sheet with 40 problems and solve as many as they can in 2 minutes.

WHAT DO THE MULTIPLE PROFICIENCY MEASURES LOOK LIKE?

Number Knowledge Test

Okamato and Case (1996) developed the Number Knowledge Test (NKT), an individually administered, untimed measure that takes approximately 10–15 minutes. The goal of this assessment is to determine kindergarten and first-grade students' procedural and conceptual knowledge of whole numbers and to identify gaps in students' knowledge of the rudimentary concepts involving quantity and number, which are critical for success in learning mathematics. The NKT identifies students who lack the basic knowledge they need to understand and master kindergarten and first-grade mathematics. Test results help educators differentiate instruction and identify students who need targeted and intensive intervention.

The NKT consists of five levels and assesses students' ability in three domains: strategic counting, magnitude comparison, and computation. Items increase in difficulty and complexity as students move through the levels. For example, the Level 1 magnitude comparison items tap students' ability to determine which single-digit numerals are larger or smaller. In Level 2, students are asked to compare double-digit numerals. A broader conception of magnitude comparison is addressed in Level 3 items where students are posed with questions such as, "Which is bigger: the difference between 98 and 91 or the difference between 28 and 11?" (Table 2.1 contains sample items.)

Table 2.1. Sample items from the Number Knowledge Test

Level	Sample item
0	Item 2: I am going to show you some more chips. (Show a mixed array of three red and four blue chips.) Count just the blue chips and tell me how many there are. (Domain: strategic counting)
	Item 4: Pretend I'm going to give you two pieces of candy and then I'm going to give you one more. (Make motions like you are giving candy to the student.) How many pieces of candy will you have altogether? (Domain: computation)
1	Item 3: What number comes two numbers after 7? (Accept either 9 or 10.) (Domain: strategic counting)
	Item 4b: Which number is bigger: 7 or 9? (Domain: magnitude comparison)
	Item 7: How much is 2 plus 4? (Domain: computation)
2	Item 1: What number comes five numbers before 60? (Domain: strategic counting)
	Item 5a: (Show visual array E.) Which number is closer to 28: 31 or 24? (Domain: magnitude comparison)
	Item 8: (Show visual array G.) How much is 47 take away 71? (Domain: computation)
3	Item 2: What number comes 9 numbers after 999? (Domain: strategic counting)
	Item 3a: Which difference is bigger: the difference between 9 and 6 or the difference between 8 and 5? (Domain: magnitude comparison)
	Item 5: (Show visual array H.) How much is 13 + 39? (Domain: computation)
4	Item 1a: How much is 42 times 3? (Domain: computation, untimed)
	Item 2a: Which item is closer to 0: –2.8 or 3.2? (Domain: magnitude comparison)

From Okamato, Y., & Case, R. (1996). Exploring the microstructure of children's centralconceptual structures in the domain of number. *Monographs of the Society for Research in Child Development,* 61, 27–59; reprinted by permission.

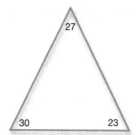

Figure 2.4.   Visual array: magnitude comparison.

Administration and Scoring

Items at all five levels, 0 to 4, are presented orally. The assessor follows the specific wording of the item in the administration and scoring guide. A visual array is provided for selected items in each domain. For example, the visual array in Figure 2.4 is similar to the visual array that accompanies the Level 2 magnitude comparison item: "Which number is closer to 27: 30 or 23?"

Each student begins at Level 0. Items answered correctly are marked with a "1," and incorrect items are marked with a "0." If a student does not respond, the protocol is marked "NR." To avoid frustration, students advance to the next level if they score above a criterion at the previous level.

WHAT IS THE NATURE OF THE EVIDENCE BASE?

In the summer of 2010, we conducted ERIC and PsycINFO searches of the literature to examine the current literature base on screening measures in mathematics administered to students in kindergarten and first grade. We described this full evidence base further in Gersten, Clarke, Jordan, et al. (under review).

In Tables 2.2 through 2.6, we summarize the current empirical evidence on screening measures in mathematics for students in the primary grades (kindergarten and first grade only). The tables include the study citation, a brief description of the screening measures, number of participants, grades at which screening assessment took place, outcome measures, and the predictive validity correlations between screeners and outcomes. We have organized the tables by the constructs assessed in each measure and have divided the measures into single proficiency measures and multiple number proficiency tests. For single proficiency measures we focused on the most commonly assessed aspects of number proficiency: magnitude comparison, strategic counting, solving simple word problems, and basic fact retrieval.

All but two of these studies provide correlations between screeners administered in the fall and mathematics outcomes administered in the spring of that same year. The two exceptions were Locuniak and Jordan (2008), which correlated the fall kindergarten screening measure with criterion measures administered in the winter of second grade; and Jordan, Glutting, and Ramineni (2008), which correlated the fall kindergarten screening measure with criterion measures

Table 2.2.　Measures of magnitude comparison

Study	Screening measure[a]	Grade	n[b]	Outcome measure	Predictive validity[c]
Baglici, Codding, and Tryon (2010)	Name the larger of two items: number sets 0 to 20	K	61	Timed mathematics computation	.02 (ns)
Chard, Clarke, Baker, Otterstedt, Braun et al. (2005)	Name the larger of two items: number sets 0 to 20	K 1st	436 483	Number Knowledge Test	.50 .53
Clarke, Baker, Smolkowski, and Chard (2008)	Name the larger of two items: number sets 0 to 10	K	254	Stanford Early School Achievement Test	.62
Clarke and Shinn (2004)	Name the larger of two items: number sets 0 to 20	1st	52	Woodcock-Johnson Applied Problems Timed computation	.79 .70
Gersten, Clarke, Dimino, and Rolfhus (2011)	Name the larger of two items: number sets 0 to 20 for K and 0 to 99 for 1st	K 1st	323 348	Terra Nova	.49 .62
Lembke and Foegen (2009)	Name the larger of two items: number sets 0 to 10 and 0 to 20 (i.e., 13:8)	K 1st	44 28	Test of Early Mathematics Ability-3	.35 .43
Seethaler and Fuchs (2010)	Name the larger of two items: number sets 0 to 10	K	196	Early Math Diagnostic Assessment: 　Math Reasoning 　Numerical Operations Key Math–Revised: 　Numeration 　Estimation	 .53 .75 .34 .65

Note: All coefficients $p < .05$ unless noted otherwise.
[a]All measures were timed.
[b]All study samples were from a single district except for Lembke and Foegen, which sampled three districts in two states, and Gersten et al., which sampled four districts in two states.
[c]All predictive validity measured screeners administered in the fall and mathematics outcomes administered in the spring of that same year. Although Seethaler & Fuchs calculated two predictive validity coefficients, only the coefficients from fall and spring of kindergarten were used in this table.

administered in the spring of third grade. All coefficients were statistically significant at the .05 level with the exception of the magnitude comparison measure used by Baglici et al. (2010), which was nonsignificant. Note that the number of participants varied from 28 to 483, with a median of 197. The majority of studies we reviewed used single proficiency screeners rather than multiple proficiency screeners. However, across studies, predictive validity was similar for the single versus multiple proficiency screeners, with correlations ranging from .02 to .79 with a median of .62 for single proficiency and .40 to .74 with a median of .63 for multiple proficiency measures. With the exception of the correlation of .02, the set of validity coefficients are, in general, quite acceptable.

Single Proficiency Measures

The single proficiency measures tend to be quite brief, often only taking 1 or 2 minutes. Thus, all are efficient screeners.

Screeners are always validated by performance on some end-of-the-year measure of mathematics proficiency. Typically, these outcome measures are broad measures of mathematics proficiency, such as the widely used Terra Nova (CTB/McGraw-Hill, 2008) or Woodcock-Johnson Applied Problems test (Woodcock, McGrew, & Mather, 2001), and the Test of Early Mathematics Ability (TEMA-3; Ginsburg & Baroody, 2003), a test that covers a wide array of concepts and procedures involving whole numbers, the major curriculum emphasis in the primary grades. The question we always ask in conducting predictive validity studies is this: How well does the screener predict student performance in mathematics at the end of the school year?

Of the single proficiency assessments, magnitude comparison was the one most frequently used (Chard et al., 2005; Clarke et al., 2008; Clarke & Shinn, 2004; Gersten et al., 2011; Lembke & Foegen, 2009; Seethaler & Fuchs, 2010). Most of these measures (see Table 2.2) require students to name the larger of two items, with number sets ranging from 0 to 10 for kindergarten students and 0 to 20 for first-grade students. For kindergarten measures, a range of numbers

Table 2.3.   Measures of strategic counting

Study	Screening measure[a]	Grade	n[b]	Outcome measure	Predictive validity[c]
Baglici, Codding, and Tryon (2010)	Name the missing number in a string of numbers between 0 and 20	K	61	Timed mathematics computation	.47
Clarke, Baker, Smolkowski, and Chard (2008)	Name the missing number in a string of numbers between 0 and 10	K	254	Stanford Early School Achievement Test	.64
Clarke and Shinn (2004)	Name the missing number in a string of numbers between 0 and 20	1st	52	Woodcock-Johnson Applied Problems	.72
				Math computation probes	.67
Gersten, Clarke, Dimino, and Rolfhus (2011)	Name the missing number in a string of numbers between 0 and 20 for K and 0 and 99 for 1st	K 1st	323 348	Terra Nova	.48 .55
Lembke and Foegen (2009)	Name the missing numbers in a pattern: counting by ones to 20, by fives to 50, and by tens to 100 (i.e., 6 _ 8 9). Exact same items for K and 1st.	K 1st	44 28	Test of Early Mathematics Ability–3	.37 .68
Methe, Hintze, and Floyd (2008)	Students "count on" four numbers from a given number between 1 and 20 (e.g., experimenter says 8 and student says 9, 10, 11)	K	64	Test of Early Mathematics Ability–3	.46

Note: All coefficients $p < .05$ unless noted otherwise.
[a]All measures were timed.
[b]All study samples were from a single district except for Lembke and Foegen, which sampled three districts in two states, and Gersten et al., which sampled four districts in two states.
[c]All predictive validity measured screeners administered in the fall and mathematics outcomes administered in the spring of that same year.

Table 2.4. Fact retrieval

Study	Screening measure[a]	Grade	n[b]	Outcome measure	Predictive validity[c]
Bryant, Bryant, Gersten, Scam-macca, and Chavez (2008)	TEMI: addition/subtraction (sums or minuends range from 0 to 18)	1st	126	Stanford Achievement Test–10	.55
Gersten, Clarke, Dimino, and Rolfhus (2011)	Basic facts: Students are presented 40 problems that can be composed and decomposed in base-10 system	1st	329	Terra Nova	.50

Note: All coefficients $p < .05$ unless noted otherwise.
Key: TEMI = Texas Early Mathematics Inventories.
[a]All measures were timed.
[b]All study samples were from a single district except for Gersten et al., which sampled four districts in two states.
[c]All predictive validity measured screeners administered in the fall and mathematics outcomes administered in the spring of that same year.

beyond 10 is likely to be too difficult for students, particularly during fall administrations, and results in lower predictive validity. The study with the lowest predictive validity (Baglici et al., 2010) used a timed mathematics computation outcome, which is weakly related to the skills required for magnitude comparison.

For the strategic counting measures (see Table 2.3), students name the missing number in a sequence of numbers, typically between 0–10 or 20. The Lembke and Foegen (2009) measure requires students to count by ones to 20, fives to 50, and tens to 100 and, unlike the other measures noted in the table, uses the same items for kindergarten and first grade. Counting by fives and tens is an advanced skill for most kindergarten students and may account for the low predictive validity (.37) obtained for the kindergarten sample. In addition, the coefficient obtained for the first-grade sample was moderately strong (.68), which demonstrates the need for screening measures to differentiate items for varying grade levels.

The fact retrieval measures (see Table 2.4) included both addition and subtraction, with sums and minuends ranging from 0 to 18, and placed the problems in rows. Students were asked to answer as many of the problems as they could in 1 minute. Only one study measured story problems as a single proficiency (see Table 2.5). Locuniak and Jordan (2008) presented the word problems orally

Table 2.5. Exploratory measures: Word problems as a reasonable long-term predictor

Study	Screening measure[a]	Grade	n[b]	Outcome measure	Grade outcome	Predictive validity[c]
Locuniak and Jordan (2008)	Eight-item story problems with four addition and four subtraction story problems	K	198	Calculation fluency	Middle of 2nd	.51

Note: All coefficients $p < .05$ unless noted otherwise.
[a]Untimed measure.
[b]Study samples were from a single district.
[c]Correlated the fall of kindergarten screening measure with criterion measures administered in the winter of second grade.

Table 2.6. Multiple number proficiency tests

Study	Screening measure[a]	Grade	n	Outcome measure	Grade outcome	Predictive validity[b]
Baker, Gersten, Flojo, Katz, Chard, and Clarke (2002)	Number Knowledge Test: (takes about 10 to 15 minutes)	K	64	Stanford Achievement Test–9	1st	.73
Jordan, Glutting, and Ramineni (2008)	Number Sense Brief: 33 items assessing counting, one-to-one correspondence, number recognition, nonverbal addition and subtraction	K	200	Woodcock-Johnson–III	3rd	.63
Seethaler and Fuchs (2010)	Number Sense: 30 items	K	196	Early Math Diagnostic Assessment:	K	
				Math Reasoning		.56
				Numerical Operations		.62
				Key Math–Revised:		
				Numeration		.40
				Estimation		.74

Notes: All coefficients $p < .05$.
[a]All measures were timed except Number Sense and Number Knowledge Test.
[b]Although Seethaler and Fuchs calculated two predictive validity coefficients, only the fall and spring of kindergarten were used in this table.

because few of the kindergarteners could read at this point in the school year. The measure included four addition and four subtraction problems and was phrased as "Jim has 3 pennies. Jill gives him 6 more pennies. How many pennies does Jim have now?"

This type of quick assessment proved to demonstrate reasonable long-term predictive validity. It also seems a good screening measure to use because it targets a key focal area for kindergarten and first grade—use of mathematics to solve simple problems that occur in everyday life. Another reason that this seems a good idea for screening is that earlier researchers discovered that many kindergartners have a much easier time solving the problem in the previous paragraph than the purely symbolic representation, $6 + 3 = ?$ (Riley, Greeno, & Heller, 1983).

Single proficiency measures can quickly identify students whose mathematics achievement is on track or at risk in one or more critical areas related to development of number sense/number proficiency, the most critical component of the early elementary grade mathematics curriculum. However, as with any screening measure, these brief measures cannot provide a full diagnostic profile.

Multiple Proficiency Measures

In contrast, multiple proficiency measures address a wide array of whole number concepts and procedures including counting and skip counting, magnitude comparisons, simple arithmetic word problems, simple addition and subtraction, and estimation. These measures typically provide only a total or composite score. Although one might expect multiple proficiency measures to demonstrate better predictive validity than the single proficiency measures because they attempt to encompass a wide range of proficiencies and skills and cover numerous aspects of mathematical skills, the research we have reviewed showed them to be comparable.

Much of the research in this area is quite new, but appears to be equally promising. Research to date demonstrates that measures encompassing multiple aspects of number competence, such as the NKT (Okamato & Case, 1996) and Number Sense Brief (Jordan et al., 2008), tend to demonstrate comparable, predictive validity (median of .63) to the briefer, single proficiency measures (median of .62). This is impressive because most of these studies look at longer-term prediction (12 months to almost 3 years, and typically predictive validity decreases for longer time intervals). The NKT seems to be the strongest in the set, but larger scale research is necessary to confirm this.

WHAT THINGS SHOULD WE CONSIDER WHEN SELECTING MEASURES AND INTERPRETING SCORES?

Predictive Validity

Predictive validity is the sine qua non of screening measures. The index, a correlation coefficient that ranges from 0 to 1, tells us how well the screener accurately predicts subsequent mathematics performance.

According to the U.S. Department of Education's *RTI Practice Guide for Math*,[1] "Greater predictive validity means that schools can be more confident that decisions based on screening data are accurate" (Gersten et al., 2009, p. 14). Obviously, the higher the predictive validity, the better. Ideally, measures would predict at .70 or higher and the developer would supply information on mathematics achievement 2 or even 3 years after the screener is administered. However, given the current state of the field, we recommend that schools and districts employ measures with predictive validity coefficients of at least .50 within a school year.

The tables in this chapter provide up-to-date information on screening measures that could be gleaned from the extant research. However, there currently is a good deal of work going on in the field, and we urge readers to also consult the Screening Tools Chart of the National RTI Center (http://www.rti4 success.org/screeningTools) for current information.

Reliability

"Reliability is an index of the consistency and precision of a measure" (Gersten et al., 2009, p. 14). For screening measures, we want to ensure that two testers will give the same student very similar scores. Thus, we need to ensure that intertester reliability is at least .80. This is rarely a problem in this field at the

---

[1]The *RTI Practice Guide for Math*, a resource available online at http://ies.ed.gov/ncee/wwc/pdf/practiceguides/rti_math_pg_042109.pdf, is a practical guide for educators on the evidence-based features of any solid RTI framework. The practice guide, produced by an expert panel convened by the (Gersten R. et al., 2009) U.S. Department of Education's What Works Clearinghouse, offers recommendations for providing remediation in math through the RTI process to students in elementary and middle school.

current point in time. We also want to ensure that scores do not vary much when alternate forms are given. We want alternate form reliability to be at least .80. In this chapter, we do not actually report reliabilities for the various screening measures because all of them demonstrate reliabilities above .80, and often above .90.

Efficiency

The term *efficiency* refers to how quickly a screening measure can be administered, scored, and analyzed for all of the students. Screening measures vary in efficiency, with some taking as little as 5 minutes to administer and others as long as 20 minutes. When selecting screening measures, schools need to consider both the efficiency and the intended use. For example, multicomponent measures tend to be time-consuming for administering to an entire school population.

As a rule, we recommend that a screening measure require no more than 20 minutes to administer; this enables collection of a substantial amount of information in a reasonable time frame. In addition, schools should select screening measures that have greater efficiency if their technical adequacy (predictive validity, reliability) is roughly equivalent to less-efficient measures.

Cut Scores

A predetermined cut score is a necessary component of a screening measure used to identify at-risk students. However, it is important to remember that screening is just a way of determining which students are *likely* to need help. If a student scores poorly on a screening measure or screening battery, especially if the score is at or near a cut point, then it is beneficial to continue to monitor his or her progress to determine whether additional instruction is necessary. The What Works Clearinghouse panel recommended:

> Schools alleviate concern about students just above or below the cut score by screening students twice during the year. The second screening in the middle of the year allows another check on these students and also serves to identify any students who may have been at risk and grown substantially in their mathematics achievement—or those who were on-track at the beginning of the year but have not shown sufficient growth. (Gersten et al., 2009, p. 14).

Some of the measures we describe have already developed cut scores from samples that encompass districts from around the United States. In that case, it is reasonable to use those cut scores. However, it is certainly possible to develop your own by seeing how well the screener predicts end-of-year achievement on some measure of mathematics achievement. This would probably entail work with the research department of the school district or the school psychologist. Some districts choose an at-risk criterion as scoring below the 35th percentile on a nationally normed test of mathematics achievement. We then would find the score on the screener that corresponds to at least 75% of students reaching this criterion.

Because this field is changing so quickly, we urge visits to the web site of the National RTI Center for updates on cut scores and screening strategies. We suspect that more developers will establish cut scores based on national samples in the very near future.

HAVE WE BEEN SUCCESSFUL IN EARLY MATHEMATICS SCREENING MEASURES?

Even though the empirical evidence on mathematics screeners is still in the beginning stages, we have gained some important insights from the studies that have been conducted thus far. On the one hand, the research to date shows that measures of magnitude comparison and strategic counting serve as valid and quick screeners for students in kindergarten and first grade, on the other hand, single-proficiency screeners that assess fact retrieval are not developmentally appropriate for students in kindergarten or the beginning of first grade. Fact retrieval measures are better used as a screener at the middle and end of first grade, when retrieval has become more automatic for many students. In addition, research by Locuniak and Jordan (2008) demonstrated that measures of word problems administered in kindergarten can be used as a reasonable long-term predictor. This measure predicted second-grade calculation fluency.

We also know that measures encompassing multiple aspects of number competence, such as the NKT (Okamato & Case, 1996) and Number Sense Brief (Jordan et al., 2008) show promise. We were surprised that they did not seem to predict better than the single proficiency measures, at least for kindergartners and first graders. We suspect that the multiple proficiency measures are the best way to go for third grade and beyond, however.

In the near future, we envision advances in several directions. The first is the development of screening batteries that not only demonstrate predictive validities in the .70 range and above, but also are efficient. We also envision more research attention paid to issues of *classification accuracy*, of determining the percentage of students who are false positives (i.e., score below the cutoff score and yet do fine without any intervention) and false negatives (students who really need help but who score above the cutoff). These improvements will require large sample research and use of increasingly sophisticated statistical techniques. We also envision increased use of technology to provide students with items of appropriate difficulty. At the current time, however, we do possess screening measures that are efficient and useful for implementation of RTI in mathematics while future refinement and development work occurs.

REFERENCES

Baglici, S.P., Codding, R., & Tryon, G. (2010). Extending the research on the tests of early numeracy: Longitudinal analyses over two school years. *Assessment for Effective Intervention, 35*(2), 89–102.

Baker, S., Gersten, R., Flojo, J., Katz, R., Chard, D., & Clarke, B. (2002). *Preventing mathematics difficulties in young children: Focus on effective screening of early number sense delays* (Technical Report No. 0305). Eugene, OR: Pacific Institutes for Research.

Bryant, D.P., Bryant, B.R., Gersten, R., Scammacca, N., & Chavez, M. (2008). Mathematics intervention for first and second grade students with mathematics difficulties: The effects of tier 2 intervention delivered as booster lessons. *Remedial and Special Education, 29*(1), 20–32.

Chard, D.J., Clarke, B., Baker, S., Otterstedt, J., Braun, D., & Katz, R. (2005). Using measures of number sense to screen for difficulties in mathematics: Preliminary findings. *Assessment for Effective Intervention, 30,* 3–14.

Clarke, B., Baker, S., Smolkowski, K., & Chard, D.J. (2008). An analysis of early numeracy curriculum-based measurement: Examining the role of growth in student outcomes. *Remedial and Special Education, 29,* 46–57.

Clarke, B., Gersten, R., Dimino, J., & Rolfhus, E. (in press). *Assessing Student Proficiency in Early Number Sense* (working title). Longmont, CO: Cambium Learning Sopris.

Clarke, B., & Shinn, M. (2004). A preliminary investigation into the identification and development of early mathematics curriculum-based measurement. *School Psychology Review, 33,* 234–248.

CTB/McGraw-Hill. (2008). *Terra Nova, Third Edition Complete Battery.* Monterey, CA: Author.

Duncan, G.J., Dowsett, C.J., Claessens, A., Magnuson, K., Huston, A.C., Klebanov, P., et al. (2007). School readiness and later achievement. *Developmental Psychology, 43,* 1428–1446.

Geary, D.C. (2004). Mathematics and learning disabilities. *Journal of Learning Disabilities, 37,* 4–15.

Gersten, R., Beckmann, S., Clarke, B., Foegen, A., Marsh, L., Star, J.R., et al. (2009). *Assisting students struggling with mathematics: Response to intervention (RtI) for elementary and middle schools* (NCEE 2009-4060). Washington, DC: National Center for Education Evaluation and Regional Assistance, Institute of Education Sciences, U.S. Department of Education. Retrieved from http://ies.ed.gov/ncee/wwc/publications/practiceguides/

Gersten, R., Clarke, B., Dimino, J., & Rolfhus, E. (2011). *Universal screening measures of number sense and number proficiency for K-1: Preliminary findings* (Report No. 2011-1). Los Alamitos, CA: Instructional Research Group.

Gersten, R., Clarke, B., Jordan, N.C., Newman-Gonchar, R., Haymond, K., & Wilkins, C. Universal screening in mathematics for students in the primary grades. *Exceptional Children* (under review).

Gersten, R., Clarke, B., & Mazzocco, M. (2007). Historical and contemporary perspectives on mathematical learning disabilities. In D.B. Berch & M.M.M. Mazzocco (Eds.), *Why is math so hard for some children? The nature and origins of mathematical learning difficulties and disabilities* (pp. 7–29). Baltimore: Paul H. Brookes Publishing Co.

Ginsburg, H.P., & Baroody, A.J. (2003). *Test of Early Mathematics Ability—Third Edition.* Los Angeles: Western Psychological Services.

Goldman, S.R., Pellegrino, J.W., & Mertz, D.L. (1988). Extended practice of basic addition facts: Strategy changes in learning disabled students. *Cognition and Instruction, 5,* 223–265.

Hasselbring, T., Sherwood, R., Bransford, J., Fleenor, K., Griffith, D., & Goin, L. (1988). Evaluation of a level-one instructional videodisc program. *Journal of Educational Technology Systems, 16,* 151–169.

Jordan, N.C., Kaplan, D., Ramineni, C., & Locuniak, M.N. (2009). Early math matters: Kindergarten number competence and later mathematics outcomes. *Developmental Psychology, 45,* 850–867.

Jordan, N.C., Glutting, J., & Ramineni, C. (2008). A number sense assessment tool for identifying children at risk for mathematical difficulties. In A. Dowker (Ed.), *Mathematical difficulties: Psychology and intervention* (pp. 45–58). San Diego: Academic Press.

Kalchman, M., Moss, J., & Case, R. (2001). Psychological models for the development of mathematical understanding: Rational numbers and functions. In S. Carver & D. Klahr (Eds.), *Cognition and instruction: Twenty-five years of progress* (pp. 1–38). Mahwah, NJ: Lawrence Erlbaum Associates.

Lembke, E.S., & Foegen, A. (2009). Identifying early numeracy indicators for kindergarten and grade 1 students. *Learning Disabilities Research & Practice, 24,* 12–20.

Locuniak, M.N., & Jordan, N.C. (2008). Using kindergarten number sense to predict calculation fluency in second grade. *Journal of Learning Disabilities, 41,* 451–459.

Methe, S.A., Hintze, J.M., & Floyd, R.G. (2008). Development and validation of early numeracy skill indicators. *School Psychology Review, 37,* 359–373.

Morgan, P.L., Farkas, G., & Wu, Q. (2009). Five-year growth trajectories of kindergarten children with learning difficulties in mathematics. *Journal of Learning Disabilities, 42,* 306–321.

National Center on Response to Intervention. (n.d.). *Screening tools chart*. Retrieved from http://www.rti4success.org/screeningTools

Okamato, Y., & Case, R. (1996). Exploring the microstructure of children's central conceptual structures in the domain of number. *Monographs of the Society for Research in Child Development, 61*, 27–59.

Riley, M.S., Greeno, J.G., & Heller, J.H. (1983). Development of children's problem solving ability in arithmetic. In H. Ginsburg (Ed.), *The development of mathematical thinking* (pp. 109–151). New York: Academic Press.

Seethaler, P.M., & Fuchs, L.S. (2010). The predictive utility of kindergarten screening for math difficulty. *Exceptional Children, 77*(1), 37–60.

Siegler, R.S., & Robinson, M. (1982). The development of numerical understandings. In H. Reese & L. Lipsitt (Eds.), *Advances in Child Development and Behavior* (pp. 241–311). New York: Academic Press.

Stock, P., Desoete, A., & Roeyers, H. (2010). Detecting children with arithmetic disabilities from kindergarten: Evidence from a 3-year longitudinal study on the role of preparatory arithmetic abilities. *Journal of Learning Disabilities, 43*(3), 250–268.

Woodcock, R.W., McGrew, K.S., & Mather, N. (2001). *Woodcock-Johnson III Normative Update Tests of Achievement*. Rolling Meadows, IL: Riverside Publishing.

3 Understanding the *R* in RTI

What We Know and What We Need to Know About Measuring Student Response in Mathematics

Ben Clarke, Erica S. Lembke,
David D. Hampton, and Elise Hendricker

Explain the concepts underlying response to intervention (RTI) to most educators—or even noneducators—and RTI immediately makes sense. Students receive research-based instruction and their response, or nonresponse, to that instruction determines whether they receive additional, more intensive intervention (Clarke et al., 2010). But underlying this relatively simple concept are a number of critical assumptions that require further examination.

There are two pillars upon which any RTI model rests:

1. Research-based instruction
2. The ability to measure response to research-based instruction in a valid and reliable fashion

A number of chapters in this book will cover evidence-based approaches to instructional interventions, but this chapter will delve more deeply into the other aspect of RTI. That is, it will cover the "response" in "response to intervention" and, specifically, how we measure a student's response to intervention in an accurate and educationally meaningful way.

Step into any school today and you are likely to see a number of critical supports designed to improve student achievement in the area of reading. Schools may utilize a protected 90-minute block of reading instruction, screen students for reading difficulties, provide research-based interventions, monitor student progress toward critical goals, and use reading coaches or specialists to support teachers. Take a second look and you are likely to recognize that the same level of support is often missing in the area of mathematics. Although this is the case today, it is quickly changing. Recent interest in mathematics (National Mathematics Advisory Panel [NMAP], 2008) and implementing

RTI models in mathematics (Gersten et al., 2009) coupled with the revision of the Individuals with Disabilities Education Act (IDEA [PL 108-446]; 2004) and subsequent changes to state regulations suggest that soon many schools and educators will begin to pay renewed attention to mathematics instruction and the support educators provide in their schools to students struggling with mathematics. As this process begins, what do educators need to know about progress monitoring in mathematics? This chapter will attempt to summarize where the field stands today—what tools are in use, what is the evidence supporting their use, what are current shortcomings, and what next steps we believe the field must take for RTI in mathematics to truly encapsulate the *R* in RTI.

THE RELATIONSHIP BETWEEN SCREENING AND PROGRESS MONITORING

As detailed in Chapter 2 (Gersten et al., this volume), screening students for difficulties in mathematics is a critical component of any effective RTI model. This chapter on progress monitoring is closely linked to screening because many screening measures are also used as progress monitoring measures (e.g., AIMSweb Mathematics Measures).

Fuchs (2004) proposed a framework for assessing the quality of screening and progress monitoring measures. The first stage is an appraisal of technical characteristics of the measure based on only one administration of the measure. This is the best way to examine whether the measure is reliable. Two types of reliability should be examined for progress monitoring measures: interrater and alternate forms. The first provides data on the extent to which a student's score remains the same when two different testers administer the same test. Because progress monitoring occurs on a frequent basis, alternate forms of the same measure are used to measure growth. Alternate form reliability tells us whether or not the score of a given student varies across the different forms.

The essential validity information for progress monitoring measures differs slightly from screening measures. For screening, our major interest is *predictive* validity—how well the measure predicts future performance and classifies children as at risk or not at risk. For progress monitoring, we are most interested in *concurrent* validity—how well the measure correlates with an assessment of mathematics performance administered at approximately the same point in time.

In addition, one aspect of *construct* validity is absolutely critical for progress monitoring measures—how sensitive the measure is to growth. Growth data usually are provided in the form of weekly or biweekly growth rates, which are comparable to the slope of the student growth line. Because growth is the central emphasis in progress monitoring, measures must show that they are sensitive to growth over relatively brief periods of time.

In addition to the evaluation of progress monitoring measures based on their technical characteristics (i.e., reliability, validity, capacity to detect growth), important consideration should be given to other design features. Of particular importance is the efficiency of the measure. Because progress monitoring occurs on a regular basis (e.g., weekly), schools must weigh factors such as whether measures are timed or untimed and whether they are administered to a group or individually. When other factors are equal, we recommend using measures that provide quality data in the most efficient manner possible (Gersten et al., 2009). (For a detailed review on the process of implementing progress monitoring and the selection and evaluation of progress monitoring goals, see Shapiro, 2008.)

CURRENT PROGRESS MONITORING MEASURES

Progress monitoring measures currently available for use are reviewed here and presented based on student grade level. In a recent review of 32 studies that were deemed technically adequate (Foegen, Jiban, & Deno, 2007), Foegen and her colleagues found that the majority of research on progress monitoring measures focused on the elementary level, with a few studies at the middle-school level and no studies at the high-school level.[1] The National Center on Response to Intervention (http://www.rti4success.org) recommends screening and progress monitoring tools based on expert review. Because this web site is updated at least once a year, we strongly recommend use of this resource for updated research findings and information on progress monitoring measures. A brief review of measures in early, elementary, and secondary mathematics follows.

Early Mathematics Measures (Grades K–1)

Research in the area of early mathematics screening and progress monitoring has focused on students' general understanding of mathematical concepts and their development of number sense. Measures typically focus on discrete dimensions of mathematics proficiency such as the ability to compare magnitudes or to use strategic counting (e.g., Lembke & Foegen, 2009). The focus on discrete proficiencies differs from later grades, in which more broad-based measures that sample the year's key topics are typically used. (For a more detailed review of the construction of early screening measures, see Gersten et al., this volume.) Table 3.1 summarizes the data on these measures, including reliability, criterion validity, and weekly growth rates.

Across the various studies, there appears to be a consensus that three aspects of number knowledge make the most sense for progress monitoring measures of kindergartners and first graders. These three areas are number identification, magnitude comparison (sometimes called *quantity discrimination*), and strategic counting knowledge (such as the missing number assessment by Clarke & Shinn [2004]). These tasks all have adequate reliability and acceptable concurrent validity, with validity increasing as students move into first grade. Criterion validity was in the range of .49 to .80 across all measures and stronger for first-

---

[1]Foegen, Jiban, and Deno (2007) conducted an extensive review of progress monitoring measures in mathematics, and should be referred to for more information, specifically on technical adequacy of the measures.

Table 3.1. Technical adequacy of early mathematics measures, Grades K–1

Study	Grade level	Alternate form reliability	Criterion validity	Growth rates (weekly)
		Counting knowledge		
Baglici, Codding, and Tryon (2010; using TEN measures)	K–1			.65 digits (K) .34 digits (1st)
Clarke, Baker, Smolkowski, and Chard (2008)	K		Concurrent: SESAT: .55–.59	1.23 units
Clarke and Shinn (2004; using TEN measures)	1	.93; test–retest: .78–.80	Number Knowledge Test: .70 WJ-AP: .60–.64 M-CBM: .49–.50	.55 units
		Number identification		
Baglici et al. (2010; using TEN measures)	K–1	.71–.84		.11 digits (K) .15 digits (1st)
Lembke and Foegen (2009)	K–1	K: .91–.92 1st: .87–.90 Test–retest (median of three scores): K: .83–.87	MBA: K: .52; 1st: .49 Teacher ratings: K: .47–.61; 1st: .46–.60 TEMA: K: .33; 1st: .52 SESAT: 1st: .52	.79 digits (K) .25 digits (1st)
Clarke et al. (2008)	K		Concurrent: SESAT: .53–.61	.80 units
Lembke, Foegen, Whittaker, and Hampton (2008)	K–1	K: .79–.93 1st: .77–.89	Teacher ratings: K: .44–.66; 1st: .03–.70 SESAT: 1st: .47,	.34 digits (K) .24 digits (1st)
Chard, Clarke, Baker, Otterstadt, Braun, and Katz (2005)	K–1		Number Knowledge Test: K: .58–.65; 1st: .56–.58	1.3 digits (K) .88 digits (1st)
Clarke and Shinn (2004; using TEN measures)	1	.89–.93 Test–retest: .76–.85	Number Knowledge Test: .70 WJ-AP: .63–.65 M-CBM: .60–.66	.47 units
		Magnitude comparison (quantity discrimination)		
Baglici et al. (2010; using TEN measures)	K–1	.89–.91		.21 digits (K and 1st)
Lembke and Foegen (2009)	K–1	K: .83–.89 1st: .81–.89 Test–retest (median of three scores): K: .84–.86; 1st: .84–.91	MBA: K: .38–.50; 1st: .31–.48 Teacher ratings: K: .46–.59; 1st: .56–.66 TEMA: K: .45; 1st: .57 SESAT: 1st: .60	.49 digits (K) .12 digits (1st)
Clarke et al. (2008)	K		Concurrent: SESAT: .62	.51 units
Lembke et al. (2008)	K–1	K: .83–.91 1st: .70–.85	Teacher ratings: K: .55–.62; 1st: .04–.75 SESAT: 1st– .50	.27 digits (K) .12 digits (1st)
Chard et al. (2005)	K–1		Number Knowledge Test: K: .50–.55; 1st: .45–.53	.28 digits (K) .42 digits (1st)

Study	Grade level	Alternate form reliability	Criterion validity	Growth rates (weekly)
Clarke and Shinn (2004; using TEN measures)	1	.92–.93 Test–retest: .85–.86	Number Knowledge Test: .80 WJ-AP: .71–.79 M-CBM: .71–.75	.36 units
Missing number				
Baglici et al. (2010; using TEN measures)	K–1	.81–.86		.33 digits (K) .02 digits (1st)
Lembke and Foegen (2009)	K–1	K: .59–.75 1st: .73–.81 Test–retest (median of three scores): K: .79–.82; 1st: .78–.88	MBA: K: .49–.57; 1st: .44–.45 Teacher ratings: K: .57–.64; 1st: .56–.70 TEMA: K: .48; 1st: .54 SESAT: 1st: .75	.17 digits (K) .03 digits (1st)
Clarke et al. (2008)	K		Concurrent: SESAT: .60–.64	.28 units
Lembke et al. (2008)	K–1	K: .76–.82 1st: .61–.79	Teacher ratings: K: .50–.64; 1st: .21–.61 SESAT: 1st: .21	.15 digits (K) .11 digits (1st)
Chard et al. (2005)	K–1		Number Knowledge Test: K: .64–.69; 1st: .61,	.33 digits (K) .35 digits (1st)
Clarke and Shinn (2004; using TEN measures)	1	.78–.83 Test–retest: .79–.81	Number Knowledge Test: .74 WJ-AP: .68–.69 M-CBM: .74–.75	.23 units

Key: TEN, Test of Early Numeracy; M-CBM, Mathematics Curriculum Based Measures; OC, oral counting; WJ-AP, Woodcock-Johnson Applied Problems; SESAT, Stanford Early School Achievement Test; MBA, Mini Battery of Achievement.

grade students, particularly for the quantity discrimination (.71 to .80) and missing number measures (.68 to .75).

Of greatest importance for purposes of progress monitoring is the sensitivity to growth. Weekly growth rates are available for the majority of measures in Table 3.1; they vary across studies, but are typically below 1 point per week, with most falling between .25 and .5 points per week. The growth rates found across the studies are particularly problematic given that they are used to evaluate RTI. For example, if a first-grade student is receiving an intervention and having his or her progress monitored with a measure of quantity discrimination (estimated growth of .3 per week), it would take roughly 3 weeks to document a gain of 1 point and 6 weeks to document a gain of 2 points if the measure were perfectly reliable. However, these measures are far from perfectly reliable, with alternate-form reliabilities ranging from .78 to .99. Thus, the confidence educators would have in making a decision about student progress would be limited by the time it would take to see a gain of 1 or 2 points and, even more so, severely constrained by knowledge that an increase of 1 or 2 points on a measure could be attributable to either a true change in the student's understanding of mathematics or fluctuation because of nonequivalence between alternate forms of a measure.

Researchers have begun to examine the equivalence of forms used to monitor progress in the area of reading (e.g., Oral Reading Fluency) and their impact on the shape of growth trajectories and estimates of growth (Francis et al., 2008) but to date this question has not been examined in the area of mathematics.

Elementary Mathematics Measures (Grades 2–6)

In the area of mathematics progress monitoring at the elementary level (Grades 2–6), the primary domains assessed include computation and concepts and applications. A summary of the measures that have been validated as measures of progress over time can be found in Table 3.2. As mentioned earlier in the discussion of the early mathematics measures, only those measures with validated growth rates are listed here.

Development of progress monitoring measures in mathematics with elementary-age students dates back to the late 1970s (Deno, 1985). Much of the early work involved measures of computational fluency. Most current systems

Table 3.2. Elementary mathematics measures

	Grade	Alternate form reliability	Criterion validity	Growth rates
Computation				
MBSP	2–6	.73–.93	.77–.87 (Math Computation Test) .55–.93 (Stanford Achievement Test, Math Computation Subtest)	.20–.77
Concepts and applications				
MBSP	2–6	.45–.93	.71–.81 (CTBS: Total Math) .67–.74 (CTBS: Computation) .64–.81 (CTBS: Concepts/Application)	.12–.69
AIMSweb M-CAP	2–6	.83–.89		.4 points (2nd: 50th percentile) .2 points (3rd: 50th percentile) .1 points (4th/5th: 50th percentile)

Key: MBSP, Monitoring Basic Skills Progress; CTBS, Comprehensive Test of Basic Skills; M-CAP, Mathematics Concepts and Applications.

reflect a framework first developed by Fuchs, Hamlett, and Fuchs (1990) with their development of the Monitoring Basic Skills Progress (MBSP) measures. These measures were developed by sampling proficiencies from the Tennessee state curriculum standards at that time at each grade level and formulating a representation of what mathematical skills students should master each year. Probes were based on two types of problems: 1) computation and 2) concepts and applications. Most systems based on this model have placed a heavy emphasis on computation and the use of standard algorithms to solve grade-level computation problems. Factor analytic data indicate that, although the two types of measures are highly related, they are also distinct and measure separate constructs (Thurber, Shinn, & Smolkowski, 2002).

An example of a slightly different approach to the Fuchs approach is the set of measures developed by AIMSweb. AIMSweb offers computational probes for students in Grades 1 through 6 composed of either single operations (addition, subtraction, multiplication, or division) or a mixed set of skills. Measures were developed after the identification of computational problems across grade-level curricula; advanced weighting was done to give higher importance to those problems representing computational objectives as specified in the National Council of Teachers of Mathematics (NCTM) Principles and Standards (2000). According to the AIMSweb web site (http://www.aimsweb.com/), the concepts and applications (M-CAP) measures that are accessible on the site are based on the NCTM Principles and Standards of number sense, measurement, operations, patterns and relationships, and data interpretation and analysis. Recently researchers (Alonzo, Tindal, Ulmer, & Glasgow, 2006) have begun to develop progress monitoring measures more reflective of current documents such as the NCTM Curriculum Focal Points (2006). Thus, most contemporary progress monitoring assessments include measures that assess growth in knowledge of concepts and mathematical principles and/or ability to solve word problems. It should be noted that the move in the majority of states (39 at the time of preparation of this chapter) to adopt the Common Core State Standards (2010) would seem to indicate that progress monitoring measures linked to older state standards (such as MBSP) or older NCTM documents are likely to be replaced with versions linked to Common Core State Standards or newer progress monitoring assessments linked to the Common Core State Standards.

Numerous studies have examined weekly growth rates for typically developing students on progress monitoring measures; as reported by Foegen, Jindal, and Deno (2007), the mean growth rates range from 0.25 to 0.75 units per week. For students with documented disabilities, overall mean growth across grades was 0.38 units per week (Shapiro, Edwards, & Zigmond, 2005). Additional technical adequacy data are provided in Table 3.2. The problems of low growth rates and stability of scores are also concerns for progress monitoring in the elementary grades.

Beyond the MBSP and AIMSweb measures, there are a number of commercially available measures. As mentioned previously, the National Center on RTI (http://www.rti4success.org) has a technical review committee that reviews the extant literature and then provides recommendations for both screening and progress monitoring measures based on the quality of the normative sample; availability of alternate forms; and reliability, validity, and growth data. In the area of mathematics, four additional progress monitoring tools are suggested, with varying technical adequacy: easyCBM (http://easycbm.com), mClass math (http://wirelessgeneration.com), STAR math (http://renlearn.com), and Yearly Progress Pro (YPP; http://ctb.com/yearlyprogresspro).

Secondary Mathematics Measures

Very little research is available in the area of secondary mathematics, resulting in few technically valid measures available for use with middle- and high-school students. Foegen (2000) and Deno (Foegen & Deno, 2001) have developed a basic facts measure and a timed estimation measure requiring students to choose the most accurate estimate of computational and mathematical word problems. Reliability data have been strong overall (near or above .80). However, the criterion validity for the majority of measures has been in the low-to-moderate range, with the majority of coefficients between .40 and .50 (Foegen, Jiban, & Deno, 2007). Growth rates have also been analyzed, producing a weekly growth rate of .25 for the estimation measure and .55 for basic facts, quite similar to growth rates of other mathematics measures used with younger students.

Foegen and colleagues have a promising line of research in the development of algebra- and prealgebra-based progress monitoring measures for middle and secondary school. Measures were developed by examining current algebra curricula, state standards in algebra, and high-stakes test items in algebra, with additional feedback provided by algebra teachers. Three measures (Basic Skills, Algebra Foundations, and Content Analysis–Multiple Choice) in middle school have been found to have adequate reliability and criterion validity (Foegen, 2008). Monthly data from across three school districts indicated that weekly growth rates ranged from .32 to .87 points correct, with higher growth rates found for students in more advanced algebra courses (e.g., algebra vs. prealgebra). At a minimum, all students (even those with identified disabilities) were growing at a weekly rate of .25 points correct, indicating the usefulness of these measures to detect progress in average- and low-achieving students.

GENERAL FRAMEWORK FOR IMPLEMENTING PROGRESS MONITORING

Commonly, progress monitoring data are only collected on those students who are identified as at risk during the screening process and provided intervention services. The frequency of progress monitoring is matched to the degree of a student's instructional needs (Gersten et al., 2009). For example, students receiving Tier 2 services might have their progress monitored a minimum of once per month, whereas students with more intensive instructional needs (i.e., Tier 3) would have their progress monitored on a weekly basis. If students appear to be on grade level based on screening data, in most cases, their monthly progress need not be monitored. However, all students' learning should be assessed with curriculum-embedded assessments, informal measures, and formative assessment.

Student progress is evaluated in relation to instructional goals set at the beginning of a cycle based on both the student's initial performance and the desired level of performance in the future (e.g., what score is expected after a certain period of time). In most cases, the time frame is the entire school year, although some prefer to use shorter time frames, such as 10–12 weeks, for students who are struggling. Once a goal has been selected, a set of decision rules is utilized to evaluate the effectiveness of the supplemental or intervention program. For example, a simple evaluation metric is used to consider instructional changes when a student has four consecutive data points below the expected rate of progress or the trend of data is below the expected rate of progress (Shinn et al., 2002).

Consider a first-grade student, Jim, who is identified as at risk based on screening data. The starting point, 5, for Jim's progress monitoring goal is his score on the initial screening assessment (see Figure 3.1, Jim's progress monitoring graph). The approximate weekly rate of growth for a first-grade student in quantity discrimination is .3 digits, or correct answers per week. Jim's teacher multiplies the number of weeks left in the school year (36) by .3 to find Jim's expected amount of growth across the year. She adds the expected amount of growth she would like Jim to make (a 12-digit increase) to his initial data point from the screening starting point (5) to derive a long-term goal of 17 digits correct. Because Jim is significantly behind his peers, his teacher decides to monitor his progress weekly. Jim's teacher tracks his progress based on a set of decision-making rules evaluating his actual progress against his expected progress. After 8 weeks, she implements an instructional change (labeled "Instructional Phase 2" on the graph) because his *actual* growth rate (the trend

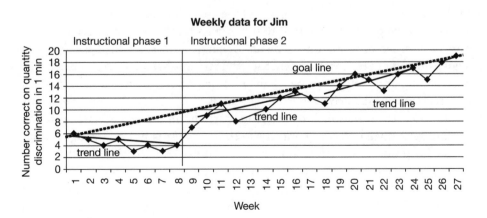

Figure 3.1.   Jim's progress monitoring graph showing weekly data on two instructional phases.

line) is not meeting his expected rate of progress (the goal line). She continues to monitor his progress, evaluating his trend line compared with his goal line to make sure his progress is on track.

LIMITS OF PROGRESS MONITORING AND SUGGESTIONS FOR THE FIELD

Although numerous mathematics measures have been found to be technically acceptable for use with students for progress monitoring purposes, we would be remiss if we did not discuss current criticisms or limits of these measures.

Measuring Conceptual Understanding

A main flaw from the perception of those within the mathematics education field is that progress monitoring measures fail to measure students' conceptual mathematical understanding, and instead identify the level of student performance under timed conditions with a greater emphasis on computation procedures than on conceptual understanding (Seeley, 2009; Woodward & Howard, 1994). In part, this reflects what we would consider a false dichotomy between conceptual understanding and procedural fluency (Wu, 1999), but some concern is valid.

Many of the most common assessments used to monitor progress are based on older state standards with a heavy emphasis on computation. We see two potential solutions to this issue. The first is to evaluate and select measures based on a more contemporary understanding of the mathematics children need to acquire. The second is to not only use progress monitoring measures reflecting more sophisticated content but also to use them in conjunction with other types of assessments. Potential sources of additional data include curriculum-embedded assessments, in-time formative assessments, and diagnostic interviews.

Curriculum-embedded assessments are found in almost all curricula or instructional programs. Typically, they occur after a period of time in which students are exposed to a particular topic and the goal is to assess whether a student has mastered the particular content that has been taught. This may occur after a lesson, a set of lessons, or a unit. The use of curriculum-embedded assessments provides immediate feedback on whether the student has mastered the content of instruction, and results can be used to refine and target instruction in cases where mastery is not achieved. One caveat is that research from the 1980s revealed that the relationship between curriculum-embedded assessments and more generalized achievement in the content area is not as strong as what is found for progress monitoring measures (Tindal et al., 1985). A reasonable approach is to use both progress monitoring measures and curriculum-embedded assessments to evaluate a student. Curriculum-embedded assessments provide immediate feedback highly related to specific instructional targets, whereas progress monitoring links mastery of specific knowledge to overall growth in the content domain (Gersten et al., 2009).

There is some confusion about the term *formative assessment* because it is also used to describe progress monitoring. However, in this case, when we refer to formative assessment, we mean teachers assessing students in real time as students are solving problems in the classroom (Heritage, 2010). The approach relies on teachers asking students probing questions to assess knowledge of the concepts underlying student actions and to build that understanding as students think about and explain their approach to problem solving (National Research Council, 2001). It should be noted that, although this is considered a valuable instructional technique, no empirical studies have validated its use in affecting student outcomes (NMAP, 2008).

A third approach we consider useful is completing a detailed skill analysis on a student's understanding of mathematics (Howell & Nolet, 2000). For example, Herb Ginsburg and his colleagues at Columbia University Teachers College developed a diagnostic interview protocol that attempts to provide detailed analyses of the thinking that underlies children's mathematical performance. The interviews are based on the idea that proficiency in mathematics requires both conceptual and procedural fluency and that these fluencies are intertwined (Ginsburg, 1997). Domains assessed include young children's counting and enumeration and older children's methods for obtaining number facts, mental calculation, written calculation, and conceptual understanding of place value and base-10. Both informal mathematics (such as mental calculation or spontaneously generated ideas about commutativity) and formal mathematics (such as use of the algorithms, bugs, and understanding of base-10 ideas) are assessed and administrators are able to create a profile of student learning by indicating strategy use, nonuse, or misuse as the student completes problems.

Although procedures such as this show promise for use in the classroom, diagnostic interviews in general can be time consuming for the classroom teacher to perform frequently with a group or subgroup of students within a classroom. Thus, it is recommended that diagnostic interviews and assessments be used judiciously and in conjunction with progress monitoring and other assessment approaches detailed previously.

Small Growth Rates

Another issue for measuring progress in mathematics is that current progress monitoring measures in mathematics, unlike progress monitoring measures in reading, have yielded very small average growth rates. Further complicating the matter of small growth rates is the notion of measurement error. Every assessment has some degree of error, but, when measurement error is great, educational decision making is negatively affected. Because a student's growth (or slope) is used to evaluate responsiveness to instruction, it is critical that any change in student performance is attributable to an increase in the student's understanding of mathematics and not caused by error in the measurement.

Measurement error can occur for many reasons, including lack of standardized procedures, but the biggest concern is that alternate forms used in progress monitoring are not of equal difficulty. When there is measurement error present, it becomes harder to interpret the results of progress monitoring. A contrasting example is in the area of weight loss, in which a long-term goal (the loss of weight) is evaluated over a period of time by using a scale. Because a scale is incredibly reliable and accurate, we can attribute any weight loss as a true change and not a function of the measure (the scale). In education if we have inaccurate measures, those that have low reliability and large measurement error, schools may make decisions about programs or students that are incorrect. For example, schools may continue ineffective programs or change effective programs (Hintze & Marcotte, 2010).

Developers and researchers of progress monitoring materials have begun to address this concern in the area of reading in two ways. Developers of many oral reading fluency measures now attempt to equate forms used in progress monitoring (Adroin & Christ, 2009). Using readability formulas to evaluate alternate forms is now common practice as well as conducting extensive field testing of passages to select materials that are roughly equivalent, thereby reducing measurement error (Yovanoff & Alonzo, 2010). Researchers have begun to calculate how much error is present in slope estimates and have used those findings to suggest durations of time that progress should be measured before making educational decisions (Christ, 2006). We suggest that developers and researchers of materials used in mathematics progress monitoring engage in similar efforts.

Other Problems with Growth Rates

Two additional considerations related to growth are important to consider. First, when growth occurs on progress monitoring measures, that growth needs to be correlated with a greater understanding of mathematics. In other words, growth has to mean something. If a student shows growth on a narrow progress monitoring measure, that growth should be accompanied by a greater understanding of mathematics as measured by a broader assessment of mathematical knowledge (e.g., a high-stakes state test).

Second, progress monitoring materials need to be sensitive to effective instructional programs (Fuchs, 2004). In other words, not only should students show growth over time, but also that growth should occur at a higher rate if the student is receiving an intervention program that has evidence of a positive impact. Again, work in evaluating oral reading fluency provides a template for similar work in mathematics.

CONCLUSION

From the early work in mathematics progress monitoring to the time of this publication, much progress has been made. Across grade levels, with more evidence in the early elementary grades, we have options for progress monitoring measures that have evidence of reliability and concurrent validity. Yet, as we move forward, there are a number of key areas that need attention. First, as a more contemporary perspective takes hold on the critical content that students must learn in mathematics, we expect new measures to be developed based on new standards and expectations for student learning. We hope that the extensive work that has been completed in the early elementary grades continues and is paired with increased interest in developing and researching measures for use in middle school and high school.

Second, we believe that to build effective progress monitoring systems, developers need to use state-of-the-art procedures to develop equivalent alternate forms to reduce measurement error, and researchers need to investigate the impact of measurement error on educational decision making. Last, serious consideration should be given to the use of technology in progress monitoring. The use of computer-based measures shows great promise, as more sophisticated assessments that allow for efficient data collection could be developed.

REFERENCES

Alonzo, J., Tindal, G., Ulmer, K., & Glasgow, A. (2006). *EasyCBM online progress monitoring assessment system.* Eugene, OR: Center for Educational Assessment Accountability. (Available at http://easycbm.com)

Ardoin, S.P., & Christ, T.J. (2009). Curriculum-based measurement of oral reading: standard errors associated with progress monitoring outcomes from DIBELS, AIMSweb, and an experimental passage set. *School Psychology Review, 38*(2), 266–283.

Baglici, S.P., Codding, R., & Tryon, G. (2010). Extending the research on the tests of early numeracy: Longitudinal analyses over two school years. *Assessment for Effective Intervention, 35*(2), 89–102.

Chard, D.J., Clarke, B., Baker, S., Otterstedt, J., Braun, D., & Katz, R. (2005). Using measures of number sense to screen for difficulties in mathematics: Preliminary findings. *Assessment for Effective Intervention, 30*(2), 3–14. doi: 10.1177/073724770503000202

Christ, T.J. (2006). Short-term estimates of growth using curriculum-based measurement of oral reading fluency: Estimating standard error of the slope to construct confidence intervals. *School Psychology Review, 35*(1), 128–133.

Clarke, B., Baker, S., Smolkowski, K., & Chard, D.J. (2008). An analysis of early numeracy curriculum-based measurement: Examining the role of growth in student outcomes. *Remedial and Special Education, 29*(1), 46–57. doi: 10.1177/0741932507309694

Clarke, B., Gersten, R., & Newman-Gonchar, R. (2010). RtI in mathematics. In T.A. Glover & S. Vaughn (Eds.), *The promise of response to intervention: Evaluating current science and practice* (pp. 187–202). New York: Guilford Press.

Clarke, B., & Shinn, M.R. (2004). A preliminary investigation into the identification and development of early mathematics curriculum-based measurement. *School Psychology Review, 33,* 234–248.

Council of Chief State School Officers. (2010). *Common core state standards initiative: Designing common state assessment systems.* Retrieved from http://www.nga.org/files/pdf/1004ngaccsso assessments.pdf

Deno, S.L. (1985). Curriculum-based measurement: The emerging alternative. *Exceptional Children, 52*(3), 219–232.

Foegen, A. (2000). Technical adequacy of general outcome measures for middle school mathematics. *Assessment for Effective Intervention, 25*(3), 175–203.

Foegen, A. (2008). Algebra progress monitoring and interventions for students with learning disabilities. *Learning Disability Quarterly, 31,* 65–78.

Foegen, A., & Deno, S. (2001). Identifying growth indicators of low-achieving students in middle school mathematics. *Journal of Special Education, 35*(1), 4–16.

Foegen, A., Jiban, C., & Deno, S. (2007). Progress monitoring measures in mathematics. *Journal of Special Education, 41*(2), 121–139.

Francis, D.J., Santi, K.L., Barr, C., Fletcher, J.M., Varisco, A., & Foorman, B.R. (2008). Form effects on the estimation of students' oral reading fluency using DIBELS. *Journal of School Psychology, 46*(3), 315–342. doi: 10.1016/j.jsp.2007.06.003

Fuchs, L. (2004). The past, present, and future of curriculum-based measurement research. *School Psychology Review, 33*(2), 188–193.

Fuchs, L., Hamlett, C., & Fuchs, D. (1990). *Monitoring basic skills progress: Basic math computation and concepts and applications programs.* Austin, TX: PRO-ED.

Gersten, R., Beckmann, S., Clarke, B., Foegen, A., March, L., Star, J.R., et al. (2009). *Assisting students struggling with mathematics: Response to intervention (RtI) for elementary and middle schools.* Washington, DC: National Center for Education Evaluation and Regional Assistance, Institute of Education Sciences, U.S. Department of Education.

Ginsburg, H.P. (1997). Mathematics learning disabilities: A view from developmental psychology. *Journal of Learning Disabilities, 30*(1), 20–33.

Heritage, M. (2010). *Formative assessment and next-generation assessment systems: Are we losing an opportunity?* Washington, DC: Council of Chief State School Officers.

Hintze, J.M., & Marcotte, A.M. (2010). Student assessment and data-based decision making. In T.A. Glover & S. Vaughn (Eds.), *The promise of response to intervention: Evaluating current science and practice* (pp. 57–77). New York: Guilford Press.

Howell, K., & Nolet, V. (2000). *Curriculum-based evaluation: Teaching and decision making* (3rd. ed.) Atlanta, GA: Wadsworth.

Individuals with Disabilities Education Improvement Act (IDEA) of 2004, PL 108-446, 20 U.S.C. §§ 1400 *et seq.*

Lembke, E., & Foegen, A. (2009). Identifying early numeracy indicators for kindergarten and first grade students. *Learning Disabilities Research & Practice, 24*(1), 12–20.

Lembke, E., Foegen, A., Whittaker, T., & Hampton, D. (2008). Establishing technically adequate measures of progress in early numeracy. *Assessment for Effective Intervention, 33*(4), 206.

National Council of Teachers of Mathematics. (2006). Curriculum focal points for prekindergarten through grade 8 mathematics: A quest for coherence. Retrieved from http://www.nctm.org/standards/focalpoints.aspx?id=282

National Council of Teachers of Mathematics. (2000). *Principles and standards for school mathematics.* Reston, VA: National Council of Teachers of Mathematics.

National Mathematics Advisory Panel. (2008). *Foundations for success: The final report of the National Mathematics Advisory Panel.* Washington, DC: U.S. Department of Education.

National Research Council. (2001). *Adding it up: Helping children learn mathematics.* In J. Kilpatrick, J. Swafford, and B. Findell (Eds.). Mathematics Learning Study Committee, Center for Education, Division of Behavioral and Social Sciences and Education. Washington, DC: National Academy Press.

Seeley, C. (2009). *Faster isn't smarter: Messages about math, teaching, and learning.* Sausalito, CA: Math Solutions.

Shapiro, E. (2008). Best practices in setting progress monitoring goals for academic skill improvement. In A. Thomas & J. Grimes (Eds.), *Best practices in school psychology* (5th ed., Vol. 2, pp. 141-158).Bethesda, MD: National Association of School Psychologists.

Shapiro, E., Edwards, L., & Zigmond, N. (2005). Progress monitoring of math among students with learning disabilities. *Assessment for Effective Instruction, 30*(2), 15–23.

Shinn, M.R., Shinn, M.M., Hamilton, C., & Clarke, B. (2002). Using curriculum-based measurement in general education classrooms to promote reading success. In M.R. Shinn, H.M. Walker, & G. Stoner (Eds.), *Interventions for academic and behavior problems II: Prevention and remedial approaches* (pp. 113–142). Bethesda, MD: National Association of School Psychologists.

Thurber, R.S., Shinn, M., & Smolkowski, K. (2002). What is measured in mathematics tests? Construct validity of curriculum-based mathematics measures. *School Psychology Review, 31*(4), 498–513.

Tindal, G., Fuchs, L.S., Fuchs, D., Shinn, M.R., Deno, S.L., & Germann, G. (1985). Empirical validation of criterion-referenced tests. *The Journal of Educational Research, 78*(4), 203–209.

Woodward, J., & Howard, L. (1994). The misconceptions of youth: Errors and their mathematical meaning. *Exceptional Children, 61*(2), 126–136.

Wu, H. (1999, Fall). Basic skills versus conceptual understanding. *American Educator,* 14–19, 50–52.

Yovanoff, P., & Alonzo, J. (2010, February). *ORF scores: Are we getting a raw deal: Equating ORF scores.* Paper presented at the Pacific Coast Research Conference, Coronado, CA.

4

Pursuing Instructional Coherence

Can Strong Tier 1 Systems Better Meet the Needs of the Range of Students in General Education Settings?

Ben Clarke, Chris T. Doabler, Scott K. Baker,
Hank Fien, Kathleen Jungjohann, and Mari Strand Cary

Response to intervention (RTI) models begin with research-based instruction delivered in the general education setting (Gersten et al., 2009). This simple statement is in fact one of the most complex challenges schools face in implementing RTI service delivery models (Fuchs, Fuchs, & Stecker, 2010; Gersten & Dimino, 2006; Vaughn & Fuchs, 2003). Schools are often left to decipher mixed messages about the role of a core program, or Tier 1, in RTI models and to deal with specific questions for which they may not have answers. Does a core program require evidence of effectiveness or is it sufficient that the program describes itself as containing material designed to reflect the current research base? What content should a core program cover? What students should receive and benefit from instruction in the general education setting?

Answers to these questions and countless others are not easy, particularly in mathematics where the research base, although it is growing, is still scant (National Research Council, 2004). A recent review of research in mathematics compared with research in reading found a ratio of 15 reading studies to every 1 math study (Gersten, Clarke, & Mazzocco, 2007). But beyond mere numbers, consider what happens every day in schools across the country. Imagine stepping into any school and examining the support provided to assist all students in becoming competent readers. It would not be uncommon to see the use of a core program that attempts to incorporate current research, a dedicated block for reading instruction of 90 minutes, supplementary and intervention programs for at-risk students at each grade level, and the use of a reading specialist or coach working with teachers and struggling students. The same visit would likely reveal dissimilar support in mathematics.

It is not that mathematics is seen as unimportant. In fact, ask any lay individual or educator what the two most critical subjects in elementary school are and you are likely to hear a response that includes reading and mathematics. So, the question becomes, how do we start building the same systems of support in mathematics as in reading so that all children develop the skills necessary to be successful in school mathematics?

The goal of this chapter is to detail our work in developing and field testing a kindergarten mathematics curriculum. Through a detailed overview of the Early Learning in Mathematics (ELM) program, we hope to answer some of the questions we posed, and at the very least begin to shed some light on how we have begun to approach some of these difficult issues. In particular, we will focus on how we think about the use of a core program in general education supporting the goals of RTI.

STARTING OFF RIGHT IN MATHEMATICS: WHY KINDERGARTEN AND WHY TIER 1?

When we began the development of ELM, we chose to focus on creating a core (Tier 1) kindergarten math program. But why? In part, we selected kindergarten on the basis of our experience working with struggling students in reading. Over the past two decades, significant changes have occurred in how schools approach reading instruction. As evidence accumulated that students who exited the early primary grades as poor readers continued to remain poor readers and developed deficits that were increasingly difficult to remediate (Lyon et al., 2001), educators and researchers began to pay greater attention to the idea of preventing these difficulties before the onset of reading failure.

The importance of prevention was also reflected in the revision of the Individuals with Disabilities Education Act (IDEA [PL 108-446]; 2004) where RTI was first formalized into law. Although RTI was initially conceptualized as a means to determine special education eligibility, equal weight was given to the prevention of academic difficulties (Fuchs et al., 2010). Response to intervention is premised upon and linked to the idea of providing intensive early intervention with struggling students to increase their chances of being successful in general education and to avoid later special education placement.

Utilizing longitudinal databases, researchers have documented the long-term math trajectories of students who struggle in the early elementary grades (i.e., kindergarten and first grade). Results across multiple studies have shown that students who do not have a successful start in mathematics during kindergarten and first grade are likely to continue struggling with mathematics in the upper elementary grades (Bodovski & Farkas, 2007; Guarino, Hamilton, Lockwood, & Rathbun, 2006; Hanich, Jordan, Kaplan, & Dick, 2001; Morgan, Farkas, & Wu, 2009; Princiotta, Flanagan, & Germino Hausken, 2006). For students with the greatest need, the consequences are severe. Findings from a study involving data from the Early Childhood Longitudinal Study–Kindergarten Cohort (ECLS-K) suggest that kindergarten students entering and exiting kindergarten who score below the 10th percentile at both time points have a 70%

likelihood of scoring below the 10th percentile at the end of fifth grade, and their achievement at the end of fifth grade is roughly 2 standard deviations below that of their peers (Morgan et al., 2009). In addition, a meta-analysis of longitudinal databases indicated that the association between early and later mathematics proficiency exceeded that of reading achievement (Duncan et al., 2007).

The findings from these studies and the preventive focus of RTI provide a compelling case that the early elementary grades offer a critical window in which to focus intensive instructional efforts to improve student mathematics achievement. However, a number of challenges are present in kindergarten. Because of practical considerations (e.g., time constraints) or tradition, many schools allocate a minimum of time to mathematics instruction for all students and do not offer intervention support to students struggling in mathematics. The time constraint is particularly vexing in half-day kindergartens where, in a mere 2.5- to 3-hour, day schools are expected to provide, at a minimum, instruction in reading (often for a mandated time period—e.g., 60 minutes), additional support in reading for struggling students, mathematics, and social skills. In our experience, a philosophical shift has taken place in the instruction of reading and the prevention of reading difficulties through targeted interventions for at-risk students; however, the same shift has not yet fully occurred in mathematics.

One approach to improving math achievement for all kindergarten students, including those at risk for math difficulties, is the delivery of effective core instruction. Effective core instruction represents the first tier in any tiered RTI model. Surprisingly enough, it is this first tier of the multitier model that is often overlooked. In part, this may be the result of the weak knowledge base about curricula typically used in Tier 1 (National Research Council, 2004) and conflicting views about what content should be covered in general education classrooms (National Mathematics Advisory Panel [NMAP], 2008). However, the first tier represents an opportunity to ensure that at-risk students receive a solid mathematical foundation that would prevent the development of more serious mathematics difficulties that in the later grades would require the use of Tier 2 or Tier 3 interventions. In kindergarten, Tier 1 may represent the only mathematics instruction that students have the opportunity to receive.

CRITICAL FEATURES OF TIER 1 CORE PROGRAMS

If a Tier 1 core program is to be implemented successfully in kindergarten, what elements need to be present? At a minimum, two key elements should form the foundation of an effective Tier 1 core program:

1. A focus on covering critical math content
2. The incorporation of research-based instructional design principles.

Schmidt, Houang, and Cogan (2002) noted that curricula used in the United States were plagued by a mile-wide, inch-deep approach, where textbooks attempt to cover a wide array of mathematical concepts, because they are based, in large part, on current state standards in mathematics. In direct contrast, a number of curricula in countries with superior achievement in mathematics to the United States take the opposite approach. In particular, the curricula of these so-called "A+" countries cover a limited number of topics and exercise greater instructional depth, resulting in students mastering foundational concepts that lay the groundwork for the more advanced mathematical content they will encounter in later grades.

Recognizing the fallacy in the mile-wide, inch-deep approach, the National Council of Teachers of Mathematics (2006) released a set of curricular focal points for each grade level with the intent of helping educators focus on the critical content students should learn at each grade level and correspondingly the type of content that should form the core of instructional programs used in classrooms. Whereas the focal points provide general guidelines, the recently released Common Core State Standards (National Governors Association, 2010) provide more specific guidance. Even though the Common Core State Standards are fewer in number than traditional state standards, they are more focused and coherent in their expectations for developing mathematical knowledge across the K–12 grade span.

Although there is only a sparse number of studies about the impact of specific mathematics programs or interventions (Agodini et al., 2009; Chard et al., 2008; Newman-Gonchar, Clarke, & Gersten, 2009; Slavin & Lake, 2008) there is a burgeoning body of research about the types of instructional or curricular design features that are most effective for students with low achievement and learning disabilities (see Gersten et al., 2009). By the term instructional design, we mean the way academic information is organized and sequenced before teacher delivery (Coyne, Kame'enui, & Carnine, 2007). Recent meta-analyses on interventions for teaching mathematics identified a number of instructional design features that were effective for enhancing the mathematics achievement of low-achieving students (Baker, Gersten, & Lee, 2002) and students with learning disabilities (Gersten et al., 2009; Kroesbergen & Van Luit, 2003). These design features include explicit and systematic instruction, and scaffolding of instruction through visual representations of mathematical ideas (for a more detailed review see Jayanthi & Gersten, Chapter 7). We briefly describe these features here, but provide greater detail of their application in ELM, later in the chapter.

- *Explicit and systematic instruction:* refers to clear teacher demonstrations, structured practice opportunities for students, verbalization of thought processes, and academic feedback. A consistent finding of math intervention research is that explicit and systematic instruction improves math outcomes for students at risk for failure (NMAP, 2008).
- *Scaffolding instruction through visual representations of math ideas:* refers to temporary instructional support to facilitate student conceptual understanding around critical mathematical content and ideas. As students achieve conceptual understanding, scaffolds are gradually removed to promote learner independence.

A curriculum that includes well-designed instructional features increases the probability that at-risk students will have access to and success with the mathematical concepts presented. And, although instructional design features are present in most, if not all, of current math curricula, accruing evidence indicates their presence can vary in both quantity and rigor (Chard & Jungjohann, 2006; Jitendra et al., 2005; Schmidt et al., 2002). For instance, in a study of four first-grade programs, Sood and Jitendra (2007) found that textbooks varied in scaffolding instruction for teaching the construct of number sense. An investigation of four widely used mathematics textbooks revealed that programs provided inadequate opportunities for students to practice new and recently acquired mathematical skills (Bryant, Bryant, Gersten, Scammacca, & Chavez, 2008). Similarly, in a recent curricular review, Doabler, Fien, Nelson-Walker, and Baker (2010) found few opportunities for explicit instruction and superficial coverage of key topics in three U.S. market-leading programs at second and fourth grades. Taken together, these findings have implications for teaching those at risk for academic failure (Carnine, 1997; Hirsch, 2002; Porter, 1989). When programs contain shortfalls in their instructional design, they adversely affect struggling learners in mastering the key topics and concepts of early mathematics. Moreover, a weak core program can undermine the effectiveness of a multitiered service-delivery model. Central to increasing the effectiveness of an RTI service delivery model is a Tier 1 math program built around critical math content and key instructional design features that research has empirically validated to increase student achievement.

ELM OVERVIEW

ELM is a comprehensive mathematics curriculum specifically designed to support a wide range of learners in kindergarten classrooms. The program consists of 120, 45-minute lessons, with supplemental 15-minute calendar activities. Every fifth lesson comprises a whole-class problem-solving activity. A cornerstone of ELM is a focus of learning to mastery. Therefore, lessons revisit content in a variety of math contexts so children engage in multiple learning opportunities and experience high rates of success.

Table 4.1 presents ELM's yearlong scope and sequence. Broken down by school quarters and content areas, the table shows the critical objectives of ELM. Table 4.1 also provides a progression of learning for each objective. For instance, in learning to rote count to 100, lessons from the first and second quarters focus on numerals up to 10 and 30, respectively. With a strong focus on learning to mastery, ELM expects students to achieve conceptual understanding and procedural fluency in these objectives. For example, students are expected to have a firm understanding of writing numbers 1 to 30 and identifying simple ordinal numerals by the end of the third quarter.

On average, lessons contain four or five activities, each of which has a primary focus on one of three content areas: number and operations, measurement, and geometry. Typically, the first activity introduces or reviews a math concept

Table 4.1. Early Learning in Mathematics instructional objectives by school year quarter

	1st Q	2nd Q	3rd Q	4th Q
Numbers and operations				
Rote counts	1–10	1–30	1–60	1–100
Reads numbers	1–10	1–30	1–60	1–100
Counts objects and pictures	1–10	1–20		
Counts on from a number	# <5	# <10	# <20	# <30
Skip counts		10s to 100	5s to 50	25s to 100
Sequences numbers	1–10	11–30	31–60	61–100
Matches sets to number	1–10	1–30		
Writes numbers	1–10	11–20	21–30	
Identifies quantity more or less	<10			
Identifies number more or less		<10		
Identifies ordinals		1st–4th	1st–5th	
Estimates number			√	√
Adds with objects and pictures		√	√	√
Subtracts with objects and pictures			√	√
Adds 1 to a number			√	
Subtracts 1 from a number				√
Geometry				
Identifies, extends, creates patterns	√	√	√	√
Identifies shapes	circle, square, triangle	rectangle, oval	hexagon	cube, sphere, cone, cylinder
Creates and interprets graphs	√	√	√	√
Measurement				
Identifies coins, value		penny, dime	nickel	quarter
Counts coins by value		penny, dime	nickel	quarter
Tells time to the hour			√	
Measures with inches				√
Calendar				
Says days of the week	√			
Identifies and says daily date	√			
Names current month and year	√			
Identifies seasons		√		
Identifies *yesterday*		√		
Identifies *tomorrow*		√		
Says months of the year			√	
Identifies month before and next			√	

or skill that is central to the lesson's overall objective. For this part of the lesson, the teacher provides concrete examples and makes explicit the focus of the activity's targeted content. The second and third activities involve either an extension of the first activity or a review of previously learned material. The fourth activity often targets previously learned material from a different content area. For example, if the first three activities focus on telling time to the hour (measurement), the fourth activity will address material related to geometry or number operations. The last activity in each lesson is a paper–pencil review.

Facilitated by the teacher, this 10- to 15-minute worksheet activity provides children with a cumulative review of the lesson's content. Worksheets also contain a "note home" (in both English and Spanish) to provide families with a snapshot of the day's math activities and encourage additional practice opportunities in the home.

Most activities focus primarily on one content area, but others cut across the different content areas. This way, children receive continuous practice in number, measurement, and geometry. For example, a measurement activity may have the students identify and count pennies to 20. Thus, students gain opportunities to practice their counting skills as well as to learn how to identify and compare numerical representations. Other activities that integrate measurement and whole number are the problem-solving activities. In these activities, students learn how to represent and interpret data, thereby providing practice in both content areas. For example, students learn how to build a picture graph (measurement) and tell how many more or less (number) are in each column.

ELM Instructional Content

ELM is designed to address the critical content kindergarten students must master both to succeed in kindergarten and to have a solid foundation for the advanced mathematics they will encounter in later grades. Whereas many intervention programs focus exclusively on number (Bryant et al., 2008; Fuchs et al., 2005), ELM provides a broader, although still tightly focused, coverage of key content areas because it is designed for use as a core program. ELM contains three mathematics strands that mirror the three kindergarten focal points specified in the National Council of Teachers of Mathematics Focal Points (NCTM, 2006) and the three domain areas identified in the Common Core State Standards (National Governors Association, 2010). There are three content strands comprising the ELM curriculum:

1. Whole number and number operations
2. Measurement
3. Geometry

The content focus also aligns with the recommendations of the National Mathematics Advisory Panel (NMAP, 2008), and other experts in the field (Cross, Woods, & Schweingruber, 2009; National Research Council, 2001; Wu, 2009). Although ELM contains three content strands, they are not given equal weight (i.e., 33% of content coverage to each strand). Rather, ELM places strong emphasis on the development of understanding whole number and operations, and utilizes parts of the content covered in the geometry and measurement strands to reinforce and further develop proficiency with whole numbers. The focus on whole number provides the foundation for later success in key mathematics topics, including rational number, and lays the groundwork for algebra readiness (NMAP, 2008). In the following section, we briefly describe each math strand.

Underlying the first ELM content strand, whole numbers and number operations, is a strong focus on the development of early number sense. Gersten and Chard defined the construct of number sense as "a child's fluidity and flexibility with numbers, the sense of what numbers mean, and an ability to perform mental mathematics and to look at the world and make comparisons" (1999, pp. 19-20). For example, the students who have a developed sense of number can make precise numerical magnitude comparisons (e.g., 10 is 7 more than 3) and use efficient counting strategies (e.g., counting on from the larger addend) to solve simple addition and subtraction problems. Although many students acquire a sense of number before entering kindergarten through informal learning experiences at home and at preschool, a considerable number of students lack these opportunities and enter school with immature levels of mathematical knowledge (National Research Council, 2001; West, Denton, & Germino-Hausken, 2000). Recognizing these different knowledge levels, ELM builds upon the informal understanding that students have of number and links it to formal work with the whole number system. ELM provides an in-depth focus on students developing understanding of whole number because this understanding is not only critical for success in kindergarten but also plays a major role in teaching children the knowledge they need to grasp more sophisticated content in the first and second grades. For example, composing and decomposing numbers from 1 to 10, a big idea of number sense (Resnick, 1983; Van de Walle, 2001), forms the basis of addition and subtraction and, eventually, multiplication and division. Within the operation of addition, composing and decomposing teaches children the relationship between a sum and its corresponding addends. In addition, teaching children to think about how a number is made up of two or more parts also facilitates mathematical problem solving ("change" word problems) and place-value concepts (Cross, Woods, & Schweingruber, 2009).

A second content focus of ELM is geometry. Geometric and spatial thinking are important components of early mathematics because they allow children to represent figures and understand their spatial environment (Clements & Sarama, 2007; Van de Walle, 2001). In ELM, lessons introduce the names and attributes of common two- and three-dimensional shapes. For example, an objective is to have children recognize and name circles, rectangles, hexagons, and ovals. Another part of the program is teaching children to recognize and extend basic AB and AABB patterns with numbers, and like and unlike objects (Clements, 2004). A number of the geometry activities are integrated with building an understanding of whole number so that a student's understanding of geometry is not built in isolation but rather is connected to critical elements of whole number.

The third strand of ELM is measurement. Children use measurement to describe and compare objects (Clements, 2004). ELM addresses the strand of measurement by teaching the concepts of time (telling time to the hour) and money (identifying and counting coins). Children also learn how to use nonstandard units (informal) and standard units (inches) to measure length. Lessons first introduce children to nonstandard units (e.g., Unifix Cubes) to facilitate understanding of the process of measuring length, and the relationship between the unit of measurement and number of units of which the object consists (Cross et al., 2009; Van de Walle, 2001). As children become more familiar with measuring length, lessons transition to standard units or inches. Also, to extend student learning, lessons teach the concept of using different tools for measuring different attributes. For example, lessons address how a clock and a calendar can both measure time.

The Role of Mathematics Vocabulary and Discourse in ELM

Embedded across content strands, ELM also places strong emphasis on math-related vocabulary and discourse to deepen student understanding of mathematical concepts. Previous research has found that students enter school with early differences in vocabulary size (Beck & McKeown, 2001; Biemiller & Slonim, 2001; Hart & Risley, 1995) and in the number of opportunities to use mathematical language outside school (Cross et al., 2009; Klein, Starkey, Clements, Sarama, & Iyer, 2008; NMAP, 2008). To address this critical gap, ELM embeds vocabulary unique to early mathematics by providing teachers with precise definitions and explicit teaching examples to use during instruction. For example, when the program introduces the concept of equality, a concept often misunderstood by children (Franke, Carpenter, & Battey, 2008), it provides a precise, yet kindergarten-friendly, definition. But beyond providing a specific definition of a vocabulary word, ELM attempts to develop a meaningful understanding of the concept through extended work and practice opportunities embedded across multiple lessons, incorporating different learning contexts. Students learning the concept of equality would encounter the concept through teacher-led instruction, including teacher models and responses to specific teacher questions, problem-solving activities with their peers, and, finally, independent practice.

ELM Instructional Design Principles

ELM adheres to a set of research-based principles of instruction (Chard & Jungjohann, 2006; Coyne et al., 2007; Jayanthi and Gersten, see Chapter 7). First and foremost, ELM employs an explicit and systematic model of instruction. Lessons have clear teacher demonstrations with scripted dialogue, structured opportunities for guided and independent student practice, and academic "checks" for student understanding. These components are critical to the success of ELM and the facilitation of frequent and high-quality instructional interactions among teachers and students around key math concepts and skills.

Within ELM's instructional model are opportunities for teachers to use "think alouds" as they demonstrate how to solve problems and complete procedural tasks. Verbalizing one's mathematical thinking or thought process provides a valuable model for students who may struggle to determine how to solve a variety of mathematical problems (Darch, Carnine, & Gersten, 1984; Jitendra et al., 1998; Woodward, 2006). The think-aloud process during ELM instruction makes explicit not only the procedural side of solving the problem but also the mathematical reasoning behind completing each step.

ELM also allows opportunities for students to explain and justify the solution of problems. These verbalizations help facilitate a deeper understanding of key mathematical concepts for students. At the same time, they allow the teacher to gauge student understanding and provide feedback if an error occurs (Fuchs et al., 2003; Schunk & Cox, 1986). For example, in composing combinations of 5 with yellow and red tokens (e.g., 2 red + 3 yellow), students verbalize how many reds plus how many yellows equal 5. If students make an error during the explanation, the teacher can provide feedback to address potential misconceptions.

Second, ELM scaffolds instruction (Harniss, Carnine, Silbert, & Dixon, 2007; Jitendra et al., 1998; Tournaki, 2003). Scaffolding is a way of providing instructional supports that promote learner independence. Scaffolding accomplishes this by gradually transferring the task from teacher to student (Chard & Jungjohann, 2006). As learners become more confident in their learning, the scaffolds or supports are removed.

Early in the learning process, ELM provides students with substantial teacher support to students, and systematically reduces these scaffolds as the students become proficient in the content and begin to transition to more student-driven activities. For example, when introducing a new procedure, mathematical idea, or concept, the program begins with simpler teaching examples so as to not confuse students. As students become more proficient, lessons gradually introduce more complex problems. It is important to note that, despite high levels of teacher support during initial instruction, ELM actively and meaningfully involves students in the learning process by providing frequent opportunities to respond and practice.

To facilitate student conceptual understanding, ELM scaffolds instruction through visual representations of mathematical ideas, such as number lines, tally marks, place-value models, base-10 blocks, and 10-frame models. Previous research has documented the impact of visuals across a number of areas, including general mathematics, prealgebra concepts, word problems, and whole-number operations (Gersten et al., 2009). Visual representations help students form connections between abstract symbols and conceptual models of mathematics (Hecht, Vagi, & Torgesen, 2007). For most concepts, ELM introduces concrete examples before introducing abstract representations of whole numbers (Gersten et al., 2009; Jayanthi and Gersten, see Chapter 7). This sequence of instruction is sometimes referred to as the concrete-representational-abstract approach (CRA; Bruner, 1966; Miller & Hudson, 2007).

ELM uses the CRA approach to teach a host of mathematical concepts and skills. For example, instruction incorporates CRA to teach efficient counting strategies, such as the *min strategy*, or counting on from the larger addend. Lessons first introduce the strategy with concrete examples (e.g., counting blocks). As students begin to develop a foundational understanding of the strategy, instruction fades out the counting blocks and then moves to a semicon-crete or representational model, such as tally marks. Finally, when students acquire a firm conceptual understanding of the min strategy, instruction transitions into the abstract level or to working with real numerals.

Another example of visual representations in ELM is the use of 10-frame models. Through 10-frame exercises, students can build a rich understanding of the base-10 system and learn how to apply this knowledge across multiple problem types (Van de Walle, 2001). ELM incorporates 10 frames to help students learn how to compose and decompose numbers within the base-10 system, understand number relationships, and grasp the concept of place value. Figure 4.1 shows how students count the number of dots in each 10-frame and then write the corresponding numeral. As students progress through the school year, the curriculum teaches them how to quickly recognize the numeral that is represented by the 10- frame rather than counting each dot.

Finally, ELM preteaches relevant background knowledge to increase student success in content introduced in the later parts of the curriculum. For instance, to prepare students for column alignment when working with multidigit numbers, ELM devotes a substantive amount of instruction toward reading and writing numerals accurately. Preteaching relevant background knowledge in this case consists of students tracing and writing each numeral following its introduction. As students write the numeral 13, for example, the teacher reminds the students that 13 is made up of one 10 and three 1's. Thus, learning how to read, write, and decompose numerals is based upon the written numerical placement of numbers.

 = 5   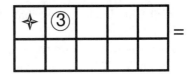 =

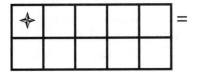 =   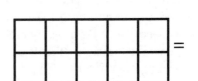 =

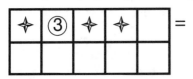 =   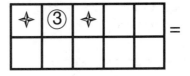 =

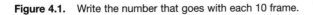

Figure 4.1.   Write the number that goes with each 10 frame.

Student Outcomes

In conducting our research, we think of ELM in terms of how it affects two types of students. The first is the student who enters kindergarten having a developed sense of number, often from informal interactions with parents or more formal instruction in a preschool setting. For this type of student, the goal of ELM is to build upon that knowledge base and help the student stay on track in developing his or her mathematical thinking. The second type of student enters kindergarten with a poorly developed sense of number and mathematics. He or she may have had limited informal interactions with mathematics and may not have attended a preschool program. For this type of student, the goal of ELM is to build his or her understanding of number and mathematics at a rate that allows the student to exit kindergarten at the same level as his or her peers or at least having reduced the gap between the student and his or her typically achieving peers. We consider the focused content of ELM and incorporation of research-based instructional design principles, detailed in the previous sections, as the key mechanisms in ELM that help us meet the needs of students without informal number sense while also ensuring the continued development of students who enter kindergarten on track.

Preliminary evidence suggests that ELM accomplishes these goals (Clarke, Smolkowski, Baker, Fien, & Chard, in press). We split our student sample into two broad categories of at risk and not at risk by using a pretest score on the Test of Early Mathematics–Third Edition (TEMA-3; Ginsburg & Baroody, 2003) corresponding to the 40th percentile. Posttest results indicated that at-risk students in ELM classrooms significantly outperformed control classroom students on both the TEMA and a set of short-duration measures of early number sense (EN-CBM), with classroom-level effects sizes of .24 and .22, respectively. The impact of ELM also meant that at-risk students were able to close the gap with their not-at-risk peers. For example, ELM at-risk students reduced the gap between themselves and their not-at-risk peers on the TEMA by 4.8 points.

From an RTI perspective, the results are also interesting because they occurred in the context of a general education setting. That is, by using a research-based core curriculum in the general education classroom, we were able to reduce the number of students who did not "respond" to Tier 1 and would thus need Tier 2 services. By meeting the needs of a greater number of students in general education, schools can be more efficient in their provision of services to struggling students. This has serious implications for schools dealing with finite resources that limit their ability to provide intervention services. If the core program addresses the needs of a larger number of students, fewer students will need Tier 2 or Tier 3 intervention services, thereby allowing schools or districts to target their intervention services to students with the most severe learning needs.

ONGOING RESEARCH

Beyond examining the impact of ELM, we are also interested in unpacking the experiences or interactions between teachers and students that influence student achievement. We used the Coding of Academic Teacher–Student interactions (CATS; Doabler, Fien, Smolkowski, et al., 2010) observation instrument to examine instructional practices in the 65 Oregon kindergarten classrooms that participated in our original study of ELM (Clarke et al., in press). The CATS instrument measures the important instructional interactions that occur between teachers and students during kindergarten mathematics instruction. In particular, observers code occurrences of teacher models, academic feedback, group and individual practice opportunities, and student errors.

Two primary purposes guided our classroom observations. First, we wanted to explore the relation between observed instructional interactions and student math outcomes. Second, we wanted to test whether the effect of specific instructional practices, such as teacher models, differed for students at risk for math difficulties. Preliminary results showed a number of interesting findings. For example, we found that students at risk for math difficulties at the start of kindergarten had stronger gains in classrooms with higher rates of teacher models. In many ways, this finding corroborates much of what is already known about teaching students struggling with mathematics (Baker et al., 2002; Gersten et al., 2009; Haas, 2005; Kroesbergen & Van Luit, 2003; NMAP, 2008; Jayanthi and Gersten, see Chapter 7) and provides further information for delivering professional development in mathematics that emphasizes key instructional practices.

CONCLUSION

In our work with ELM, we have begun to develop a framework for thinking about RTI. First, general education curricula should be tightly focused on covering the most critical mathematics content, and, second, they should do so in a manner that reflects what is currently known about instructional design for teaching students who are at risk. We believe curricula that adhere to these core principles have the possibility of improving the achievement of students who would normally need additional instructional services (i.e., Tier 2) in a general education, or Tier 1, setting. The impact should go beyond merely increasing the achievement of at-risk students to effectively allowing them to bridge the gap with their not-at-risk peers. Last, we urge teachers, schools, and districts to recognize that no one curriculum is a magic bullet for improving student achievement. Good curricula must be implemented by teachers knowledgeable in both mathematical content and pedagogical practice. It is not until we achieve all of these goals (good curricula, knowledgeable teachers, and ample supports) that the full promise of RTI can be realized.

REFERENCES

Agodini, R., Harris, B., Atkins-Burnett, S., Heaviside, S., Novak, T., & Murphy, R. (2009). *Achievement effects of four early elementary school math curricula: Findings from first graders in 39 schools* (p. 11). Washington, DC: U.S. Dept. of Education, Institute of Education Sciences, National Center for Educational Evaluation and Regional Assistance.

Baker, S., Gersten, R., & Lee, D.S. (2002). A synthesis of empirical research on teaching mathematics to low-achieving students. *Elementary School Journal, 103*(1), 51–73.

Beck, I.L., & McKeown, M.G. (2001). Text talk: Capturing the benefits of read-aloud experiences for young children. *Reading Teacher, 55*(1), 10–20.

Biemiller, A., & Slonim, N. (2001). Estimating root word vocabulary growth in normative and advantaged populations: Evidence for a common sequence of vocabulary acquisition. *Journal of Educational Psychology, 93*(3), 498–520.

Bodovski, K., & Farkas, G. (2007). Mathematics growth in early elementary school: The roles of beginning knowledge, student engagement, and instruction. *Elementary School Journal, 108*(2), 115–130.

Bruner, J.S. (1966). *Toward a theory of instruction.* Cambridge, MA: Belknap Press of Harvard University.

Bryant, D.P., Bryant, B.R., Gersten, R., Scammacca, N., & Chavez, M.M. (2008). Mathematics intervention for first- and second-grade students with mathematics difficulties: The effects of tier 2 intervention delivered as booster lessons. *Remedial and Special Education, 29*(1), 20–32. doi: 10.1177/0741932507309712

Carnine, D. (1997). Instructional design in mathematics for students with learning disabilities. *Journal of Learning Disabilities, 30*(2), 130–141.

Chard, D., Baker, S.K., Clarke, B., Jungjohann, K., Davis, K.L.S., & Smolkowski, K. (2008). Preventing early mathematics difficulties: The feasibility of a rigorous kindergarten mathematics curriculum. *Learning Disabilities Quarterly, 31*(1), 11–20.

Chard, D.J., & Jungjohann, K. (2006). *Scaffolding instruction for success in mathematics learning, intersection: Mathematics education sharing common grounds.* Houston, TX: Exxon-Mobil Foundation.

Clarke, B., Smolkowski, K., Baker, S.K., Fien, H., & Chard, D. (in press). The impact of a comprehensive tier 1 kindergarten curriculum on the achievement of students at-risk in mathematics. *Elementary School Journal.*

Clements, D.H. (2004). Major themes and recommendations. In D.H. Clements, J. Sarama, & A.M. DiBiase (Eds.), *Engaging young children in mathematics: Standards for early childhood mathematics education* (pp. 1–72). Mahwah, NJ: Lawrence Erlbaum Associates.

Clements, D.H., & Sarama, J. (2007). Effects of a preschool mathematics curriculum: Summative research on the Building Blocks project. *Journal for Research in Mathematics Education, 38*(2), 136.

Coyne, M., Kame'enui, E.J., & Carnine, D. (2007). *Effective teaching strategies that accommodate diverse learners* (3rd ed.). Upper Saddle River, NJ, Merrill Prentice Hall.

Cross, C.T., Woods, T.A., & Schweingruber, H. (2009). *Mathematics learning in early childhood: Path towards excellence and equity.* Washington, DC: National Academies Press.

Darch, C., Carnine, D., & Gersten, R. (1984). Explicit instruction in mathematical problem solving. *Journal of Educational Research, 4*(2), 155–165.

Doabler, C., Fien, H., Nelson Walker, N.J., & Baker, S.K. (2010). *Evaluating the instructional design elements of elementary mathematics programs.* Unpublished technical report, University of Oregon, Eugene, OR.

Doabler, C., Fien, H., Smolkowski, K., Baker, S.K., Clarke, B., Kosty, D., et al. (2010). *Measuring instructional interactions in kindergarten mathematics.* Paper presented at the Society for Research on Educational Effectiveness Conference, Washington, DC.

Duncan, G.J., Dowsett, C.J., Claessens, A., Magnuson, K., Huston, A.C., Klebanov, P., et al. (2007). School readiness and later achievement. *Developmental Psychology, 43*(6), 1428–1446. doi: 10.1037/0012-1649.43.6.1428

Franke, M., Carpenter, T., & Battey, D. (2008). Content matters: Algebraic reasoning in teacher professional development. In D. Carraher & M. Blanton (Eds.), *Algebra in the early grades* (pp. 5–17). Mahwah, NJ: Lawrence Erlbaum Associates.

Fuchs, L., Compton, D.L., Fuchs, D., Paulsen, K., Bryant, B., & Hamlett, C. (2005). The prevention, identification, and cognitive determinants of math difficulty. *Journal of Educational Psychology, 97,* 493–513.

Fuchs, L., Fuchs, D., Prentice, K., Burch, M., Hamlett, C., Owen, R., et al. (2003). Explicitly teaching for transfer: Effects on third-grade students' mathematical problem solving. *Journal of Educational Psychology, 95*(2), 293–305.

Fuchs, D., Fuchs, L.S., & Stecker, P.M. (2010). The "blurring" of special education in a new continuum of general education placements and services. *Exceptional Children, 76*(3), 301–323.

Fuchs, L.S., Powell, S.R., Seethaler, P.M., Fuchs, D., Hamlett, C.L., Cirino, P.T., et al. (2010). A framework for remediating number combination deficits. *Exceptional Children, 76*(2), 135–156.

Gersten, R., Beckmann, S., Clarke, B., Foegen, A., March, L., Star, J.R., et al. (2009). *Assisting students struggling with mathematics: Response to Intervention (RtI) for elementary and middle schools*. Washington, DC: National Center for Education Evaluation and Regional Assistance, Institute of Education Sciences, U.S. Department of Education.

Gersten, R., & Chard, D. (1999). Number sense: Rethinking arithmetic instruction for students with mathematical disabilities. *Journal of Special Education, 33*(1), 18–28.

Gersten, R., Clarke, B., & Mazzocco, M.M.M. (2007). Historical and contemporary perspectives on mathematical learning disabilities. In D.B. Berch & M.M.M. Mazzocco (Eds.), *Why is math so hard for some children?: The nature and origins of mathematical learning difficulties and disabilities* (pp. 7–28). Baltimore: Paul H. Brookes Publishing Co.

Gersten, R., & Dimino, J.A. (2006). New directions in research—Current issues in special education and reading instruction—RTI (Response to intervention): Rethinking special education for students with reading difficulties (yet again). *Reading Research Quarterly, 41*(1), 92.

Ginsburg, H., & Baroody, A.J. (2003). *Test of early mathematics ability* (3rd ed.). Austin, TX: PRO-ED.

Guarino, C.M., Hamilton, L.S., Lockwood, J.R., & Rathbun, A.H. (2006). Teacher qualifications, instructional practices, and reading and mathematics gains of kindergartners. Research and development report. NCES 2006-031. Jessup, MD: ED Pubs. (Available at http://www.edpubs .org)

Haas, M. (2005). Teaching methods for secondary algebra: A meta-analysis of findings. *NASSP Bulletin, 89*, 24–46.

Hanich, L.B., Jordan, N.C., Kaplan, D., & Dick, J. (2001). Performance across different areas of mathematical cognition in children with learning difficulties. *Journal of Educational Psychology, 93*(3), 615–627.

Harniss, M.K., Carnine, D., Silbert, J., & Dixon, R.C. (2007). Effective strategies for teaching mathematics. In M. Coyne, E.J. Kame'enui, & D. Carnine (Eds.), *Effective teaching strategies that accommodate diverse learners*. Upper Saddle River, NJ: Pearson Prentice Hall.

Hart, B., & Risley, T.R. (1995). *Meaningful differences in the everyday experience of young American children*. Baltimore: Paul H. Brookes Publishing Co.

Hecht, S.A., Vagi, K.J., & Torgesen, J.K. (2007). Fraction skills and proportional reasoning. In D.B. Berch & M.M.M. Mazzocco (Eds.), *Why is math so hard for some children* (pp. 121–132). Baltimore: Paul H. Brookes Publishing Co.

Hirsch, E.D.J. (2002). The benefit to equity. *American Educator*, 6–7. Individuals with Disabilities Education Improvement Act (IDEA) of 2004, PL 108-446, 20 U.S.C., subpart 614(6)(b).

Jitendra, A., Griffin, C., Deatline-Buchman, A., DiPipi, C., Sczesniak, E., Sokol, N., et al. (2005). Adherence to NCTM standards and instructional design criteria for problem-solving in mathematics textbooks. *Exceptional Children, 71*, 319–337.

Jitendra, A.K., Griffin, C.C., McGoey, K., Gardill, M.C., Bhat, P., & Riley, T. (1998). Effects of mathematical word problem solving by students at-risk or with mild disabilities. *Journal of Educational Research, 91*(6), 345–355.

Klein, A., Starkey, P., Clements, D., Sarama, J., & Iyer, R. (2008). Effects of a pre-kindergarten mathematics intervention: A randomized experiment. *Journal of Research on Educational Effectiveness, 1*(3), 155–178.

Kroesbergen, E.H., & Van Luit, J.E.H. (2003). Mathematics interventions for children with special educational needs: A meta-analysis. *Remedial & Special Education, 24*(2), 97–114.

Lyon, G.R., Fletcher, J.M., Shaywitz, S.E., Shaywitz, B.A., Torgesen, J.K., Wood, F.B., et al. (2001). Rethinking learning disabilities. In C.E. Finn, A.J. Rotherham, & C.R. Hokanson (Eds.), *Rethinking special education for a new century* (pp. 259–288). Washington, DC: Thomas B. Fordham Foundation and the Progressive Policy Institute.

Miller, S.P., & Hudson, P.J. (2007). Using evidence-based practices to build mathematics competence related to conceptual, procedural, and declarative knowledge. *Learning Disabilities Research & Practice, 22*(1), 47–57.

Morgan, P.L., Farkas, G., & Wu, Q. (2009). Five-year growth trajectories of kindergarten children with learning difficulties in mathematics. *Journal of Learning Disabilities, 42*(4), 306–321.

National Council of Teachers of Mathematics (NCTM). (2006). Curriculum Focal Points for prekindergarten through grade 8 mathematics: A quest for coherence. Retrieved from http://www.nctm.org/standards/focalpoints.aspx?id=282

National Governors Association. (2010). Common Core State Standards. Washington, DC: Author.

National Mathematics Advisory Panel (NMAP). (2008). Final report of the National Mathematics Advisory Panel. Washington, DC: U.S. Department of Education.

National Research Council. (2001). Adding it up: Helping children learn mathematics (pp. xvii, 454). J. Kilpatrick, J. Swafford, & B. Findell (Eds.). Washington, DC: Mathematics Learning Study Committee.

National Research Council. (2004). On evaluating curricular effectiveness: Judging the quality of k-12 mathematics evaluations. Washington, DC: National Academies Press.

Newman-Gonchar, R., Clarke, B., & Gersten, R. (2009). A summary of nine key studies: Multi-tier intervention and response to interventions for students struggling in mathematics. Portsmouth, NH: RMC Research Corporation, Center on Instruction.

Porter, A. (1989). A curriculum out of balance: The case of elementary school mathematics. *Educational Researcher, 18*(5), 9–15. doi: 10.3102/0013189x018005009

Princiotta, D., Flanagan, K.D., & Germino Hausken, E. (2006). Fifth Grade: Findings from the fifth grade follow-up of the early childhood longitudinal study, kindergarten class of 1998-99 [ECLS-K]. Washington, DC: U.S. Department of Education, National Center for Education Statistics.

Resnick, L.B. (1983). Mathematics and science learning: A new conception. *Science, 220*(4596), 477–478.

Schmidt, W., Houang, R., & Cogan, L. (2002). A coherent curriculum. *American Education* (Summer), 1–18.

Schunk, D., & Cox, P. (1986). Strategy training and attributional feedback with learning disabled students. *Journal of Educational Psychology, 78*(3), 201–209.

Slavin, R.E., & Lake, C. (2008). Effective programs in elementary mathematics: A best-evidence synthesis. *Review of Educational Research, 78*(3), 427.

Sood, S., & Jitendra, A.K. (2007). A comparative analysis of number sense instruction in reform-based and traditional mathematics textbooks. *Journal of Special Education, 41*(3), 145–157. doi: 10.1177/00224669070410030101

Tournaki, N. (2003). The differential effects of teaching addition through strategy instruction versus drill and practice to students with and without learning disabilities. *Journal of Learning Disabilities, 36*(5), 449–458.

Van de Walle, J.A. (2001). *Elementary and middle school mathematics: Teaching developmentally* (4th ed.). New York: Longman.

Vaughn, S., & Fuchs, L. (2003). Redefining learning disabilities as inadequate response to instruction: The promise and potential problems. *Learning Disabilities Research & Practice, 18*(3), 137–146.

West, J., Denton, K., & Germino-Hausken, E. (2000). America's kindergartners: Findings from the Early Childhood Longitudinal Study, kindergarten class of 1998-1999, fall 1998. *Education Statistics Quarterly, 2*, 7–13.

Woodward, J. (2006). Making reform-based mathematics work for academically low-achieving middle school students. In M. Montague & A.K. Jitendra (Eds.), *Teaching mathematics to middle school students with learning difficulties* (pp. 29–47). New York: Guilford Press.

Wu, H. (2009). *From arithmetic to algebra.* Paper presented at the Mathematicians Workshop Series Schedule, University of Oregon, Eugene, OR.

5

Tier 2 Early Numeracy Number Sense Interventions for Kindergarten and First-Grade Students with Mathematics Difficulties

Diane Pedrotty Bryant, Greg Roberts,
Brian R. Bryant, and Leann DiAndreth-Elkins

It is known that some children enter kindergarten demonstrating a good understanding of early number concepts. Other children come to school with limited knowledge of these basic concepts and usually fall into two categories: those who already exhibit difficulties in learning mathematical concepts and for whom these mathematical difficulties will persist into first grade and beyond (Morgan, Farkas, & Wu, 2009; Roberts & Bryant, in press) and those who enter kindergarten with limited early mathematical experiences yet do just fine in the early grades with strong instruction. Because early math ability is very predictive of later achievement (Morgan et al., 2009), rather than waiting for students to demonstrate serious mathematical learning difficulties in later grades, the response to intervention (RTI) process should be used to identify and help struggling students in the early years of school instruction.

In a series of studies over several years, we used an iterative process to develop, test, and refine a Tier 2 intervention called the Early Numeracy Booster (ENB) intervention for teaching number sense concepts and skills to kindergarten and first-grade students with identified mathematics difficulties. The purpose of this chapter is to describe the intervention, its development, and the preliminary results of the project.

This chapter was supported in part by Grant 076600157110004 from the Texas Education Agency. Statements do not support the position or policy of this agency, and no official endorsement should be inferred.

DEVELOPMENT OF A TIER 2 INTERVENTION: THE EARLY NUMERACY BOOSTER

The ENB was developed with the goal of promoting conceptual understanding, procedural knowledge, and computational fluency of early numeracy concepts, which are important areas to consider as part of the development process (Matthews & Rittle-Johnson, 2009; National Mathematics Advisory Panel [NMAP], 2008; Rittle-Johnson & Star, 2007). The concepts and skills selected for the booster intervention reflect recommendations from the National Council of Teachers of Mathematics (2000, 2006) and NMAP (2008) for kindergarten and first grade.

Mathematical Content for the Tier 2 Intervention

Examining the mathematics performance of young students over time has helped researchers identify critical mathematical ideas that are difficult for struggling students. For example, Jordan, Kaplan, Ramineni, and Locuniak (2009) found that kindergartners' performance on number sense tasks is predictive of their mathematics achievement between first and third grades. Also, in follow-along studies of students tested in kindergarten and tested again in second or third grade, findings showed that these students had problems with number constancy, reading 1-digit numerals, adding 1-digit numbers using manipulatives, and accurately judging number magnitude along a number line (Geary, Bailey, Littlefield, Wood, Hoard, & Nugent, 2009; Mazzocco & Thompson, 2005).

In yet another area, solving arithmetic facts poses many difficulties for most struggling students. For example, Geary (1990, 2004) found that persistent deficits in the retrieval of arithmetic facts among elementary-age students tend to be associated with mathematics difficulties. Students with mathematics difficulties typically display problems mastering arithmetic facts because of immature counting strategies such as relying on counting all of the objects instead of moving to a more efficient counting on strategy (e.g., 4 + 3 can be solved as start with 4 and count on 3 more to equal 7). Unfortunately, the continued use of immature counting strategies contributes to difficulties in developing computational fluency (Geary, 1990). In sum, these studies identify mathematics topics in which struggling students demonstrate difficulties at an early age. Thus, interventions that are based on a curriculum that develops number sense concepts appear to be a worthwhile goal for early numeracy instruction.

The ENB curriculum was developed with an emphasis on number sense and early numeracy concepts and skills. For kindergarten, the ENB curriculum includes the rudiments of number sense—for example, identifying and writing numerals; counting, ordering, and comparing quantities; identifying part-part-whole quantities; making groups; and solving simple change problems with the result unknown. For first grade, examples of topics in the curriculum include reading and writing numbers to 100, counting in units and multiples of tens and ones, comparing and ordering according to the magnitude of numbers, composing and decomposing numbers, using counting and cognitive strategies, learning about mathematical properties (e.g., commutative), and using the inverse relationship of addition and subtraction to solve number combinations.

To ensure that the curriculum and lessons were mathematically sound, mathematics specialists and external reviewers examined the intervention package and provided feedback on the precise use of the mathematics vocabulary and the accuracy of the mathematics content. Feedback from the reviewers focused on how the lessons were aligned with the state's mathematics standards (i.e., the content), which was a major consideration for practitioners because of the relationship between the standards and the state's high-stakes assessment. Consequently, some concepts and skills were deleted, and some mathematical vocabulary (e.g., *greater than*) that was not targeted in the state's standards was removed from the final product. Thus, the ENB intervention has undergone rigorous review and subsequent revisions.

Instructional Features

The instructional design of the lessons includes the critical features of systematic instruction that have been validated in numerous studies with struggling students and, specifically, with students who have learning disabilities (e.g., Fuchs & Fuchs, 2003; Swanson, Hoskyn, & Lee, 1999). Systematic, explicit instruction involves:

- Breaking tasks into smaller units and systematically sequencing concepts across lessons.
- Providing cumulative review of previously taught mathematical ideas.
- Modeling or demonstrating how to solve a problem by using specific procedures and then having students complete problems using the same procedures.
- Engaging students in ways to practice what they have learned, usually under the teacher's direction. Students with mathematics learning needs benefit from multiple opportunities to practice, which could be in a peer-assisted group, with virtual online practice, or with the teacher.
- Providing error correction procedures to correct mistakes and to provide feedback. For example, stopping the student if an error is made, modeling the correct response for the student, and having the student repeat the correct response.
- Providing independent practice activities that do not require direct teacher supervision or guidance. For example, students can practice information in small groups, independently at their desks, or as homework (Stein, Kinder, Silbert, & Carnine, 2006).

The lessons include a validated teaching routine: warm-up of previous skills (review), advance organizer, modeled practice to show students how to do the activity and to keep them engaged, guided practice (two types of activities), and a timed independent practice, which is the progress monitoring component of the intervention. A self-correction feature is conducted after independent practice so that students obtain immediate feedback on how well they did; errors are also corrected. Other instructional features include error diagnosis and correction and timed conditions to keep the pace moving along.

The lessons also include concrete and/or visual representations (e.g., manipulatives, number lines, 10 frames, 100s charts). Findings from research studies support the use of visual representations to help students better understand mathematical concepts (Gersten, Beckman, et al., 2009; Gersten, Chard, et al., 2009). We used visual representations to help students develop and build conceptual knowledge of concepts, operations, and properties (e.g., commutative property in both grades, associative property in first grade). The visual representations were intended to help students construct connections between mathematical concepts by using manipulatives (e.g., connecting cubes, base-10 materials), pictorial representations (e.g., 10 frames, dot configurations for facts, place-value models), and symbolic representations, which are critical components of conceptually based instruction (Baroody, 1990; Clements & Sarama, 2009; Hiebert & Wearne, 1992; NCTM, 2006; Sarama & Clements, 2009).

A lesson from the kindergarten ENB intervention is shown in Figure 5.1. The lesson illustrates, as an example, the curriculum, instructional features, and visual representations that are characteristic of the program. Information in the heading banner tells teachers how much time to allocate for this lesson, Shake and Make!, and how the lesson fits—Booster Lesson 2 Day 2—within Unit 5. The curriculum is aligned with the Texas state standards (TEKS K.1A, K.1C, K.2A, K.2B) because the intervention program was developed for Texas educators. Teachers find reference to the state's standards important for their lesson planning and instruction because they are usually held accountable for ensuring TEKS-based instruction. The kindergarten lesson focuses on number building with the instructional content focusing on the quantity of 7. Also, included at the beginning of the lesson are the objective, vocabulary, and materials. Thumbnails (smaller pictures) of the student practice sheets are included to help teachers know about accompanying materials.

Figure 5.2 contains an example of a first-grade lesson on addition and subtraction combinations. The instructional features and visual representations (pictorial in this case) are the same as the kindergarten lesson.

Two Implementations of the Intervention

First, trained mathematics interventionists from the research project implemented the experimental package. They made recommendations on ways to adjust the materials, lessons, and amount of instructional time. Second, in a scale-up project, kindergarten and first-grade teachers in schools in various regions of Texas were trained to implement the ENB intervention and asked

TEKS
K.1A, K.1C
K.2A, K.2B

(15) Total Time: 15 minutes
Instructional Time: 12 minutes
Independent Practice: 3 minutes

Unit 5
Booster Lesson 2
NB

DAY 2

Shake and Make! (7)
Number Building

Objective:	The student will be able to make part-part-whole combinations to seven and say the matching number sentence, using cubes.

Instructional Content:	7

Vocabulary:	Different, part, combination, more, altogether

Materials:	Teacher Master, pp. 4–5; tall, opaque plastic cup (T); number card (T; 7); 20 counting cubes (T; 2 colors, 10 of each); 14 counting cubes (S; 2 colors, 7 of each); 2 markers per student (that match the cube colors)

Guided Practice

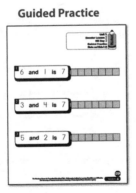

Independent Practice

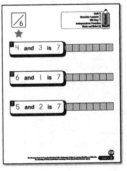

(continued)

Figure 5.1. Example of a kindergarten lesson on number building. (Reprinted with permission from 3-Tier Mathematics Model: Mathematics Institute for Learning Disabilities and Difficulties [2009]. *Kindergarten Tier 2 Intervention Manual.* Austin, TX: Meadows Center for Preventing Educational Risk.)

Figure 5.1. *(continued)*

Unit 5, Lesson 2

Time:

Set the timer for 12 minutes. Spend the majority of the time on Guided Practice.

Note to Teacher:

Students often want to make patterns with cubes. Teach that in these lessons, students will not make patterns, but instead students will count groups of colors in cube chains.

Error Diagnosis and Correction

When counting with manipulatives, a student skips numbers or counts inaccurately: ask the student to slow down his or her counting and touch each cube as it is counted.

Preview

(show the number card 7)

Today we will show 7 in different ways.

We will play a game called Shake and Make!

Modeled Practice
(My Turn, Your Turn)

❶ Show the number 7 card and the cube chains from the previous number building lesson (6 + 1, 5 + 2, 4 + 3, 0 + 7), along with 1 new cube chain (8 + 1). Have students discuss whether the new cube chain belongs with the other cube chains.

What number? *(7)*

I have the cube chains from yesterday and 1 new cube chain that does not belong.

Which cube chain does not belong? *(8 + 1)*

How do you know? *(it is more than 7; it has too many cubes)*

This cube chain has 9 cubes. It does not belong with the 7-cube chains.

❷ Show each 7-cube chain, take the chain apart, and count/place the cubes in a tall plastic cup.

The cube chains show different ways to make 7.

I will take each 7-cube chain apart and put the cubes into the cup.

(take cubes apart and put into the cup)

Ready? Count. 1, 2 ... 7.

(continue until all cube chains have been taken apart and placed in the cup)

❸ Model Shake and Make! Shake the cup, and remove 7 cubes of 2 different colors. Sort the cubes into color groups and make 2 part chains with the cubes. The following example uses 3 blue cubes and 4 yellow cubes.

The Meadows Center for Preventing Educational Risk—Mathematics Institute for Learning Disabilities and Difficulties
The University of Texas at Austin ©2009 University of Texas System/Texas Education Agency

Figure 5.1. *(continued)*

Unit 5, Lesson 2

Modeled Practice
(continued)

My Turn: Shake it. I shake the cup and take out 7 cubes: 1, 2 … 7.

Make it. I make 2 part chains with my cubes.

I have 3 blue cubes and 4 yellow cubes.

Connect it. I take the 2 parts and connect them to make 1 whole chain. *(connect 2 part chains)*

Part-part-whole! *(point to each part and whole)*

3 and 4 is 7 altogether. Say it.

Error Diagnosis and Correction

A student says the number combination incorrectly: model how to say the number combination while touching each part.

Guided Practice
(Our Turn)

 4 Play Shake and Make! as a group using the language from step 3. Call on individual students to complete each step: 1 student removes 7 cubes from the cup, 1 student makes the part chains, 1 student connects all of the cubes to make a whole chain, and 1 student says the number combination. Continue playing the game, rotating roles as time allows.

5 Distribute a Guided Practice sheet to each student. Give students 7 cubes of 1 color, 7 cubes of a different color, and 2 markers that match their cubes. Tell students to read the number combination, show it with cubes, and then mark the cube pictures on their cube chain. Continue as time allows. Use the following language:

Read the number combination together. Ready? Read. 6 and 1 is 7.

Make your cubes match the number combination by showing 6 cubes of 1 color in the cube chain and 1 cube of another color in the cube chain.

Mark the pictures of cubes. Read the number combination.

Error Diagnosis and Correction

A student cannot mark the cube chain picture correctly: have the student put the cubes on the picture of the cube chain, remove 1 cube at a time, and mark the space for each cube removed.

The Meadows Center for Preventing Educational Risk—Mathematics Institute for Learning Disabilities and Difficulties
The University of Texas at Austin ©2009 University of Texas System/Texas Education Agency

Grade K | 11

(continued)

71

Figure 5.1. *(continued)*

Unit 5, Lesson 2

Time:

Set the timer for 3 minutes.

Independent Practice/ Progress Monitoring
(Your Turn)

❶ For 3 minutes: Distribute an Independent Practice sheet to each student and tell students to complete as many items as possible.

> Look at the number combinations next to the star , and show them with cubes on the cube chain.
>
> Say the number combinations.

Note to Teacher:

For each number combination, score 1 point for correctly making it with cubes and 1 point for correctly reading it.

❷ During the 3 minutes: Go through the items with students, telling them the correct answers. They should put a check mark (√) by correct answers and correct any errors.

❸ Record their scores as the number correct / total number possible.

72

⏰ **Total Time: 8 minutes**
Instructional Time: 6 minutes
Independent Practice: 2 minutes

Unit 3
Booster Lesson 1
ASC

D A Y 1

Facts with + 2!
Addition/Subtraction Combinations

Objective: The student will be able to use pictorial representations when adding two numbers with sums to eleven when one addend is two.

Instructional Content: + 2 facts to 11

Vocabulary: Add, all, part, answer, plus, turnaround, count on, strategy, greater

Materials: Teacher Master, pp. 1–2; number line (T); + 2 fact cards

Guided Practice

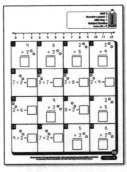

Independent Practice

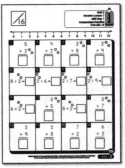

Grade 1 | 3

(continued)

Figure 5.2. Example of a first-grade lesson on addition and subtraction combinations. (Reprinted with permission from 3-Tier Mathematics Model: Mathematics Institute for Learning Disabilities and Difficulties [2009]. *First Grade Tier 2 Intervention Manual.* Austin, TX: Meadows Center for Preventing Educational Risk.)

Figure 5.2. *(continued)*

Time:

Set the timer for 6 minutes. Spend the majority of the time on Guided Practice.

Preview

Today we will learn strategies for adding + 2 facts.

What is a strategy? *(a plan to solve a problem)*

When we add, which way do we count on the number line? *(point to the number line; we count up on the number line)*

Modeled Practice
(My Turn, Your Turn)

❶ Place the 5 + 2 fact card on the table.

> **This fact is 5 + 2. It is a + 2 fact.**
>
> **My Turn: When I see a + 2 fact, I put the greater number in my head** *(point to head)* **and count on 2 more.**
>
> **Which number is greater, 5 or 2?** *(5)*
>
> **Your Turn: Say the strategy. Greater number in your head and count on 2 more.**
>
> **Count together. Ready? Count on. 5, 6, 7.**
>
> **5 + 2 = 7. Say it with me.** *(5 + 2 = 7)*

Error Diagnosis and Correction

The student has difficulty counting on 2 more: point to the number line and show the student how to count on 2 more.

❷ Place the 2 + 5 fact card on the table.

> **We can turn the numbers around and still get the same answer.**
>
> **If 5 + 2 = 7, what does 2 + 5 equal?** *(2 + 5 = 7)*
>
> **These are called turnaround facts.**
>
> **What are they called?** *(turnaround facts)*

Note to Teacher:

If your curriculum uses a different term for these types of facts, please use that term in place of "turnaround facts."

Guided Practice
(Our Turn)

❸ Using the Modeled Practice procedure, practice the + 2 strategy. Show students fact cards paired with their turnaround facts, tell students to state the strategy, and solve the fact. Use the following language:

The Meadows Center for Preventing Educational Risk—Mathematics Institute for Learning Disabilities and Difficulties
The University of Texas at Austin ©2009 University of Texas System/Texas Education Agency

Figure 5.2. *(continued)*

Guided Practice
(continued)

What strategy?

Start with the greater number in your head and count on 2.

What answer?

 Distribute a Guided Practice sheet to each student. Go through each item as a group and write the answer. Show students that the dots can be used as a scaffold to help them count on 2 more from the greater number. Model where to write the answers to both vertical and horizontal facts.

Error Diagnosis and Correction

The student has difficulty stating the strategy: model locating the number 2, stating "+ 2," and then taking the bigger number and counting on 2 more.

Independent Practice/ Progress Monitoring
(Your Turn)

Time:

Set the timer for 2 minutes. For the first minute, have students complete the Independent Practice sheet.

❶ **For 1 minute:** Distribute an Independent Practice sheet to each student and tell students to complete as many items as possible.

You will have 1 minute to complete as many items as you can. Start at the top and go across each row.

❷ **For the remaining time:** Go through the items with students, telling them the correct answers. They should put a check mark (√) by correct answers and should correct any errors.

Note to Teacher:

Score 1 point for each correctly written answer.

❸ Record their scores as the number correct / total number possible.

The Meadows Center for Preventing Educational Risk—Mathematics Institute for Learning Disabilities and Difficulties
The University of Texas at Austin ©2009 University of Texas System/Texas Education Agency

Grade 1 | 5

to provide feedback on aspects of the intervention. These teachers provided invaluable feedback on the lessons and the realities of conducting a Tier 2 intervention in the classroom.

In both implementation conditions, students were identified as being at risk based on results from the universal screener, the Texas Early Mathematics Inventories–Progress Monitoring (TEMI-PM), which has four subtests and a total score, and teacher ratings of students on mathematics state standard expectations. (See Bryant, Bryant, Gersten, Scammacca, & Chavez, 2008; Bryant, Bryant, Gersten, Scammacca, Funk, & Winter, 2008; Bryant et al. [in press] for a description of the TEMI-PM.) Students who scored below the 25th percentile on the TEMI-PM and had below-average to poor scores as rated by their teachers on mathematics performance were identified for the ENB intervention.

Implementation by Math Interventionists

The mathematics interventionists' daily routine included picking up students from their kindergarten or first-grade classrooms, going to the tutoring room, conducting the intervention and progress monitoring, and returning students to their classrooms. Of 236 kindergarten students, 45 were identified for the ENB intervention and the remaining students (n = 191) were taught in the comparison group. For first grade, of 161 students, 42 were identified for the ENB intervention and the remaining students (n = 119) were part of the comparison group. The comparison group received typical instruction, which included small-group and individualized instruction as part of whole-group core mathematics instruction.

The intervention instruction occurred in small groups of students with up to four students in kindergarten groups and four or five students in first-grade groups. The tutoring sessions occurred for 4 days per week for 20 minutes per session across 23 weeks. A period of 23 weeks was selected to allow sufficient time for Tier 2 instruction that paralleled the core curriculum in terms of when topics in number, operation, and word-problem solving were taught during the school year. Both grades included three lessons on specific concepts and skills, and a brief warm-up and cool down, which were intended to build procedural fluency on previously taught skills and concepts. For example, in kindergarten, the warm-up would be asking the students to quickly say how many dots were in a set on a flashcard and the cool down would focus on reading numerals quickly when presented on cards.

As part of the ENB intervention program, we observed the interventionists several times during the year to determine the degree to which they were implementing the intervention lessons as intended; this is often referred to as *the fidelity of implementation* (Gersten, Fuchs, Coyne, Greenwood, & Innocenti, 2005). The observation focused on the degree to which the mathematics interventionist followed a series of procedures and were rated on a 0-to-3–point scale where 0 = *not at all;* 1 = *rarely;* 2 = *some of the time;* and 3 = *most of the time.* For item (a), which followed the scripted lessons for the content (e.g., modeling, guided practice, independent practice), a median of 3.0 was achieved; for item (b), which implemented the features of explicit, systematic instruction (e.g., pacing, error correction, minimal teacher talks, engagement), the median score was 2.80; for item (c), which managed student behavior (e.g., use of reinforcers and redirection), a median of 2.80 was computed; and for item (d), which managed the lesson (e.g., use of timer, smooth transitions between booster lessons), a median of 3.0 was scored. These results across tutors showed a high degree of fidelity in the implementation of the booster lessons.

In the spring, the kindergarten results showed that students who were receiving instruction by the mathematics interventionists overall outperformed the students in the comparison group on the TEMI-PM. Also, at the end of the academic year, 27 of the 45 (60%) treatment students were exited from treatment because they scored at or above the 25th percentile on the TEMI-PM.

Also in the spring, the first-grade results on the TEMI-PM showed that students in the mathematics interventionists' groups overall outperformed the students in the comparison group. In addition, at the end of the school year, 21 of the 42 (50%) treatment students were exited from treatment because they scored at or above the 25th percentile on the TEMI-PM.

Scaling Up to Implementation by Classroom Teachers

We wanted to learn the effects of the ENB intervention on the mathematics performance of struggling students when classroom teachers taught the lessons as part of their daily routine. To do so, we provided a full day of professional development for the teachers. Training included a review of the lessons and materials, an opportunity to view a video of teachers implementing the lessons, and time to practice the lessons under the guidance of the workshop leaders. Teachers were not only given the lessons and accompanying materials, but they also received copies of student booklets. Thus, preparation time was reduced because teachers were equipped to implement the intervention when they returned to school. In addition, sufficient copies of the TEMI-PM, which they were responsible for administering, were shipped to their schools.

Teachers were responsible for teaching the ENB intervention during their already designated Tier 2 small-group instruction time. The ENB intervention small group consisted of three to five students who met 4 days per week for 25 to 28 minutes over the course of 23 weeks. Based on mathematics interventionists' feedback, we reduced the number of lessons to two per daily session, yet retained the warm-up and cool down. However, in the middle of the school year, we eliminated the cool down because classroom teachers were having difficulties getting through the lessons in the allotted time.

Coordinators from the research team visited the classroom teachers twice during the school year. These visits included a fidelity check, coaching, and meeting with the project's liaison or principal. The project's liaison conducted a fidelity-of-implementation check as well and was available to help teachers as needed. The liaison kept the project staff informed about issues that could be addressed through webcasts or newsletters. Webcasts were conducted on topics that the project coordinators thought were important based on their site visits. For example, a webcast was conducted on the topic of what to do with the rest of the class while the teacher conducts the Tier 2 intervention lessons and how to interpret progress monitoring data.

Similar to the math interventionists' procedures, fidelity-of-implementation data were collected several times during the year on four areas: following the script, implementing the features of explicit, systematic instruction, managing student behavior, and managing the lesson delivery. Overall data showed that, in the fall, teachers were "about average" in implementing the intervention. The main issues focused on instructional delivery; teachers were not familiar with systematic instructional procedures and, thus, lessons tended to run longer than expected. However, in the spring, the data revealed higher levels of fidelity of implementation, which we attributed to the site visits by the project coordinators when coaching and modeling were conducted.

There were 621 kindergarten students in the 22 schools statewide of which 76 at-risk students qualified for Tier 2 intervention. Of the 76 students, 42 students were in comparison classrooms and 34 students received the Tier 2 intervention in this quasi-experimental design. The treatment group outperformed the comparison group. Figure 5.3 illustrates the students' performance, with the lines representing students' scores across testing periods during the school year. The top line corresponds to the pattern of scores for the group of typically performing students, the middle line shows the pattern for the students receiving the ENB intervention, and the bottom line represents average scores for the control or comparison group students at each time point. Although the

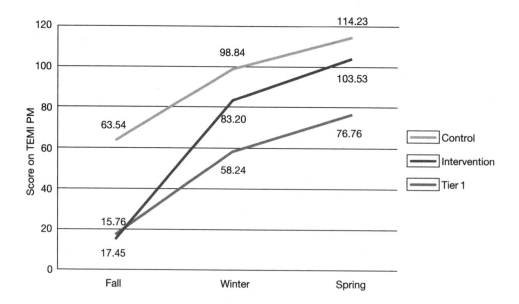

Figure 5.3. Kindergarten TEMI-PM total scores on fall, winter, and spring administrations. *Key:* TEMI-PM, Texas Early Mathematics Inventories–Progress Monitoring (University of Texas System/ Texas Education Agency, 2008).

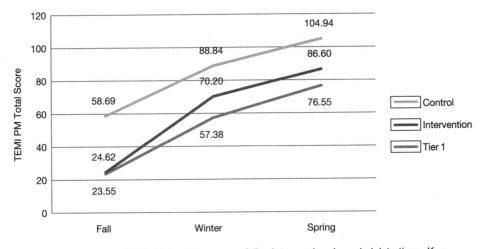

Figure 5.4. First-grade TEMI-PM total scores on fall, winter, and spring administrations. *Key:* TEMI-PM, Texas Early Mathematics Inventories–Progress Monitoring (2008).

treatment and comparison groups began the year at about the same level, change in the treatment group compared with the control group indicated that students receiving the ENB intervention were making greater progress than the group of nonparticipating students and "closing the gap" with the group of typically performing students.

In first grade, of the 587 students in the 22 participating schools who were given the TEMI-PM measures in the fall, 118 students were identified as being at risk. Fifty-two of these at-risk students participated in the ENB intervention and 66 students attended classes with the "business as usual" instruction. Figure 5.4 depicts student mathematics performance across the year. As already discussed, these lines represent the average scores for the three groups of students—typically performing, Tier 2 intervention students, and comparison or control students. The pattern of average first-grade scores in the treatment group is similar to the kindergarten data in terms of the improved performance from fall to spring, though the results are somewhat less dramatic.

INTERVENTIONIST OR CLASSROOM TEACHER?

As schools wrestle with the issue of who should provide Tier 2 intervention, a mathematics interventionist or the classroom teacher, the benefits and challenges of making this decision must be carefully weighed. The overall findings from our study suggest that teachers can be effective interventionists even in the early stages of adopting and implementing a new program and that at-risk students benefit from evidence-based, data-driven instruction when the program is a part of their daily mathematics routine across the school year. But the jury is out on who would be a better choice for teaching Tier 2 interventions.

Scheduling intervention time is a challenge for many schools. If math interventionists were responsible for delivering Tier 2 intervention, then they could conceivably see students all day, whereas classroom teachers have many other demands on their schedules to consider. However, interventionists, particularly in schools with a high rate of students who demonstrate academic struggles, are often overwhelmed with the number of students who need their services. Thus, they may have to make decisions about which students are most in need of their instructional services. In this situation, it may take both the mathematics interventionist and the classroom teacher to work with different groups of struggling students to address their needs.

The main issue voiced by the majority of teachers implementing the intervention, both in kindergarten and first grade, was the amount of time that was needed, which was beyond what we anticipated, to implement the daily sessions. Apparently, the number of materials (e.g., manipulatives, pictorial representations) needed for the lessons and the number of lessons in a daily session contributed to the time issue. However, upon closer examination during site visits, we found that the pacing of instruction, materials management, and the amount of "teacher talk" were challenging for some teachers and, thus, contributed to difficulty getting through a daily session that included a warm-up, two instructional lessons with progress monitoring (i.e., independent practice), and a cool down. In addition, first-grade teachers indicated that they needed more time to have students work with manipulatives for some of the skills and concepts (e.g., relationships of 10 and addition–subtraction combinations). In addition, kindergarten teachers were also challenged with the length of the daily session, particularly in the fall when young children's attention spans and experiences with formal schooling are limited. So, a number of factors contributed to time issues.

We recommend that teachers who are implementing a Tier 2 intervention receive ongoing coaching that involves demonstrating how to conduct systematic instruction (e.g., modeling of the lessons, pacing, error correction), managing materials, and keeping "teacher talk" within the scope of the program. These recommendations are supported by a response to a survey item, which was representative of the teachers in general: "This was the BEST part: [The] staff visit helped me get on track. I was doing so much talking that was not part of the script that I could not handle the time. [The staff member] modeled for me, and that is when I got it!" (first-grade teacher).

We also recommend that when teachers are first implementing a Tier 2 intervention, they may need to start with just a warm-up and one lesson and then layer on the second lesson. Our experiences tell us that as teachers became more adept with the instructional delivery and comfortable with the program in general, implementation issues tend to subside. This gradual layering approach potentially could help teachers achieve gradual success with the components; for kindergarten teachers, a warm-up and one lesson may be the best approach in the fall for students with short attention spans and limited formal schooling experiences.

On the one hand, we learned that keeping the rest of the class on task while implementing a Tier 2 intervention is a big issue for many classroom teachers in the area of mathematics. Surprisingly, some teachers could manage this issue with a Tier 2 reading intervention but were at a loss as to what to do with a mathematics intervention. On the other hand, we observed some teachers who were quite adept with providing learning centers to keep students engaged during the Tier 2 intervention time. One teacher commented, "Although it took some time and planning to get the center-based activities started, now the centers are up and running, and I can reuse them next year." If classroom teachers are going to implement a Tier 2 intervention, then we recommend that as part of the Tier 2 intervention training, expert teachers, who successfully create and manage learning centers, present their ideas and tips for doing so. There are numerous resources on this topic, some of which could help teachers get started. Also, a Make and Take! session where teachers are given time to create centers is imperative and is an important component that may be overlooked as part of a Tier 2 intervention.

A possible benefit of math interventionists providing the Tier 2 intervention is that this is primarily what they do all day and they do not have to keep the rest of the class engaged during Tier 2 intervention, which is a big issue. Thus, there is more potential for consistent in-depth work and delivery of instruction. There are no issues related to keeping the rest of the class engaged.

In addition, the mathematics background of elementary teachers varies as a function of their teacher preparation program and comfort level teaching math. One benefit of having trained mathematics interventionists provide Tier 2 intervention might be the in-depth instruction they can provide to build conceptual knowledge and diagnose and correct possible misconceptions about math.

FINAL THOUGHTS

The chapter described the development and validation of a Tier 2 intervention program for those students who are performing below typical achievement levels for their grade and, thus, qualify for supplemental, preventative instruction. The chapter provided recommendations, based on lessons learned with our work, for educators who are in the midst of identifying Tier 2 programs and thinking about potential issues and ways to address these issues. The content in this chapter for the most part is based on our experiences over the past few years as we tried different delivery models (i.e., mathematics interventionists and classroom teachers). We know that there are other research teams that are also developing and validating Tier 2 intervention programs, so readers should be aware of different models and ways of approaching this task.

The success with at-risk young students, as demonstrated in these data, underscores the potential of early intervention and may represent a means of affecting later math outcomes. In thinking more about the data and first-grade teachers' comments, more time with manipulatives might have strengthened the student response, although the intervention students did outperform the comparison group. For kindergarten, the strong performance is reflective of a 25-minute daily session. Although we did cut the cool-down, we do not know how students would perform with only a warm-up, one rather than two lessons, and progress monitoring.

Interestingly, when asked about the benefit of the progress monitoring to help teachers determine whether students learned the content of the lessons, on a rating scale of 1 to 5 (5 = *strongly agree*), kindergarten teachers' average rating was 4.22 and first-grade teachers' average was 4.05. So, although the progress monitoring was part of the lesson and took time, the teachers overall seemed to see value in this aspect of the intervention program.

Overall, teachers saw the benefit of the intervention on student progress and confidence. Notably, one classroom teacher commented, "My students have closed the gap. They have confidence in math, are willing to take a challenge and not shy away. They have the tools to help them when working independently." Examination of the data at the beginning of the year shows that Tier 2 students were performing well below their peers. The data reveal a closing of the gap; however, we do not yet know the type of intensive intervention that must occur to help Tier 2 students achieve the same level of performance as their peers.

REFERENCES

Baroody, A.J. (1990). When and how should place-value concepts and skills be taught? *Journal of Research in Mathematics Education, 21*(4), 281–286.

Bryant, D.P., Bryant, B.R., Gersten, R., Scammacca, N., & Chavez, M. (2008). Mathematics intervention for first- and second-grade students with mathematics difficulties: The effects of Tier 2 intervention delivered as booster lessons. *Remedial and Special Education, 29*(1), 20–32.

Bryant, D.P., Bryant, B.R., Gersten, R., Scammacca, N., Funk, C., & Winter, A. (2008). The effects of Tier 2 intervention on first-grade mathematics performance. *Learning Disability Quarterly, 31*(2), 47–63.

Bryant, D.P., Bryant, B.R., Roberts, G., Vaughn, S., Hughes, K., Porterfield, J., et al. (in press). Effects of an early numeracy intervention on the performance of first-grade students with mathematics difficulties. *Exceptional Children.*

Chard, D.J., Baker, S.K., Clarke, B., Jungjohann, K., Davis, K., & Smolkowski, K. (2008). Preventing early mathematics difficulties: The feasibility of a rigorous kindergarten mathematics curriculum. *Learning Disability Quarterly, 31*(1), 11–20.

Clements, D.H., & Sarama, J. (2009). *Learning and teaching early math: The learning trajectories approach.* New York: Routledge.

Dehaene, S. (2001). Precis of the number sense. *Mind & Language, 16,* 16–36.

Fuchs, L.S., & Fuchs, D. (2003). Enhancing the mathematical problem solving of students with mathematics disabilities. In H.L. Swanson, K.R. Harris, & S. Graham (Eds.), *Handbook of learning disabilities* (pp. 306–322). New York: Guilford Press.

Geary, D.C. (1990). A componential analysis of an early learning deficit in mathematics. *Journal of Experimental Child Psychology, 49,* 363–383.

Geary, D.C. (2004). Mathematics and learning disabilities. *Journal of Learning Disabilities, 37,* 4–15.

Geary, D.C., Bailey, D.H., Littlefield, A., Wood, P., Hoard, M.K., & Nugent, L. (2009). First-grade predictors of mathematical learning disability: A latent class trajectory analysis. *Cognitive Development, 34,* 411–429.

Gersten, R., Beckmann, S., Clarke, B., Foegen, A., Marsh, L., Star, J.R., et al. (2009). *Assisting students struggling with mathematics: Response to Intervention (RtI) for elementary and middle schools* (NCEE 2009-4060). Washington, DC: National Center for Education Evaluation and Regional Assistance, Institute of Education Sciences, U.S. Department of Education. Retrieved from http://ies.ed.gov/ncee/wwc/publications/practiceguides/

Gersten, R., Chard, D., Jayanthi, M., Baker, S., Morphy, P., & Flojo, J. (2009). Mathematics instruction for students with learning disabilities: A meta-analysis of instructional components. *Review of Educational Research, 79*(3), 1202–1242.

Gersten, R., Fuchs, L.S., Coyne, M., Greenwood, C., & Innocenti, M.S. (2005). Quality indicators for group experimental and quasi-experimental research in special education. *Exceptional Children, 71*(2), 149–164.

Hiebert, J., & Wearne, D. (1992). Links between teaching and learning place value with understanding in first grade. *Journal for Research in Mathematics, 23*(2), 98–122.

Individuals with Disabilities Education Improvement Act (IDEA) of 2004, PL 108-446, 20 U.S.C. §§ 1400 *et seq.*

Jordan, N.C., Kaplan, D., Ramineni, C., & Locuniak, M.N. (2009). Early math matters: Kindergarten number competence and later mathematics outcomes. *Developmental Psychology, 45*(3), 850–867.

Matthews, P., & Rittle-Johnson, B. (2009). In pursuit of knowledge: Comparing self-explanations, concepts, and procedures as pedagogical tools. *Journal of Experimental Child Psychology, 104*, 1–21.

Mazzocco, M.M.M., & Thompson, R.E. (2005). Kindergarten predictors of math learning disability. *Learning Disabilities & Practice, 20*(3), 142–155.

Morgan, P.L., Farkas, G., & Wu, Q. (2009). Five-year growth trajectories of kindergarten children with learning difficulties in mathematics. *Journal of Learning Disabilities, 42*, 306–321.

National Council of Teachers of Mathematics. (2000). *Principles and standards for school mathematics.* Reston, VA: Author.

National Council of Teachers of Mathematics. (2006). *Curriculum focal points for prekindergarten through grade 8 mathematics: A quest for coherence.* Reston, VA: Author.

National Mathematics Advisory Panel. (2008). *Foundations for success: The final report of the National Mathematics Advisory Panel.* Washington, DC: U.S. Department of Education.

Rittle-Johnson, B., & Star, J.R. (2007). Does comparing solution methods facilitate conceptual and procedural knowledge? An experimental study on learning to solve equations. *Journal of Educational Psychology, 99*, 561–574.

Roberts, G., & Bryant, D.P. (in press). *Early mathematics achievement trajectories: ELL and L1 population estimates using the Early Childhood Longitudinal Survey.*

Sarama, J., & Clements, D.H. (2009). *Early mathematics education research: Learning trajectories for young children.* New York: Routledge.

Stein, M., Kinder, D., Silbert, J., & Carnine, D.W. (2006). *Designing effective mathematics instruction* (4th ed.). Upper Saddle River, NJ: Pearson.

Swanson, H.L., Hoskyn, M., & Lee, C. (1999). *Interventions for students with learning disabilities. A meta-analysis of treatment outcomes.* New York: Guilford Press.

University of Texas System/Texas Education Agency. (2008). *Texas Early Mathematics Inventories: Progress Monitoring.* Austin, TX: Authors.

6

A Two-Tiered RTI System for Improving Word-Problem Performance Among Students at Risk for Mathematics Difficulty

Lynn S. Fuchs, Douglas Fuchs, and Robin F. Schumacher

With the introduction of response to intervention (RTI) multilevel prevention systems in the past decade, the context for preventing academic difficulty in schools has changed. The first level of the RTI prevention system is the Tier 1 classroom core curriculum. Many core curricula are designed using instructional principles derived from research, but few are validated because of the challenges associated with conducting controlled studies of complex, multicomponent programs. Regardless of the nature of the Tier 1 program, students who are at risk for poor learning mathematics outcomes in response to the core classroom program also receive a second level of the prevention system using small-group tutoring (e.g., three to five students per group). Some of these tutoring programs have been validated to show positive effects on student learning.

The focus of this chapter is a two-tiered RTI prevention system designed to enhance students' mathematics word-problem proficiency. This RTI work, which has been conducted at second and third grade, can serve as a model for conducting RTI for preventing difficulty with word problems at any grade level. The system comprises two coordinated tiers of prevention. The first, designed for use at Tier 1, is delivered to whole classes within general education. The second is designed for use in Tier 2 small-group tutoring. In this chapter, we begin by explaining the theoretical basis for this approach to word-problem instruction and illustrate its use with one simple word-problem type. We then describe how two companion pieces that comprise the program, one at each tier, can be used in a coordinated fashion. Finally, we summarize a randomized controlled trial

This chapter was supported in part by Grant RO1HD059179 and Core Grant P30HD15052, both from the Eunice Kennedy Shriver National Institute of Child Health and Human Development to Vanderbilt University. The content is solely the responsibility of the authors and does not necessarily represent the official views of the Eunice Kennedy Shriver National Institute of Child Health and Human Development or the National Institutes of Health.

that evaluated the efficacy of the two companion pieces. (Readers interested in obtaining manuals for Tier 1 or Tier 2 implementation should contact the first author.)

THEORETICAL AND EMPIRICAL BASIS FOR
THIS APPROACH TO PROBLEM-TYPE TRANSFER INSTRUCTION

Students who conceptualize word problems as fitting within categories or problem types are more flexible and successful problem solvers. The broader the category students have for understanding a given problem type, the greater the chance students will recognize connections between familiar and novel problems within that problem type and succeed with solving the problem. This helps them know when to apply previously learned solution methods to novel word problems, thereby transferring their learning. In this chapter, we refer to this approach to word-problem instruction as *problem-type transfer instruction.*

Developing students' understanding of a problem type involves two instructional phases. In the Problem–Solution Instructional Phase, teachers must teach students to

- Understand the essential features of the problem type
- Identify the problem type within which a problem belongs as one of the first steps in a problem solution
- Apply an efficient set of rules for solving that problem type

In the Transfer Instructional Phase, teachers help students anticipate how unexpected problem features, which we refer to as *transfer features,* can be incorporated within the problem type. The goal of this second instructional phase is to broaden the students' understanding of the problem type.

THE PROBLEM–SOLUTION INSTRUCTIONAL
PHASE OF PROBLEM-TYPE TRANSFER INSTRUCTION

Three predominant word problem types in the primary-grade curriculum are *total, difference,* and *change* problems. Several researchers use this classification system, although the labels for the problem types vary. To explain Problem–Solution Instruction, we focused on the difference problem type. Each problem type incorporates a specific action: a combination of sets for the total problem type, a comparison of sets for the difference problem type, and a change in one set over time for the change problem type. Although the computational demands of the three problem types are similar (i.e., one-step addition or subtraction), the most challenging is the difference problem type.

Difference problems describe a static relationship between sets, in which two quantities are compared to create a difference set. In difference problems, the unknown (which is asked for in the question) can be the difference set (e.g., Jill has 5 marbles. Tom has 8 marbles. How many more marbles does Tom have than Jill?), the compared set (e.g., Jill has 3 marbles. Tom has 5 more marbles than Jill. How many marbles does Tom have?), or the referent set (e.g., Jill has 8 marbles. She has 5 more marbles than Tom. How many marbles does Tom have?). We provide an overview of how teachers conduct Problem–Solution Instruction for the difference problem type when they work within the problem-type transfer instructional framework.

Promoting Understanding of the Essential Features of the Problem Type

As teachers introduce a new problem type, such as the difference problem type, they devote several lessons to helping students understand the essential features and the underlying semantic structure of the problem type and how those features and that structure differ from other problem types already taught. In our work, teachers introduce the total problem first, then the difference problem type, and finally the change problem type. To introduce the difference problem type, the teacher begins by reviewing the essential features and structure of the total problem (taught in the previous unit). Then the teacher introduces the difference problem type, explaining that in a difference problem, you compare two amounts. One amount is bigger, and the other amount is smaller. You find the difference between the bigger and smaller amounts.

The teacher then illustrates a difference problem by having students role play the scenario inherent in a difference problem. Two students, one taller than the other, come to the front of the classroom and stand back to back. The teacher shows with his or her hands the difference in their heights, telling the class that this is the difference between how tall the students are and asking the class which student is bigger, which is smaller, and how much the difference is. The teacher emphasizes that when we compare how tall they are, Student A is bigger, and Student B is smaller. Then the teacher uses a bigger and smaller box, drawing analogies between the students and the boxes and relating the scenarios back to finding the difference in the difference problem type. The teacher extends this conversation to help students understand why finding a difference between two numbers involves subtraction and gradually introduces a meta-equation, $B - s = D$ (where B is the bigger number, s is the smaller number, and D is the difference), to represent the underlying structure of the difference problem type.

The teacher gradually transitions from concrete examples to pictorial representations of the difference problem type, helping students connect specific numerals with the bigger and smaller quantities. The teacher completes worked examples to help students understand how they can use the difference problem meta-equation to represent a problem with a number sentence in the form of the meta-equation. So, for the problem, Jill has 5 marbles. Tom has 8 marbles. How many more marbles does Tom have than Jill?, $B - s = D$ is the number sentence $8 - 5 = x$. For the problem, Jill has 8 marbles. She has 5 more marbles than Tom. How many marbles does Tom have?, $B - s = D$ is the number sentence $8 - x = 5$. Of note, throughout the difference unit, the teacher and class discuss key distinctions in the essential features and structures of the total problem type versus difference problem type.

Identifying the Problem Type within Which a Problem Belongs as One of the First Steps in Problem Solution

Following the introduction of the difference problem type but taught as part of the first lesson in that unit, the teacher reminds students that, as the students previously learned in the total problem type unit, the first thing to do when faced with the word problem is to *RUN* through it (Read the problem, Underline the question, and Name the problem type). The teacher reminds students as in "Remember. You have to think hard to name the problem type. Before today, we've been learning about total problems. We look for the total and the parts anywhere in the story. Always ask yourself the 'Total Tips,' Are there two parts? Is there a total? If the answer is yes to both questions, then it's a total problem. Today we've been learning about difference problems. In difference problems, we look for two things being compared in the story. Sometimes the question asks us to find how much more or how much less. Either way, the problem is asking about the difference." The teacher then provides stories for students to classify as total and difference problems, while providing students opportunities to discuss how and why a problem fits within one or the other problem type.

Applying an Efficient Set of Rules for Solving that Problem Type

The teacher's next major task within the Problem–Solution Instructional Phase of problem-type transfer instruction is to help students master a solution strategy for solving difference problems. The teacher accomplishes this goal even as he or she continues to work to consolidate students' understanding of the essential features and structure of the difference problem type. In our work, students learned to use a five-step strategy for solving difference problems (which they used after first applying the RUN strategy, which is generic across problem types). The teacher provided elaborated discussion of and practice with each step. Step 1 is to write $B - s$ equals D. Step 2 is to identify what information is missing (B, s, or D can be missing; students use x to represent the missing quantity; depending on which variable is missing, students must add or subtract to find x). Step 3 is to find the information that is provided in the problem and enter those "given" numbers into the equation. Step 4 is to write the mathematics signs into the equation. Step 5 is to solve for x (in an introductory unit, students are taught to solve for x in addition and subtraction equations where the missing number can be in any slot of the equation).

Readers should note that after ensuring that students develop a firm understanding of the difference problem type using problems where D is the missing variable, teachers help students understand how to recognize x when it occurs in the first (B) or second position (s) of the meta-equation, even as teachers help students develop flexibility in identifying which quantity in a difference problem is the bigger or smaller value. For example, teachers conduct activities in which students produce equivalence statements using *more* and *less/fewer* (e.g., "John has 5 more cards than Mary" is the same as "Mary has 5 fewer cards than John"), encourage students to read problems without the number embedded in the relational part of the story (e.g., read "John has 5 more cards than Mary" as "John has more cards than Mary"), and (in Tier 2 tutoring) teach students to translate the relational statement in the story using *greater than* or *less than*; this reduces the load on working memory as students enter the bigger and smaller amounts (either with given numerals or with *x* to signify the missing information) into their number sentence to represent the problem.

In our work at different grades and using different problem types, we have conducted the Problem–Solution Instructional Phase in similar ways, sometimes with equations to represent the underlying structures of problem types, sometimes using other strategies to represent those structures. Working primarily at the second or third tier of the RTI prevention system in small groups, Jitendra and colleagues have enjoyed success with a conceptually similar approach that relies on diagrams rather than equations to help students represent the underlying structure of problem types. Students are taught to understand the essential features of the problem type, to identify the problem type as one of the first steps in a solution, and to apply an efficient set of rules for solving that problem type. These researchers have demonstrated acquisition, maintenance, and transfer effects for students with serious mathematics deficits or at risk for mathematics difficulty at eighth grade (Jitendra, DiPipi, & Perron-Jones, 2002), sixth grade, and third and fourth grades (Jitendra, Griffin, Haria, Leh, Adams, & Kaduvettoor, 2007; Jitendra, Griffin, McGoey, Gardill, Bhat, & Riley, 1998; Jitendra & Hoff, 1996).

THE TRANSFER INSTRUCTIONAL PHASE
OF PROBLEM-TYPE TRANSFER INSTRUCTION

Our work differs from that of Jitendra and colleagues because, in addition to the Problem–Solution Instructional Phase, we also incorporate the Transfer Instructional Phase. With the Transfer Instructional Phase, we explicitly teach students to broaden their understanding of the problem type to incorporate problems within unexpected features. These transfer features include problems with irrelevant information, problems with a novel question that requires an extra step, problems with relevant information presented in charts or graphs, problems that combine problem types, and so forth. The hope is that the addition of this Transfer Instructional Phase will lead to more flexible and successful problem-solving performance.

For irrelevant information, for example, we teach students what the phrases *relevant information* and *irrelevant information* mean. We give them practice in deciphering which information in a difference problem might be irrelevant. And we teach students to cross out irrelevant information as soon as they decide it is not needed to solve the problem. The challenge associated with deciding whether a problem incorporates irrelevant information increases when we teach students to look for the difference problem type within two-step problems, which always include more than two relevant numbers. An example of a word problem that combines a difference problem type with a total problem type is this: Tim has 4 blocks and 5 trucks. Fred has 7 race cars. How many more toys does Tim have than Fred? Helping students anticipate irrelevant information, even as they are prepared for the possibility that a word problem may involve two steps to accommodate two problem types, broadens students' understanding of the difference problem type.

We (Fuchs et al., 2003) conducted a randomized controlled study to assess whether this Transfer Instructional Phase provides significant additional benefit beyond the Problem–Solution Instructional Phase. We conducted the study in general education classrooms (i.e., Tier 1) using whole-class instruction. Classes were randomly assigned to teacher-designed word-problem instruction (business-as-usual word-problem instruction), to Problem–Solution Instruction, or to Problem–Solution Instruction plus Transfer Instruction. To teach for transfer, teachers did the following. First, they explained how transfer features can make problems seem unfamiliar without modifying the problem type or the required solution methods. Second, teachers discussed examples emphasizing the same problem type, as transfer features such as format or vocabulary changed. Third, they provided practice in sorting novel problems in terms of transfer features. Fourth, they prompted students to search novel problems for familiar problem types. Results indicated that the Transfer Instructional Phase strengthened word-problem performance over and beyond the Problem–Solution Instructional Phase and beyond teacher-designed instruction.

INCORPORATING PROBLEM-TYPE TRANSFER INSTRUCTION WITHIN A TWO-TIERED PREVENTION SYSTEM

This two-phase approach to problem-type transfer instruction can be conducted at all tiers of an RTI prevention system. In this chapter, we center on its application at Tier 1 using whole-class instruction for all students and at Tier 2 with small-group tutoring for students who are at risk for poor learning outcomes. In this section, we describe how these Tier 1 and Tier 2 companion programs operate in a coordinated fashion. Problem-type transfer instruction can be applied to any word-problem type at any grade. In this section, however, to make the methods more concrete, we focus on third grade using four problem types.

Overview of Third-Grade Problem Types Addressed in This Version of Problem-Type Transfer Instruction

Four common problem types at third grade are what we refer to as the *shopping list* problem type, the *half* problem type, the *buying bags* problem type, and the *pictograph* problem type. For shopping list problems, students identify the cost of multiple quantities of items each sold at a different price and then find a total.

Table 6.1. Sample third-grade problems that only vary the cover story, as in the Problem–Solution instructional phase

Problem type	Example 1	Example 2
Buying bags	Sarah is throwing a birthday party and needs 15 party straws for her friends. Straws are sold in bags of 4. How many bags does Sarah need to buy?	There are 18 students in Mrs. Smith's class. She wants to give each student a lollipop. Lollipops are sold in bags of 8. How many bags does Mrs. Smith need to buy?
Shopping list	Kesha went to the toy store. She bought 3 games for $5 each and 4 bouncy balls for $2 each. How much money did Kesha spend at the toy store?	Dan bought 4 bananas for $1 each, 2 peppers for $3 each, and 5 apples for $2 each. How much money did Dan spend on fruit?
Half	Grandma baked 16 cookies. If she gives half of the cookies to her grandson, how many cookies will he get?	Sue has 19 oranges. She used half of the oranges to make juice. How many oranges did she use?
Pictograph	Mrs. Green gives her class a star if they are well behaved. Each star earns the students 3 minutes of extra recess on Fridays. If the students already have 10 minutes of recess on Friday, how much time do they get now?	Mom was picking apples to make cider. Each apple she picked stands for 2 apples. She also bought 10 apples from the store. How many apples does mom have to make cider?

With half problems, students compute half. Buying bags problems involve a step-up function whereby students compute how many units, each providing a fixed quantity of items, are required to accrue the desired quantity. Pictograph problems ask students to use a pictograph to identify one quantity and then add that quantity to a second amount to find the total. In Table 6.1, we show two examples of each of these four problem types. The two example problems per problem type vary the cover story such that those two problems alter the characters, actions, and numerals in superficial ways. The goal of the Problem–Solution Instructional Phase, in which students are taught to understand the underlying structure of a problem type, to identify the problem type to which a problem belongs as the first step in the solution process, and to apply an efficient solution strategy for problems in that problem type, is that students solve problems that vary cover stories in these ways. This helps build their representations and solution strategies for the problem type.

Unfortunately, varying cover stories in these ways does little to help students broaden their understanding of a problem type. This is the goal of the Transfer Instructional Phase, in which students are taught to recognize problems with novel features—beyond the kind of cover story changes illustrated in Table 6.1—as belonging to the problem type. Novelty may occur because the problem incorporates an unfamiliar format or an unexpected question or the inclusion of irrelevant information, and so forth. See Table 6.2 for examples of problems that incorporate transfer features for each of the problem types we discuss here.

Table 6.2. Sample third-grade problems that incorporate transfer features, as in the Transfer Instructional Phase

Problem type	Transfer feature	Example problems
Buying bags	Different format and unfamiliar vocabulary	Tekia is throwing a party and needs some donuts. • Donuts are sold in **boxes** of 6. • There are 15 kids invited to the party. How many **boxes** of donuts does Tekia need to buy?
Shopping list	Different question	Sally is buying party supplies. She bought 5 party hats for $1 each and 3 poppers for $2 each. If she has $20 to spend on her party, **how much money does she have left?**
Half	Unfamiliar vocabulary	Jessica and her sister have 30 M&Ms. If they **divide them equally** between them, how many will Jessica and her sister get?
Pictograph	Irrelevant information	Lily and her mom **went to the store with $30.** They wanted to buy a board game and a puzzle. The board game was on sale and the sign looked like this: Each sun stands for $5. The puzzle cost $8. How much money did Lily and her mom spend at the store? Game sale price: ☀ ☀
Shopping list and half	Combine problem types	Jessie went shopping for her birthday. She bought 3 toys for $4 each and 2 picture frames for $5 each. She also bought 1 video game that was $16. When she got to the counter to pay, the video game was half price. How much money did Jessie spend?

Before any work on the four problem types begins, however, teachers address general problem-solving strategies. This initial three-week, six-lesson unit teaches students to make sure answers make sense, to line up numbers from text correctly to perform math operations, to check their computation, and to label their answers and work with words, monetary signs, and mathematical symbols. These lessons, each lasting 30–40 minutes, rely on worked examples with explicit instruction, dyadic practice, independent work with checking, and homework. After the three-week general mathematics problem-solving unit, four three-week units, each devoted to one of the four problem types, are delivered.

Problem-Type Transfer Whole-Class Instruction: Tier 1

Each Tier 1 whole-class instruction unit comprises six sessions, lasting 30–40 minutes. Sessions 1 through 4 address the Problem–Solution Instructional Phase using problems that only vary the cover story (see examples in Table 6.1). A poster listing the steps of the solution method is displayed in the classroom. In Session 1, the teacher addresses the underlying concepts and structural features for the problem type, role playing the scenario represented in the problem type and using problems without any missing information. Then the teacher presents a problem with a missing piece of information. The teacher works this sample problem, referring to the poster, and then explains how each step of the solution method was applied in the example. Students respond frequently to questions. After reviewing the concepts and presenting several worked examples in this way, teachers share partially worked examples while students complete the steps

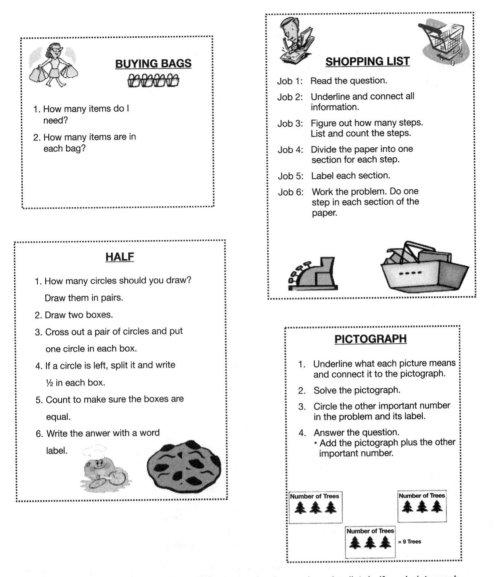

Figure 6.1. The poster for each problem type, buying bags, shopping list, half, and pictograph, listing the steps of the solution method.

of the solution strategy. Students then complete one to four problems in dyads, where stronger students help weaker students solve problems and check their work with answer keys. Sessions 2 through 4 are structured similarly, with a greater proportion of time spent on partially worked examples and dyadic practice. Also, at the end of Sessions 2 through 4, students complete one problem independently, the teacher checks work against an answer key, and students graph their scores. See Figure 6.1 for poster examples for instruction on each problem type.

Sessions 5 and 6 address the Transfer Instructional Phase. These lessons, which are designed to broaden students' understanding about the problem type, vary each problem not only in terms of the cover story (as in the Problem–

Solution Phase) but also in terms of one transfer feature (see examples in Table 6.2). Teachers first teach the meaning of the word *transfer,* and then teach five transfer features that change a problem without altering its problem type or general solution strategy. That is, students are taught that a familiar problem type, for which they know a solution, can be presented in a different format, can use unfamiliar vocabulary, can pose a different question, can incorporate irrelevant information, or can combine problem types. A poster, titled "Transfer" is displayed to remind students of the five ways problems can change (see Figure 6.2). In Session 5, teachers explain the poster, illustrating each transfer feature with a

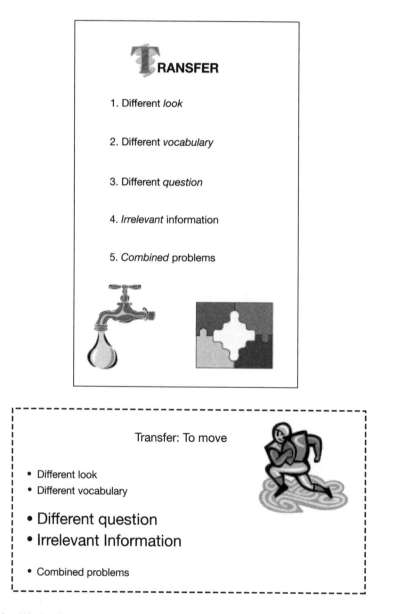

Figure 6.2.   Whole-class transfer poster (top) and tutoring transfer poster (bottom).

worked example. They gradually move to partially worked examples. Then, students work in pairs to apply the solution method to problems that vary transfer features. In Session 6, teachers review the five transfer features using similar procedures, except students spend more time working in dyads and then complete a problem independently and score work against a key.

Problem-Type Transfer Tutoring: Tier 2

Tier 2 problem-type transfer tutoring begins after the initial 3-week unit on general math problem-solving. Each three-week unit addresses one of the four problem types in a coordinated fashion with Tier 1 whole-class instruction. In this way, when Tier 1 is working on the shopping list problem type, Tier 2 tutoring is also working on the shopping list problem type. In fact, the content of problem-type transfer tutoring mirrors the content covered in Tier 1 problem-type transfer instruction whole-class instruction. In fact, it targets the most difficult concepts from Tier 1 problem-type transfer instruction whole-class instruction.

Consider the task of identifying the problem type with which many at-risk students struggle. The Tier 2 problem-type transfer tutoring supplements the Tier 1 strategies for identifying problem types. At the beginning of each unit, tutors incorporate concrete objects to help students understand the action associated with the word problem. This helps students identify the problem type so that the correct solution procedures will be applied. In the Buying Bags unit, for example, tutors bring party straws (which are sold in bags of four) to accompany the following problem (see Table 6.1): "Sarah is throwing a birthday party and needs 15 party straws for her friends. Straws are sold in bags of 4. How many bags does Sarah need to buy?" This helps students visualize the problem and recognize the problem as fitting the Buying Bags problem type. Students also use the straws to check their solution procedures for this problem. Also, after students have practice with concrete objects, tutors use examples of those completed problems as "templates" for students to reference when identifying the problem type and deciding which solution procedures to apply (see Figure 6.3).

In addition, two-dimensional visual representations are incorporated more frequently, additional scaffolding is employed to support student learning, and self-regulated learning strategies with tangible reinforcement are incorporated. With self-regulated learning strategies, students earn "tutoring dollars" in three ways. First, they monitor their daily word-problem performance by charting that day's score on a word-problem from individual work; an example of the Buying Bags unit series of charts is shown in Figure 6.4. A student earns one tutoring dollar for meeting or beating his or her score from the previous session. Second, each student earns a tutoring dollar if all group members are on task whenever a timer (set at varying time intervals throughout each session) beeps. Third, students earn points for getting selected problems correct throughout the session; only the tutor knows which problems have dollar-earning capacity. Students "bank" their tutoring dollars at the end of each session in their checking account. Each week, they have an opportunity to "shop," at which time they can spend their tutoring dollars on small prizes or save their dollars for more costly items.

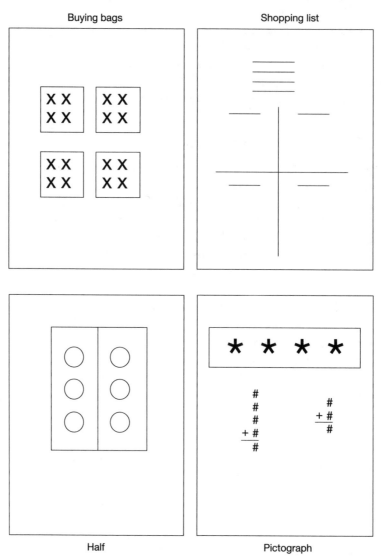

Figure 6.3. Examples of templates for students to reference when identifying problem types.

In this way, students are encouraged to self-monitor their on-task behavior, hard work, and accurate word-problem performance.

Tier 2 tutoring occurs three times per week in groups of two to four students; each session lasts 20–30 minutes. During the first five sessions of each unit, teachers deliver the Problem–Solution Instructional Phase using problems that vary only cover stories (see Table 6.1). A poster listing the steps of the solution method is displayed during the tutoring session. In Session 1, tutors address the underlying concepts and structural features for the problem type, using concrete objects. Together with the students, tutors work several examples and, as they refer to the poster (see Figure 6.1) and the concrete objects, they explain why and how each step of the solution method is applied in the examples. Next, students respond frequently to questions as they work two to four problems with

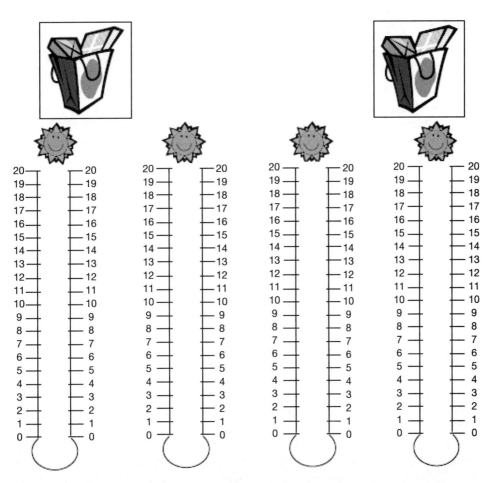

Figure 6.4. Thermometers (one for each day) for the Buying Bags Unit; students chart their score on the "Problem of the Day" and try to beat their score from the subsequent session.

the tutor. Beginning in Session 2, students complete one problem independently, which the tutor reviews and scores.

Sessions 6 through 9 address the Transfer Instructional Phase designed to broaden students' understanding of the problem type, with each problem varying the cover story as well as one of two transfer features: different question or irrelevant information (see Table 6.2). These transfer features were chosen because they present the greatest challenges for students to recognize the underlying problem type and apply previously taught solution methods. Tutors first teach the meaning of the word *transfer*, and then teach the two transfer features, utilizing a poster, "Transfer: To Move" (see Figure 6.2). Although five bulleted types of transfer features are included on the poster for continuity with Tier 1 problem-type transfer whole-class instruction, the two transfer features covered in tutoring sessions are bolded and in larger font for emphasis. In Session 6, tutors explain the poster, illustrating both transfer features by working examples. In Sessions 6 through 9, students still complete a problem independently.

EVALUATING THE EFFICACY OF
PROBLEM-TYPE TRANSFER INSTRUCTION

Fuchs, Fuchs, Craddock, Hollenbeck, Hamlett, and Schatschneider (2008) conducted a randomized controlled trial to assess the effects of Tier 2 problem-type transfer tutoring when it occurs with and without Tier 1 problem-type transfer whole-class instruction on at-risk students' word-problem solving and their learning relative to not-at-risk peers. We also examined the prevalence of mathematics difficulty with and without one or two tiers of problem-type transfer instruction.

Who Was in the Study?

Working in the Metropolitan Nashville public schools, we randomly assigned 120 third-grade classrooms to receive Tier 1 problem-type transfer whole-class instruction or to receive the conventional word-problem instruction their teachers normally provided. We did the random assignment while stratifying by school so that each condition was represented approximately equally in each school. One teacher in the problem-type transfer instruction condition left the study for personal reasons during the first month of the study. In the remaining 119 classrooms, we identified a representative sample of 1,200 students to be pre- and posttested for the study and designated them as not at risk ($n = 912$). Among these students, we identified 288 students as at risk of poor problem-solving outcomes based on their incoming mathematics scores (all 1,200 students in the problem-type transfer instruction classrooms participated in the instruction). To derive a parsimonious equation for predicting word-problem outcomes in response to Tier 1 problem-type transfer instruction, we conducted regression analyses on a previous database of third-grade students who had received the study's problem-type transfer instruction. The final prediction equation included pretest performance on The Algorithmic Word-Problem Test (Fuchs, 2004) and on the Test of Computational Fluency as predictors (Fuchs, Hamlett, & Fuchs, 1990). We selected the 288 students with the lowest predicted outcome in response to the Tier 1 version of problem-transfer instruction. At the end of third grade, 898 not-at-risk students and 243 at-risk students remained (i.e., had not moved during the school year).

Within each Tier 1 classroom (i.e., problem-type transfer instruction and conventional word-problem instruction classrooms), we randomly assigned at-risk students to continue in their classroom conditions with or without Tier 2 problem-type transfer tutoring. In this way, at-risk students received one of four conditions:

1. No problem-type transfer whole-class instruction and no problem-type transfer tutoring

2. Tier 1 problem-type transfer instruction alone (without Tier 2 problem-type transfer tutoring)

3. Tier 2 problem-type instruction tutoring alone (without problem-type transfer whole-class instruction)

4. Tier 1 problem-type transfer whole-class instruction plus Tier 2 problem-type transfer tutoring.

Teachers in the two whole-class conditions (problem-type transfer whole-class instruction versus conventional word-problem instruction) were demographically comparable and provided comparable amounts of instructional time on word problems. Not-at-risk students in the two whole-class conditions were comparable on demographics and incoming word-problem performance, as were at-risk students in the four conditions.

How We Measured Effects

We pretested students in a 3-week window before intervention began, and we posttested students in a 3-week window after 16 weeks of intervention. Intervention included 3 weeks of general problem-solving strategies (i.e., teaching students to make sure answers made sense, to line up numbers from text correctly to perform math operations, to check their computation, and to label their answers and work with words, monetary signs, and mathematical symbols), which all at-risk and not-at-risk students—those in conventional word-problem instruction and in problem-type transfer instruction whole-class instruction—received. It also included 13 weeks of word-problem instruction on the four problem types (including 1 week of review following winter break). During these 13 weeks, students in classrooms randomly assigned to conventional word-problem instruction received the word-problem instruction designed by their teachers, and students randomly assigned to problem-type transfer received the Problem–Solution and Problem–Transfer Instructional phases. At-risk students received tutoring in accord with their random assignment.

To assess the effects of problem-type transfer instruction on students' word-problem proficiency, we used three measures, all of which sampled novel problems (i.e., students had never seen the problems before and none of the problems had been used for instruction). The problems targeted the four problem types taught both as part of problem-type transfer instruction and as part of their schools' larger mathematics' curriculum, but the measures differed from each other in terms of transfer distance in relation to problems that only varied cover stories as found in the Problem–Solution Instructional Phase of problem-type transfer instruction. We refer to the three measures as immediate transfer, near transfer, and far transfer (increasing numbers signify greater transfer distance from problems that only varied cover stories).

Immediate transfer incorporated novel problems in the same format as the problems used in problem-type transfer instruction's Problem–Solution Instructional Phase; that is, they relied on new cover stories never before seen during instruction (see Appendix 6.1 for problem examples with student work). Near transfer incorporated novel problems that differed from the problems used for the Problem–Solution Instructional Phase in terms of one or more of the transfer features addressed in problem-type transfer instruction: different format, unfamiliar vocabulary, different question, irrelevant information, or combination of problem types (see Appendix 6.2 for examples with student work). Far transfer, which was designed to mirror real-life problems, differed from problems used for instruction in multiple ways. It was formatted to look like a commercial, standardized test; it presented a multiparagraph narrative with four questions; some of the information needed to answer the questions was removed from the multiparagraph narrative and placed in figures or question stems; it contained multiple pieces of numeric and narrative irrelevant information; it provided opportunities for students to formulate decisions; it combined all four problem types; and it varied all four problem-type transfer instruction transfer features.

None of the cover stories had been used for instruction. Each measure had two alternate forms; problems on both forms required the same operations and presented text with the same number and length of words. Immediate-transfer alternate forms incorporated the same numbers, near-transfer alternate forms incorporated the same numbers, and far-transfer alternate forms used similar numbers. In half the classes in each condition, we used Form A at pretest and Form B at posttest; in the other half, forms were reversed.

In addition, to gauge the effects of problem-type transfer instruction on students' risk for mathematics difficulty, we also administered Woodcock-Johnson III Applied Problems (Woodcock, McGrew, & Mather, 2001) at the end of the study. This tool, which is widely used in the schools for identifying math difficulty, assessed a wider domain than word-problem performance. It assessed proficiency in analyzing and solving practical math problems, such as counting, telling time or temperature, and problem solving. On this measure, we operationalized math difficulty with a relatively stringent cut-point of the 15th percentile.

What We Found

In this large-scale randomized field trial, we assessed the effects of problem-type transfer instruction small-group tutoring with and without validated whole-class instruction on at-risk third graders' math problem solving. The issue of how Tier 2 small-group tutoring interacts with Tier 1 validated classroom instruction among students at risk for poor learning outcomes is important for designing efficient and effective RTI prevention systems. If tutoring works better when combined with validated classroom instruction, then both tiers are critical and classroom instruction needs to be designed deliberately with at-risk students in mind, even when they receive tutoring.

By contrast, if tutoring promotes comparable outcomes regardless of the classroom instructional context, then findings may suggest that tutoring occur as a replacement for, rather than as a supplement to, classroom instruction. This would make RTI prevention systems easier to implement, facilitating the scheduling of small-group tutoring sessions.

What we found, however, was that Tier 2 problem-type transfer tutoring was significantly and substantially more effective when it occurred in combination with validated Tier 1 problem-type transfer whole-class instruction than when that tutoring occurred with conventional classroom instruction. The effect size was a large 1.34 standard deviations on a range of word problems, from those closely aligned problems within problem-type transfer instruction to real-life problems that were quite distal from the kinds of problems addressed during problem-type transfer instruction. This suggests that two tiers are better than one tier of prevention (i.e., Tier 1) and indicates the importance of providing at-risk students validated instruction in the classroom and then supplementing that instruction with high-quality tutoring. It is important to note, however, that in our study, the two tiers of problem-type transfer instruction were closely aligned, both addressing the same types of word problems at the same time and both relying on the same theoretical and operational approach to instruction.

It is possible that when the two tiers of instruction are less well aligned, as is often the case, results would differ. Moreover, it is possible that aligning Tier 1 and Tier 2 instructional content may differ as a function of academic domain. Consequently, more research is needed to assess the value-added of validated classroom instruction that is more and less aligned with tutoring and for different academic content.

It is also important to note that Tier 2 problem-type transfer tutoring was effective, even for students who were *not* receiving Tier 1 problem-type transfer whole-class instruction. For at-risk students whose classroom teachers were designing their own word-problem instruction, those who received Tier 1 problem-type transfer tutoring achieved 1.13 standard deviations beyond what at-risk students in those same classrooms who did not receive Tier 2 problem-type transfer tutoring achieved. Therefore, schools considering implementing Tier 2 problem-type transfer tutoring without taking on the added challenge of incorporating problem-type transfer instruction into Tier 1 can expect substantial benefits from simply implementing Tier 2 problem-type tutoring for students at risk for poor learning outcomes.

Moreover, the prevalence of math difficulty was clearly associated with Tier 2 problem-type transfer tutoring—and *not* with the provision of Tier 1 problem-type transfer whole-class instruction. At-risk tutored students were significantly and dramatically less likely than at-risk nontutored controls to be designated as having math difficulty at the end of the study, regardless of whether they received Tier 1 problem-type transfer whole-class instruction. Tier 2 problem-type transfer tutoring cut the proportion of students with math difficulty in half: from 26.6% of at-risk nontutored students (or 6.8% of the general population) to 12.8% of at-risk tutored students (or 3.9% of the general population). So, it appears that Tier 2 small-group tutoring, not validated Tier 1 classroom instruction, is the active agent that reduces math difficulty status for at-risk students.

CONCLUSION

As shown in this randomized controlled trial, problem-type transfer instruction is an effective practice for enhancing word-problem performance. Across three problem-solving measures and across tutoring conditions, the effect favoring Tier 1 problem-type transfer whole-class instruction over teachers' conventional mathematics problem-solving instruction on the performance of not-at-risk students was a large (and significant) 1.51 standard deviations. Findings also illustrate the disappointing efficacy of conventional math word-problem instruction and the need for improved methods to teach math problem-solving in general education classrooms. Problem-type transfer whole-class instruction represents one potentially strong approach for achieving that goal.

At the same time, Tier 2 problem-type transfer tutoring—even when conducted without Tier 1 problem-type transfer whole-class instruction—is an effective practice for improving the word-problem learning of at-risk students. In this case, the (significant) effect size was a substantial 1.13 standard deviations. Even so, the study suggests that for at-risk students, two tiers of prevention are more effective than one tier: When these students received Tier 2 tutoring closely aligned and theoretically compatible with validated Tier 1 classroom instruction, their learning exceeded that of students who received Tier 2 tutoring without validated Tier 1 classroom instruction—by a practically important effect size of 1.34 standard deviations.

Nonetheless, results indicate that small-group tutoring is the more essential tier of the prevention system. Tier 2 tutoring, not validated classroom instruction, reduced the prevalence of mathematics difficulty. Therefore, schools may consider implementing problem-type transfer tutoring as a second tier of prevention even when they do not have the resources to conduct problem-type transfer whole-class instruction for all students within the general education program.

REFERENCES

Fuchs, L.S. (2004). *The Algorithmic Word Problem Test*. Available from L.S. Fuchs, 228 Peabody, Vanderbilt University, Nashville, TN 37203.

Fuchs, L.S., Fuchs, D., Craddock, C., Hollenbeck, K.N., Hamlett, C.L., & Schatschneider, C. (2008). Effects of small-group tutoring with and without validated classroom instruction on at-risk students' math problem solving: Are two tiers of prevention better than one? *Journal of Educational Psychology, 100,* 491–509.

Fuchs, L.S., Fuchs, D., Prentice, K., Burch, M., Hamlett, C.L., Owen, R., et al. (2003). Explicitly teaching for transfer: Effects on third-grade students' mathematical problem solving. *Journal of Educational Psychology, 95,* 293–304.

Fuchs, L.S., Hamlett, C.L., & Fuchs, D. (1990). *Curriculum-based math computation and concepts/applications*. Available from L.S. Fuchs, 228 Peabody, Vanderbilt University, Nashville, TN 37203.

Jitendra, A., DiPipi, C.M., & Perron-Jones, N. (2002). An exploratory study of schema-based word problem solving instruction for middle school students with learning disabilities: An emphasis on conceptual and procedural understanding. *Journal of Special Education, 36,* 23–38.

Jitendra, A.K., Griffin, C.C., Haria, P., Leh, J., Adams, A., & Kaduvettoor, A. (2007). A comparison of single and multiple strategy instruction on third-grade students' mathematical problem solving. *Journal of Educational Psychology, 99,* 115–127.

Jitendra, A.K., Griffin, C.C., McGoey, K., Gardill, M.C., Bhat, P., & Riley, T. (1998). Effects of mathematical word problem solving by students at risk or with mild disabilities. *Journal of Educational Research, 91,* 345–355.

Jitendra, A.K., & Hoff, K. (1996). The effects of schema-based instruction on the word-problem-solving performance of students with learning disabilities. *Journal of Learning Disabilities, 29,* 421–431.

Woodcock, R.W., McGrew, K.S., & Mather, N. (2001). *Woodcock-Johnson III.* Itasca, IL: Riverside Publishing.

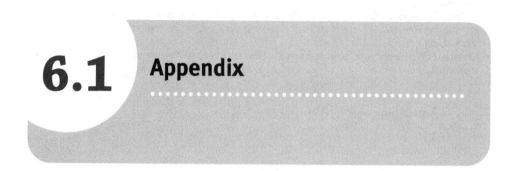

6.1 Appendix

HALF PROBLEM—WITH STUDENT WORK

3. Sharon is driving to Disney World. It takes 9 hours to drive there. She got tired of driving, so she stopped to rest after driving ½ of the trip. How many hours did she drive before she stopped?

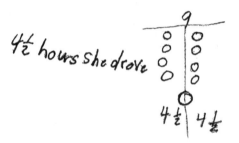

PICTOGRAPH PROBLEM—WITH STUDENT WORK

8. Kim painted Easter eggs. She made a chart of how many Easter eggs she painted. Each picture of an egg stands for 2 eggs Kim painted.

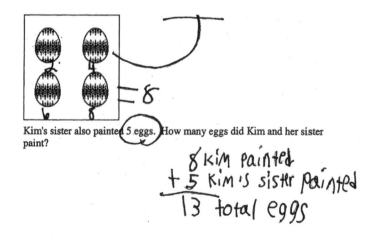

Kim's sister also painted 5 eggs. How many eggs did Kim and her sister paint?

BUYING BAGS PROBLEM—WITH STUDENT WORK

9. You want to buy some toy soldiers. Toy soldiers come in bags with 6 soldiers
    in each bag. How many bag. How many bags of toy soldiers do you need to
    buy to get 17 toy soldiers?

3 bags

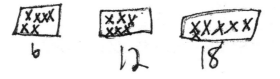

**BUYING BAGS TRANSFER PROBLEM—
DIFFERENT QUESTION—WITH STUDENT WORK**

4. You need 15 red pens. Red pens come in bags of 4 for $1. They also come in bags of 7 for $2. To save money, should you buy red pens in bags of 4 or in bags of 7?

The Best For Saving Money

**SHOPPING LIST TRANSFER PROBLEM—
DIFFERENT QUESTION—WITH STUDENT WORK (TWO EXAMPLES)**

2. Lance is going to camp. He has $40 to spend on supplies. He needs 2 lamps and 5 tents. Lamps cost $10 each. Tents cost $3 each. After he buys his camp supplies, how much money will Lance have left?

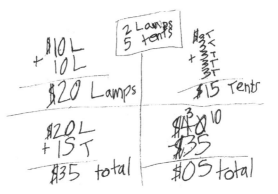

2. Lance is going to camp. He has $40 to spend on supplies. He needs 2 lamps and 5 tents. Lamps cost $10 each. Tents cost $3 each. After he buys his camp supplies, how much money will Lance have left?

$$
\begin{array}{cccc}
\begin{array}{r} 10 \\ \times\ 2 \\ \hline 20 \end{array} \text{ lamps} &
\begin{array}{r} 5 \\ \times\ 3 \\ \hline 15 \end{array} \text{ tents} &
\begin{array}{r} 15 \\ +\ 20 \\ \hline 35 \end{array} &
\begin{array}{r} 40 \\ -\ 35 \\ \hline 05 \end{array}
\end{array}
$$

5 dollars left

7

Effective Instructional Practices in Mathematics for Tier 2 and Tier 3 Instruction

Madhavi Jayanthi and Russell Gersten

Using evidence-based instructional practices to teach students is intuitively appealing and sensible. The idea has gained traction in recent years with the acceptance and widespread use of multitier response to intervention (RTI) systems (Glover, 2010; Riccomini & Witzel, 2010; Vaughn & Fuchs, 2003). But do we have sufficient high-quality research on effective instruction in mathematics to inform and guide practice? The concern is understandable given that research in mathematics has traditionally lagged behind research in other areas such as reading (Gersten, Clarke, & Mazzocco, 2007). However, in the past decade, a sufficient body of research has emerged because of a dramatic increase in the number of quality studies conducted in mathematics, from which valid conclusions can be drawn to inform and guide practice.

In this chapter we present and discuss effective research-based instructional practices in mathematics for use in Tier 2 and Tier 3 interventions. To pull together this resource, we tapped into a recent meta-analysis of causal research in mathematics (Gersten, Chard, et al., 2009) that helps summarize and highlight key instructional practices for improving students' mathematics outcomes. A meta-analysis is a statistical method by which research studies on a particular method of instruction are summarized for the purpose of determining the effectiveness of that instructional method. A meta-analysis helps combine findings from several disparate studies so that we are able to determine the effectiveness of a particular method of instruction. The methodology used in the meta-analysis is presented in Table 7.1.

Based on the findings, we present and discuss six instructional practices for teaching mathematics to students with learning disabilities and for students who are at risk of math failure—essentially Tier 2 and Tier 3 students. Although the meta-analysis focused on effective instructional practices for students with learning disabilities, we believe that many of these findings may be applicable to both students with learning disabilities and students with low achievement in mathematics.

Table 7.1. A brief description of the methodology used in the meta-analysis

Study	Gersten, Chard, Jayanthi, Baker, Morphy, and Flojo (2009)
Methodology	Meta-analysis and hierarchical multiple regressions
Sample	Students with an identified learning disability (LD)
Search dates	January 1971–August 2007
Search terms	*Mathematics achievement, mathematics education, mathematics research, elementary education, secondary education, learning disabilities, learning problems, mathematics and LD, arithmetic and LD*
Total number of studies included in the meta-analysis	42
Research design of included studies	Randomized controlled trials and quasi-experimental designs
Sample in the included studies	Students with an identified LD
Focus of the included studies	The study had to be an evaluation of the effectiveness of a well-defined method for improving mathematics proficiency.
Studies were excluded if	• Only one teacher or school was assigned per condition • Differential attrition exceeded 30% • The design was confounded • The dependent measure was poorly aligned with the intervention
Coding categories	Four major categories: 1) approaches to instruction and/or curriculum design, 2) providing ongoing formative assessment data and feedback to teachers on students' mathematics performance, 3) providing data and feedback to students with LD on their mathematics performance, and 4) peer-assisted mathematics instruction
Dependent variable	Mathematics achievement
Effect size calculation	Effect sizes for each contrast were calculated as Hedges *g*. The Wortman correction was used for studies that reported both pretest and posttest scores, and Hedges correction was used to correct for small sample size bias.

In Table 7.2, we present the effect sizes for the six suggested practices. We also indicate which of these six instructional practices are validated by other bodies of work such as the National Mathematics Advisory Panel (NMAP) reports (NMAP, 2008a, 2008b) and the practice guide on RTI in mathematics (Gersten, Beckmann, et al., 2009), and finally by synthesis of empirical research on teaching mathematics to low-achieving students (Baker, Gersten, & Lee, 2002).

EFFECTIVE INSTRUCTIONAL PRACTICES

Routinely Teach Mathematics Procedures, Ideas, and Concepts Explicitly and Systematically

Teaching students explicitly and systematically is a core feature of many special education programs (e.g., Fuchs & Fuchs, 2003; Gersten, Baker, Pugach, Scanlon, & Chard, 2001; Swanson & Hoskyn, 1998). The effectiveness of explicit instruction is demonstrated by the Gersten, Chard, et al. (2009) meta-analysis. Overall, the 11 studies that used explicit instruction as an instructional delivery tool resulted in significant effects and produced a mean effect size of 1.22 ($p < .001$).

In these 11 studies, explicit instruction was used to teach a variety of procedures, ideas, and concepts, such as one-step addition and subtraction word problems (Lee, 1992), how to find half of a given quantity (Owen & Fuchs, 2002), word problems involving multiplication and division (Xin, Jitendra, & Deatline-Buchman, 2005), how to use specific visual representations (Jitendra et al., 1998; Xin et al., 2005), and how to verbalize while solving a problem (Marzola, 1987; Ross & Braden, 1991; Tournaki, 1993, 2003). Data from the multiple regression analysis, which provide evidence on the relative impact of the instructional components included in the meta-analysis, strongly suggest that explicit instruction consistently resulted in gains regardless of whether it was paired with other instructional components.

The use of explicit instruction with both students with learning disabilities and students who are at risk of math failure is supported by additional reviews: the NMAP (2008a, 2008b) reports, the practice guide on RTI in mathematics (Gersten, Beckmann, et al., 2009), and the Baker et al. (2002) review of instructional practices with low-achieving students (see Table 7.2). Data from these research reviews lend credence to the viability of this instructional approach in teaching a variety of procedures, ideas, and concepts in a variety of situations and confirm that explicit instruction is an important tool for teaching mathematics to students with learning disabilities and those who are at risk of math failure.

Explicit instruction encompasses a series of teaching components such as modeling, opportunities for students to respond, guided practice, and corrective feedback (Silbert, Carnine, & Stein, 1989). However, the mainstay of this instructional method is modeling and demonstrating. This is not simply telling students the steps you take in

WHAT ARE OTHER REVIEWS SAYING ABOUT EXPLICIT INSTRUCTION?

Assisting Students Struggling with Mathematics: Response to Intervention (RtI) for Elementary and Middle Schools (Gersten, Beckmann, et al., 2009)

"Our panel judged the level of evidence supporting this recommendation to be *strong....* [The six] studies have shown that explicit and systematic instruction can significantly improve proficiency in word problem solving and operations across grade levels and diverse student populations." (p. 21)

Foundations for Success: The Final Report of the National Mathematics Advisory Panel (National Mathematics Advisory Panel, 2008a)

"Explicit instruction with students who have mathematical difficulties has shown consistently positive effects on performance with word problems and computation. Results are consistent for students with learning disabilities, as well as other students who perform in the lowest third of a typical class." (p. xxiii) "The Panel recommends that students with learning disabilities and other students with learning problems receive, on a regular basis, some explicit systematic instruction...." (p. 48) The Panel suggests "that teachers provide clear models for solving a problem type using an array of examples...." (p. xxiii)

Baker, Gersten, and Lee (2002) research synthesis
"[O]verall, the approaches that used explicit instruction had a positive, moderately strong effect on the mathematics achievement of at-risk students." (p. 64)

Table 7.2. Support for the six effective instructional practices

Instructional practice		Gersten, Chard, et al. (2009) meta-analysis of instructional practices in mathematics for students with learning disabilities		The National Mathematics Advisory Panel (2008a, 2008b)		Practice guide on response to intervention in mathematics (Gersten, Beckmann, et al., 2009)		Baker, Gersten, and Lee (2002) synthesis of empirical research on teaching mathematics to low-achieving students	
		Number of studies included in the meta-analysis	Mean effect size	Number of studies included in the review	Support	Number of studies included in the review	Support[a]	Number of studies included in the synthesis	Mean effect size
Explicit instruction		11	1.22***	13	√[b]	6	Strong	4	0.58*
Student verbalizations		8	1.04***	2	√[c]				
Sequence and/or range of examples		9	0.82***	—	√[d]				
Visuals for teacher and student		12	0.47***	5	√[e]	13	Moderate		
Providing teachers with feedback on student performance	Feedback plus instructional guidance	3	0.34~	11	√[f]			1	0.51
	Feedback only	7	0.21*	9	√[g]			4[h]	0.57*
Peer-assisted instruction	Peer-assisted learning within a classroom	6	0.14	11	√[i]			5	0.66*
	Cross-age tutoring	2	1.02***						

112

~$p < .10$; *$p < .05$; **$p < .01$; ***$p < .001$.

[a]Three levels of ratings are provided based on the strength of the research evidence: strong, moderate, and low. Additional information on the evidence levels can be obtained from Gersten, Beckmann, et al. (2009).

[b]For students with learning disabilities (LD), pooled effect sizes included 1.152*** for word problem outcomes (six studies) and 1.285*** for computation outcomes (three studies). For low-achieving students, effect sizes for the four studies ranged from 0.569* to 1.914.***

[c]Two studies with students with LD were reviewed in which thinking aloud was the sole independent variable. The effect sizes were 0.135 (Ross & Braden, 1991) and 1.005*** (Schunk & Cox, 1986). The panel also looked at other studies in which thinking aloud was used within the context of explicit instruction (e.g., Hutchinson, 1993; Van Luit & Naglieri, 1999) and found thinking aloud to be beneficial.

[d]The importance of example selection was discussed within the framework of explicit instruction. In some of the studies included under this category—for example, Jitendra et al. (1998; effect size [ES] = 0.557) and Owen and Fuchs (2002; ES = 3.385***)—careful selection of examples to highlight critical differences and similarities in the problems was a component of the instructional intervention.

[e]Effect sizes for the five studies with students with LD ranged from –0.153 to 0.826.*

[f]All 11 studies included students with LD and/or low-achieving students. Six studies examined feedback to teachers plus enhancements versus control. The pooled effect size was 0.383** (student-level analyses); one study was analyzed at the classroom level (ES = 0.657). Five studies examined the impact of teacher feedback plus enhancement versus teacher feedback only. These studies resulted in a pooled effect size of 0.194 (four studies with student-level analyses); one study analyzed at the classroom level resulted in an effect size of 0.750~.

[g]All studies except two included students with disabilities and/or low-achieving students. The pooled effect size for student level analyses (six studies) was 0.206~ and for classroom analyses (three studies) was 0.408~.

[h]In the four studies, feedback was provided to students and/or teachers.

[i]Studies reviewed under cooperative learning strategies included samples of general education students, students with LD, and/or low-achieving students. For computation outcome: Pooled effect size for team assisted individualization = 0.377** (four studies; student-level analyses) and 0.633*** (two studies, classroom-level analyses); pooled effect size for peer-assisted learning = 0.238~ (three studies; student-level analyses) and 0.431** (two studies, classroom-level analyses).

113

Problem: John has 3 apples and 2 oranges. How many pieces of fruit does he have in all?

Teacher writes the problem on the board and thinks aloud how to solve the problem:

"I am first going to read the problem. *John has 3 apples and 2 oranges. How many pieces of fruit does he have in all?*
How many pieces of fruit? I know that apples and oranges are fruits.
In all? That tells me that I have to add.
How many fruits does he have in all? I know what I have to do. I have to add all the fruits he has. I will add the number of oranges and the number of apples.
3 + 2 = 5. And that gives me 5 fruits."

Problem: In her pencil box, Sally found 3 red pencils, 1 blue pencil, 1 black pencil, and 1 eraser. How many more red pencils were there in all than blue pencils?

Teacher writes the problem on the board and thinks aloud how to solve the problem:

"I am first going to read the problem. *In her pencil box, Sally found 3 red pencils, 1 blue pencil, 1 black pencil, and 1 eraser. How many more red pencils were there in all than blue pencils?*
Mmm, there is a lot of information in this problem, and I am getting confused. Let me read this problem again. *In her pencil box, Sally found 3 red pencils, 1 blue pencil, 1 black pencil, and 1 eraser. How many more red pencils were there in all than blue pencils?*
In all? Hey, in the problem I just did, I added. But I don't think that is what I need to do here.
I will read this again: *How many more red pencils were there in all than blue pencils?* I know that I have 3 red pencils and 1 blue pencil. So, the question is: *How many more red pencils than blue pencils?* OK, I know that I have subtract to find out how many more red pencils I have.
3 − 1 = 2. So, I have 2 more red pencils than blue pencils."

Figure 7.1.   Sample think alouds.

computing an answer. Good modeling requires teachers to *think aloud* the steps they take to solve the problem and, more important, the decisions they make as they navigate their way toward the solution. Thus, the emphasis is on the teacher making obvious and clear all the implicit procedures and decisions involved in solving the problem.

Asking teachers to model and think aloud is a task that is easier said than done. Teachers will need professional development opportunities in which they can see some examples of effective modeling and thinking aloud and will have opportunities to practice them. See sample think alouds in Figure 7.1.

Carefully Select a Range of Instructional Examples to Include in the Lesson

The importance of example selection in teaching new math procedures, ideas, and concepts is a seminal idea that is well emphasized in the effective instruction literature (e.g., Engelmann & Carnine, 1982; Ma, 1999; Rittle-Johnson & Star, 2007; Silbert et al., 1989). The Gersten, Chard, et al. (2009) meta-analysis provides evidence in support of careful example selection while one is planning lessons. Overall, nine studies on example selection were included in the meta-analysis. The mean effect size was .82 ($p < .001$).

The nine studies looked at example selection in two ways. Some studies focused on sequencing examples to either highlight the distinctive features of a given problem type (e.g., Xin et al., 2005) or to progress systematically from easy to more complex and difficult problems (Wilson & Sindelar, 1991; Woodward, 2006) or from concrete examples to abstract notations (Witzel, Mercer, & Miller, 2003). In some other studies, the focus was on selecting a range of examples (Fuchs, Fuchs, & Prentice, 2004; Kelly, Gersten, & Carnine, 1990; Owen & Fuchs, 2002) for the purpose of highlighting common features of seemingly disparate problems.

Data from the Gersten, Chard, et al. (2009) meta-analysis indicate that, by carefully selecting and sequencing instructional examples, we can have an impact on mathematics performance of students. The NMAP reports (2008a, 2008b) also provide support for this effective practice (see Table 7.2). The NMAP recommends that teachers carefully sequence problems so that critical features and differences in the problems are highlighted (NMAP, 2008a).

Teachers need to spend some time planning their mathematics instruction, particularly focusing on selecting and sequencing their instructional examples. We believe that it is necessary for teachers to carefully sequence the problems they are planning on teaching during early acquisition of new procedures, ideas, and concepts when scaffolding is critical for student success. Teachers can present multiple examples in a specified sequence or pattern such as concrete to abstract, easy to hard, or simple to complex. For example, fractions or algebraic equations can be taught first with concrete examples, then with pictorial representations, and finally in an abstract manner (Butler, Miller, Crehan, Babbitt, & Pierce, 2003; Witzel et al., 2003). Teachers can also systematically introduce problems they teach to control the difficulty level of the task being learned. For instance, they can initially teach only proper fractions rather than introduce both proper and improper fractions at the same time.

Another goal while one is planning lessons is to expose students to all possible variations of the problem and at the same time highlight the common but critical features of seemingly disparate problems. For example, while teaching students to solve problems that require them to divide a given unit into half, a variety of problems can be presented that differ in the way the critical task of half is addressed in the problems (e.g., use symbol for half, use the word *half*, use the words *one half*, Owen & Fuchs, 2002).

Be particularly aware of textbooks that only provide examples of how to solve the easy problems and leave all of the difficult ones for students to work on independently. Allocate time while planning lessons to demonstrate solutions for some difficult problems from each lesson. Intentionally think aloud the steps and decisions while demonstrating these solutions.

Have Students Verbalize Decisions and Solutions to the Math Problem

Many struggling students lack focus and persistence when solving problems, and, rather than implementing a step-by-step solution, they often approach the problem haphazardly, randomly combining numbers to arrive at the solution (Fuchs et al., 2003; Raghubar et al., 2009). In such cases, verbalizing the decisions and steps while solving a problem may facilitate students' self-regulation and help them stay focused on the task.

In the Gersten, Chard, et al. (2009) meta-analysis, the eight studies that examined the impact of student verbalizations on mathematics performance resulted in a significant mean effect size of 1.04 ($p < .001$). The studies revealed differences in the amount of student verbalization encouraged, the specificity of the verbalizations, and the type of verbalizations. Some studies gave students very specific questions to ask themselves. Others were based on cognitive behavior modification and provided students with very general guidance. For example, Hutchinson taught students to ask themselves: "Have I written an equation?" and "Have I expanded the terms?" (1993, p. 39). Schunk and Cox (1986) provided even broader guidance to students—instructing them to verbalize what they were thinking as they solved the problems.

Student verbalizations are also supported by the research reviewed in the NMAP Report (NMAP, 2008a; see Table 7.2). The NMAP felt that students should be "provided with opportunities to think aloud (i.e., talk through the decisions they make and the steps they take)" (p .48) and that student think alouds are most beneficial when they are integrated with explicit instruction.

Teachers should encourage their students to verbalize as they solve problems both in class and at home. Students can verbalize the specific steps that lead to the solution of the problem (e.g., *I need to divide by two to get half*) or they can verbalize generic heuristic steps that are common to problems (e.g., *Now I need to check my answer*). Students can verbalize the steps in a solution format (*First add the numbers in the units column. Write down the answer. Then add numbers in the tens column...*; Tournaki, 2003) or in a self-questioning and -answering format (*What should I do first? I should...*; Pavchinski, 1988). To facilitate student verbalizations, teachers will need to model some verbalizations to the students first. Teachers can solve a problem on the board and think aloud the verbalizations that they would like to hear from the students.

Student verbalizations benefit both teachers and students. Verbalization can help students by anchoring their mathematical knowledge. By having students verbalize their thinking as they approach the problem, teachers can get an insight into student understanding, specifically misconceptions and errors, which will enable them to determine the level of support or scaffolds and additional instruction they will need to provide to the students (e.g., Palincsar, 1986).

Teach Students to Visually Represent the Information in the Math Problem

Teachers use visual representations (drawings, graphic representations) to explain and clarify problems and students use them to understand and simplify problems. Such use of visual representations has been consistently recommended in the literature on mathematics instruction (e.g., Griffin, Case, & Siegler, 1994; National Research Council, 2001; Witzel et al., 2003).

Findings from the meta-analysis (Gersten, Chard, et al., 2009) do support the use of visual representations by teachers and students. Twelve studies were reviewed in this meta-analysis to examine the impact of visual representations on student mathematics achievement. In seven of these studies, teacher use of the visual representation was followed by *mandatory* student use of the same visual while solving problems; in the remaining five studies, only the teacher used the visual representations. Both of these variations resulted in similar effect sizes (0.46 for teacher and student use; 0.41 for teacher use only), indicating that use of visuals during instruction leads to consistent significant effects (overall mean $g = 0.47$).

Data from the multiple regression analysis, which provide evidence on the relative impact of the instructional components included in the meta-analysis, suggest that better effects are obtained when visuals are used in combination with other instructional components than when used alone. For example, studies in which visuals were not paired with other instructional components (Baker, 1992; Lambert, 1996; Manalo, Bunnell, & Stillman, 2000) resulted in lesser impacts than studies in which visuals were paired with other instructional components such as explicit instruction.

The NMAP reports (2008a, 2008b) and the practice guide on RTI in mathematics (Gersten, Beckmann, et al., 2009) also provide support for use of visual representations with students with learning disability (LD) (see Table 7.2). Thus, the findings from all of these reviews confirm what teachers have sensed for many years—using graphic representations and teaching students how to understand them can help students with LD.

Various types of visual representations are evident in the literature. For example, number lines are beneficial in scaffolding learning and facilitating the transition to a more abstract mental number line, which would help with problems involving magnitude comparisons and estimation, two critical mathematical proficiencies (Gersten, Beckmann, et al., 2009; Okamato & Case, 1996). They also set the stage, as early as kindergarten, for students' ability to use and interpret graphs of functions in middle school and high school. In recent years, strip diagrams have been increasingly used to solve a variety of problems (e.g., Ng & Lee, 2009; Parker, 2004).

WHAT ARE OTHER REVIEWS SAYING ABOUT VISUAL REPRESENTATIONS?

Assisting Students Struggling with Mathematics: Response to Intervention (RtI) for Elementary and Middle Schools (Gersten, Beckmann, et al., 2009)

"The panel judged the level of evidence supporting this recommendation to be *moderate.* . . . [The 13] studies provide support for the systematic use of visual representatives or manipulatives to improve achievement in general mathematics, prealgebra concepts, word problems, and operations." (p. 30)

Foundations for Success: The Final Report of the National Mathematics Advisory Panel (National Mathematics Advisory Panel, 2008a)

"Most of the small number of studies that investigated the use of visual representations yielded nonsignificant effects. However, studies that included visual representations along with the other components of explicit instruction tended to produce significant positive effects." (p. 48)

• •

Often, visual representations are used to represent the information in problems graphically, so as to organize and make sense of the information before translating it into a mathematical notation. For example, in the study by Jitendra et al. (1998), students first identified what type of problem they had been given (e.g., compare, change) and then used a corresponding diagram (taught to them) to represent essential information and the mathematical procedure necessary to find the unknown. Then they translated the diagram into a math sentence and solved it.

Visual representations can also be used to arrive at a solution, as in the case of using a number line to solve simple addition problems. Another way to use visual representations was demonstrated by Owen and Fuchs (2002). They taught students how to determine half of a given quantity without having to translate their problem into mathematical notation (e.g., half of 6 = draw a rectangle and divide it into half to make two boxes; distribute 6 circles, representing the number 6, evenly into the two boxes; determine the number of circles in one box to determine the answer). Their goal was to use the visual representations so that students actually understood the concept of halving a quantity, and thus they could solve problems involving this concept.

It is likely that students receiving interventions in mathematics will need to be taught how to use visual representations in an explicit manner and be provided ample guidance as they begin to use visual representations. It appears to be more beneficial when students use a visual representation prescribed by the teacher and that has been designed specifically to address a particular problem type, rather than one that is self-selected (Baker, 1992; Xin et al., 2005). It appears that when students select visual representations on their own, they are often not clearly linked to mathematical ideas or critical mathematical relationships.

Mathematics coaches and specialists can be excellent sources for teachers. Teacher study groups can also be a great venue for sharing ideas with other teachers or interventionists.

Provide Teachers with Options for Addressing Instructional Needs Along with Ongoing Formative Assessment Data

Ongoing formative assessment and evaluations of students' progress in mathematics can help teachers measure the pulse and rhythm of their students' growth in mathematics, and also help them in fine-tuning their instruction to meet the needs of their students. The importance of formative assessment data was evidenced by the findings of the Gersten, Chard, et al. (2009) meta-analysis. The seven studies that were included in the meta-analysis resulted in a mean effect size of 0.23 ($p = .01$). The meta-analysis also provided information on the type of feedback that is beneficial for teachers. For instance, providing teachers with specific information on how each student was performing clearly enhanced student math achievement (mean $g = 0.21$; $p = .04$). However, the findings from the meta-analysis indicated that greater benefits on student performance will be observed if teachers are provided with not only performance feedback information but also instructional tips and suggestions that can help teachers with decisions such as what to teach, when to introduce the next skill, and how to group or pair students. Three studies allowed us to examine the "value added" by providing teachers with additional information for addressing instructional needs. The mean effect size for this set of studies was 0.34 (p = .10) and approached significance, thus indicating that additional information that provided instructional guidance to the teachers made the formative assessments more effective.

Similar conclusions were reached by two other reviews: the NMAP review (2008a) and the Baker et al. review (2002). Data from both of these reviews demonstrated the importance of providing teachers with some guidance on how to use the data from the formative assessments more effectively in making adjustments to their teaching (see Table 7.2). Note that, because of the limited number of studies included in the review, the findings of the Baker et al. review are only suggestive in nature regarding the importance of additional data to guide instruction. However, the NMAP's findings are more promising and wide reaching because the review focused on studies that included a range of students (general education students, students with disabilities, and low-achieving students).

To facilitate more effective use of formative assessment data and to help teachers in planning and fine tuning their instruction, teachers need to be provided routinely with guidance for addressing their students' instructional needs. For example, teachers can be given a set of written questions to help them use the formative assessment data for adapting and individualizing instruction. These written questions could include "On what skill(s) has the student improved compared with the previous 2-week period?" and "How will I attempt to improve student performance on the targeted skill(s)?" Teachers can respond to these questions and readdress these questions when new assessment data become available

WHAT ARE OTHER REVIEWS SAYING ABOUT FORMATIVE ASSESSMENT DATA?

Foundations for Success: The Final Report of the National Mathematics Advisory Panel (National Mathematics Advisory Panel, 2008a)

"Teachers' regular use of formative assessment improves their students' learning, especially if teachers have additional guidance on using the assessment to design and to individualize instruction. Although research to date has only involved one type of formative assessment (that based on items sampled from the major curriculum objectives for the year, based on state standards), the results are sufficiently promising that the Panel recommends regular use of formative assessment for students in the elementary grades." (p. xxiii)

Baker, Gersten, and Lee (2002) research synthesis
"[T]he small number of studies and comparisons supported the practice of providing feedback to students and recommendations to them on what problems to work." (p. 61)

. . . .

(Allinder, Bolling, Oats, & Gagnon, 2000). Teachers can also be provided with a specific set of recommendations to address instructional planning issues such as which mathematical topics require additional instructional time for the entire class, which students require additional help via some sort of small group instruction or tutoring, and which topics to include in small group instruction (Fuchs, Fuchs, Hamlett, Phillips, & Bentz, 1994).

The findings from the Gersten, Chard, et al. (2009) meta-analysis also alluded to the role special and general education teachers play in having an impact on student performance. Providing instructional guidance information to special educators produced better effects on student outcomes than when similar information was provided to general education teachers. Regarding the added benefit with special educators, it may be that because special education teachers are prepared to use detailed student performance data to set individual goals for students, their familiarity with using information on performance is particularly useful for this group. General education teachers, being less familiar with formative assessment data than special education teachers, might need assistance interpreting and using the data in fine tuning their instruction. As schools or districts begin developing and implementing progress monitoring systems in mathematics, it might be beneficial if they include not only graphs of student performance but also specific instructional guidelines and curricular materials for teachers or other relevant personnel (e.g., special educators who may co-teach or provide support services, adults providing extra support) so that they can immediately modify instruction as needed for their students.

A PROMISING INSTRUCTIONAL PRACTICE

Peer-Assisted Instruction

Students with LD and at-risk students are often provided with some type of assistance or one-to-one tutoring in areas for which they need help. Sometimes students' peers provide this assistance or one-to-one tutoring. There are two types of peer tutoring. The more traditional is *cross-age*, wherein a student in a higher grade functions primarily as the tutor for a student in a lower grade (Robinson, Schofield, & Steers-Wentzell, 2005). In the newer within-classroom approach, two students in the same grade essentially tutor or assist each other. In many cases, a higher performing student is strategically paired with a lower performing student, but typically both students work in the role of the tutor (who provides the tutoring) and the tutee (who receives the tutoring; Fuchs, Fuchs, Yazdian, & Powell, 2002). For example, in working on a set of problems, the higher performing child will work on the problems first and the lower performing child will provide feedback. Then roles will be reversed and the lower performing child will work on problems for which he or she just had a model for how to solve them. Or in providing explanations for math solutions, the higher performing child will provide the explanation first and the lower performing child will have had a model for a strong explanation (Fuchs, Fuchs, Phillips, Hamlett, & Karns, 1995).

Generally, students use their time in peer-assisted instruction practicing math problems for which they have received previous instruction from their teacher. Results from the Gersten, Chard, et al. (2009) meta-analysis do not support the use of peer-assisted instruction with students with LD. Six studies focused on peer-assisted learning within a class were included in the meta-analysis. They resulted in a mean effect size of 0.14, which was not statistically significant ($p = .27$). In sharp contrast, the two studies that investigated cross-age tutoring yielded impressive effect sizes (1.15 and 0.75). The tutees in both studies were elementary students, and the tutors were well-trained upper-elementary students.

It seems that peer-assisted instruction may fall short of the level of explicitness and scaffolding necessary to effectively help students with LD progress in the general classroom. Students with LD may be 2 or more years below grade level proficiency in mathematics, and typical peer-assisted instruction formats do not allow for "backtracking" to foundational procedures, ideas, and concepts. This interpretation is supported by the more positive effects of cross-age peer tutoring wherein the tutor is an older student who has received extensive training in how to tutor and is trained in how to build critical foundational proficiencies

> ## WHAT ARE OTHER REVIEWS SAYING ABOUT PEER-ASSISTED INSTRUCTION?
>
> *Foundations for Success: The Final Report of the National Mathematics Advisory Panel* (National Mathematics Advisory Panel, 2008a)
>
> "Research has been conducted on a variety of cooperative learning approaches. One such approach, Team Assisted Individualization (TAI), has been shown to improve students' computation skills. This highly structured instructional approach involves heterogeneous groups of students helping each other, individualized problems based on student performance on a diagnostic test, specific teacher guidance, and rewards based on both group and individual performance. Effects of TAI on conceptual understanding and problem solving were not significant. There is suggestive evidence that peer tutoring improves computation skills in the elementary grades. However, additional research is needed." (p. 46)
>
> Baker, Gersten, and Lee (2002) research synthesis
> "It is safest to conclude that the peer-assisted learning approaches demonstrated a consistent, moderately strong positive effect on the computation abilities of low achievers." (p. 61)

necessary to function at grade level. Practically speaking, however, cross-age tutoring presents practical logistical difficulties for implementation.

The NMAP (2008a, 2008b) concluded that peer-assisted instruction is promising, but that the results were not conclusive enough to recommend its use. In contrast, the Baker et al. (2002) review of peer-assisted learning interventions for low-achieving students led to positive effects on student achievement, especially in the area of computation outcomes (mean effect size = 0.62; see Table 7.2).

Peer tutoring or some form of peer-assisted instruction intuitively makes sense. Because a teacher cannot be available to provide individual help to all students in a timely manner, having students work with each other allows for students' questions to be clarified and answered in a timely manner. Because of the inconclusive nature of the evidence at this time, especially for students with disabilities, we recommend that teachers use peer tutoring judiciously and monitor its impact on student performance.

CONCLUSION

In this chapter, we have addressed the issue of how to teach, rather than what to teach. For information on what needs to be taught in Tiers 2 and 3, we suggest that the reader gain access to sources such as the practice guide in RTI in mathematics (Gersten, Beckmann, et al., 2009) and Curriculum Focal Points (National Council of Teachers of Mathematics, 2006), and the final report of the NMAP (2008a).

The effective instructional strategies identified in this chapter are not cutting-edge ideas. Instead, they are seminal ideas that have been mentioned in the literature and have been part of some teachers' repertoires for years. However, concerted efforts are necessary to ensure that their use is more common and sustained.

Professional development opportunities are essential for making these instructional practices routine. To pave the way for better implementation of these strategies, math coaches can focus on quality teaching issues. They can facilitate effective implementation by asking probing questions, such as, Are we modeling the strategies and concepts appropriately? Are we thinking aloud not only the steps but also the decisions we are making as we solve a problem? Are we having children solve a random selection of problems, or are we carefully selecting and sequencing the problems to highlight the commonalities and distinguishing features? Are we asking students to verbalize their decisions and solution steps consistently? Have we modeled how to verbalize? Are we explicitly teaching students how to visualize the content of a problem and facilitating the use of visuals with a larger set of problems?

The instructional strategies highlighted in this chapter can be incorporated within the existing approaches to RTI: the standard protocol approach (a scripted supplemental program) and problem-solving approach (program designed and tailored to an individual student's needs; see Clarke, Gersten, & Newman-Gonchar, 2010). While selecting the standard protocol programs, one should look for curricula that incorporate these strategies. If the program does not include these elements of effective instruction, one should incorporate them into the existing programs to enhance their effectiveness. Likewise, while designing a program for a student, one should incorporate elements of effective instruction to ensure that the tailored intervention is being taught effectively.

These effective instructional strategies provide a starting point in meeting the needs of struggling students. There is so much more that still needs to be studied specifically with students who are struggling in math. For instance, what is the impact of the numerous inquiry-based and project-based instructional approaches in mathematics on students with disabilities and at-risk students? What are the best instructional strategies for building understanding of the mathematical principles and ideas in the curriculum? What are the best ways to promote transfer of the strategies taught to novel situations? How do struggling students fare in problem-solving activities when exposed to multiple ways of solving a problem?

In addition, we need to figure out the nature of the content to teach during Tier 2 and Tier 3 interventions. We have a good deal of compelling research indicating that content should always be a mix of procedural and conceptual material. Earlier beliefs to first work on the "basics" (e.g., computation fluency) and to save problem solving and work on mathematical concepts and ideas for "later on" were rarely successful in promoting proficiency. Most recent interventions contain procedures, ideas, and concepts (e.g., Bryant, this volume; Fuchs, this volume; Jitendra, this volume). Also, we know little about how to link the content taught during Tier 2 and Tier 3 interventions with topics covered in core mathematics instruction. Is a tight linkage productive? Is it productive enough to justify all of the time and energy necessary to organize and orchestrate such a linkage? Should we, instead, systematically build foundational skills in mathematics for students in Tier 2 and Tier 3 interventions and not worry so much about alignment issues?

These are but a few of the topics that should be studied in the new generation of research on teaching mathematics to struggling students using a variety of Tier 2 and Tier 3 interventions. The rapid acceleration of research on interventions for students struggling in mathematics would seem to indicate that (at least partial) answers to some of these questions are on the horizon.

In summary, the need for effective mathematics instruction in Tiers 2 and 3 cannot be emphasized enough. In essence, mathematics instruction in these tiers needs to be approached as seriously and as intensively as reading instruction is approached within the RTI framework, with the basic goal of addressing student mathematics deficiencies on all fronts. Teaching students by using evidence-based strategies, routinely monitoring student performance, and fine tuning instruction based on student performance are essential elements that pave the way for mathematics proficiency in Tiers 2 and 3.

REFERENCES

Allinder, R.M., Bolling, R., Oats, R., & Gagnon, W.A. (2000). Effects of teacher self-monitoring on implementation of curriculum-based measurement and mathematics computation achievement of students with disabilities. *Remedial and Special Education, 21*, 219–226.

Baker, D.E. (1992). *The effect of self-generated drawings on the ability of students with learning disabilities to solve mathematical word problems* (Unpublished doctoral dissertation). Texas Tech University.

Baker, S., Gersten, R., & Lee, D. (2002). A synthesis of empirical research on teaching mathematics to low-achieving students. *Elementary School Journal, 103*, 51–73.

Butler, F.M., Miller, S.P., Crehan, K., Babbitt, B., & Pierce, T. (2003). Fraction instruction for students with mathematics disabilities: Comparing two teaching sequences. *Learning Disabilities Research and Practice, 18*, 99–111.

Clarke, B., Gersten, R., & Newman-Gonchar, R. (2010). RTI in mathematics: Beginnings of a knowledge base. In T.A. Glover & S. Vaughn (Eds.), *The promise of response to intervention: Evaluating current science and practice* (pp. 187–203). New York: Guilford Press.

Engelmann, S., & Carnine, D. (1982). *Theory of instruction.* New York: Irvington.

Fuchs, D., & Deshler, D.D. (2007). What we need to know about responsiveness to intervention (and shouldn't be afraid to ask). *Learning Disabilities Research & Practice, 22*, 129–136.

Fuchs, L.S., & Fuchs, D. (2003). Enhancing the mathematical problem solving of students with mathematics disabilities. In H.L. Swanson, K.R. Harris, & S.E. Graham (Eds.), *Handbook on learning disabilities* (pp. 306–322). New York: Guilford Press.

Fuchs, L.S., Fuchs, D., Hamlett, C.L., Phillips, N.B., & Bentz, J. (1994). Classwide curriculum-based measurement: Helping general educators meet the challenge of student diversity. *Exceptional Children, 60*, 518–537.

Fuchs, L.S., Fuchs, D., Phillips, N.B., Hamlett, C.L., & Karns, K. (1995). Acquisition and transfer effects of classwide peer-assisted learning strategies in mathematics for students with varying learning histories. *School Psychology Review, 24*, 604–620.

Fuchs, L.S., Fuchs, D., & Prentice, K. (2004). Responsiveness to mathematical problem-solving instruction: Comparing students at risk of mathematics disability with and without risk of reading disability. *Journal of Learning Disabilities, 37*, 293–306.

Fuchs, L.S., Fuchs, D., Prentice, K., Burch, M., Hamlett, C.L., Owen, R., et al. (2003). Enhancing third-grade students' mathematical problem solving with self-regulated learning strategies. *Journal of Educational Psychology, 95*, 306–315.

Fuchs, L.S., Fuchs, D., Yazdian, L., & Powell, S.R. (2002). Enhancing first-grade children's mathematical development with peer-assisted learning strategies. *School Psychology Review, 31*, 569–583.

Gersten, R., Baker, S.K., Pugach, M., Scanlon, D., & Chard, D. (2001). Contemporary research on special education teaching. In V. Richardson (Ed.), *Handbook for research on teaching* (4th ed., pp. 695–722). Washington, DC: American Educational Research Association.

Gersten, R., Beckmann, S., Clarke, B., Foegen, A., Marsh, L., Star, J.R., et al. (2009). *Assisting students struggling with mathematics: Response to intervention (RtI) for elementary and middle schools (NCEE 2009-4060)*. Washington, DC: National Center for Education Evaluation and Regional Assistance, Institute of Education Sciences, U.S. Department of Education.

Gersten, R., Chard, D., Jayanthi, M., Baker, S., Morphy, P., & Flojo, J. (2009). *A meta-analysis of mathematics instructional interventions for students with learning disabilities: Technical Report*. Los Alamitos, CA: Instructional Research Group. Retrieved from http://www.inresg.org

Gersten, R., Clarke, B., & Mazzocco, M.M.M. (2007). Historical and contemporary perspectives on mathematical learning disabilities. In D.B. Berch & M.M.M. Mazzocco (Eds.), *Why is math so hard for some children? The nature and origins of mathematical learning difficulties and disabilities* (pp. 7–29). Baltimore: Paul H. Brooks Publishing Co.

Glover, T.A. (2010). Key RTI service delivery components: Considerations for research-informed practice. In T.A. Glover & S. Vaughn (Eds.), *The promise of response to intervention: Evaluating current science and practice* (pp. 7–22). New York: Guilford Press.

Griffin, S.A., Case, R., & Siegler, R.S. (1994). Rightstart: Providing the central conceptual prerequisites for first formal learning of arithmetic to students at risk for school failure. In K. McGilly (Ed.), *Classroom lessons: Integrating cognitive theory and classroom practice* (pp. 24–49). Cambridge, MA: MIT Press.

Hutchinson, N.L. (1993). Effects of cognitive strategy instruction on algebra problem solving of adolescents with learning disabilities. *Learning Disability Quarterly, 16*, 34–63.

Jitendra, A.K., Griffin, C.C., McGoey, K., Gardill, M.G., Bhat, P., & Riley, T. (1998). Effects of mathematical word problem solving by students at risk or with mild disabilities. *The Journal of Educational Research, 91*(6), 345–355.

Kelly, B., Gersten, R., & Carnine, D. (1990). Student error patterns as a function of curriculum design: Teaching fractions to remedial high school students with learning disabilities. *Journal of Learning Disabilities, 23*, 23–29.

Lambert, M.A. (1996). *Teaching students with learning disabilities to solve word-problems: A comparison of a cognitive strategy and a traditional textbook method* (Unpublished doctoral dissertation). Florida Atlantic University, Boca Raton, FL.

Lee, J.W. (1992). *The effectiveness of a novel direct instructional approach on math word problem solving skills of elementary students with learning disabilities* (Unpublished doctoral dissertation). Ohio State University, Columbus, OH.

Ma, L. (1999). *Knowing and teaching elementary mathematics*. Mahwah, NJ: Lawrence Erlbaum Associates.

Manalo, E., Bunnell, J., & Stillman, J. (2000). The use of process mnemonics in teaching students with mathematics learning disabilities. *Learning Disability Quarterly, 23*, 137–156.

Marzola, E. (1987). *An arithmetic verbal problem solving model for learning disabled students*. New York: Columbia University Teachers College.

National Council of Teachers of Mathematics. (2006). *Curriculum focal points for prekindergarten through grade 8 mathematics: A quest for coherence*. Reston, VA: Author.

National Mathematics Advisory Panel. (2008a). *Foundations for success: The final report of the National Mathematics Advisory Panel*. Washington, DC: U.S. Department of Education.

National Mathematics Advisory Panel. (2008b). *Foundations for success: Reports of the task groups and subcommittees*. Washington, DC: U.S. Department of Education.

National Research Council. (2001). Adding it up: Helping children learn mathematics. In J. Kilpatrick, J. Swafford, & B. Findell (Eds.), *Mathematics Learning Study Committee, Center for Education, Division of Behavioral and Social Sciences and Education*. Washington, DC: National Academy Press.

Ng, S.F., & Lee, K. (2009). The model method: Singapore children's tool for representing and solving algebraic word problems. *Journal for Research in Mathematics Education, 40*(3), 282–313

Okamato, Y., & Case, R. (1996). Exploring the microstructure of children's central conceptual structures in the domain of number. *Monographs of the Society for Research in Child Development, 61*, 27–59.

Owen, R.L., & Fuchs, L.S. (2002). Mathematical problem-solving strategy instruction for third-grade students with learning disabilities. *Remedial and Special Education, 23*, 268–278.

Palincsar, A.S. (1986). The role of dialogue in providing scaffolded instruction. *Educational Psychologist, 21*, 73–98.

Parker, M. (2004). Reasoning and working proportionally with percent. *Mathematics Teaching in the Middle School, 9*(6), 326–330.

Pavchinski, P. (1988). *The effects of operant procedures and cognitive behavior modification on learning disabled students' math skills* (Unpublished doctoral dissertation). University of Florida.

Raghubar, K., Cirino, P., Barnes, M., Ewing-Cobbs, L., Fletcher, J., & Fuchs, L. (2009). Errors in multi-digit arithmetic and behavioral inattention with children with math difficulties. *Journal of Learning Disabilities, 42*(4), 356–371.

Riccomini, P.J., & Witzel, B.S. (2010). *Response to intervention in math*. Thousand Oaks, CA: Corwin Press.

Rittle-Johnson, B., & Star, J.R. (2007). Does comparing solution methods facilitate conceptual and procedural knowledge? An experimental study on learning to solve equations. *Journal of Educational Psychology, 99*(3), 561–574.

Robinson, D., Schofield, J., & Steers-Wentzell, K. (2005). Peer and cross-age tutoring in math: Outcomes and their design implications. *Educational Psychology Review, 17*, 327–362.

Ross, P.A., & Braden, J.P. (1991). The effects of token reinforcement versus cognitive behavior modification on learning-disabled students' math skills. *Psychology in the Schools, 28*, 247–256.

Schunk, D.H., & Cox, P.D. (1986). Strategy training and attributional feedback with learning disabled students. *Journal of Educational Psychology, 78*, 201–209.

Silbert, J., Carnine, D., & Stein, M. (1989). *Direct instruction mathematics*. Columbus, OH: Merrill.

Swanson, H.L., & Hoskyn, M. (1998). Experimental intervention research on students with learning disabilities: A meta-analysis of treatment outcomes. *Review of Educational Research, 68*, 277–321.

Tournaki, N. (1993). *Comparison of two methods of teaching addition to learning disabled and regular education students* (Unpublished doctoral dissertation). New York University, New York.

Tournaki, N. (2003). The differential effects of teaching addition through strategy instruction versus drill and practice to students with and without disabilities. *Journal of Learning Disabilities, 36*, 449–458.

Van Luit, J.E.H., & Naglieri, J.A. (1999). Effectiveness of the MASTER program for teaching special children multiplication and division. *Journal of Learning Disabilities, 32*, 98–107.

Vaughn, S., & Fuchs, L.S. (2003). Redefining learning disabilities as inadequate response to instruction: The promise and potential problems. *Learning Disabilities: Research & Practice, 18*, 137–146.

Wilson, C.L., & Sindelar, P.T. (1991). Direct instruction in math word problems: Students with learning disabilities. *Exceptional Children, 57*, 512–518.

Witzel, B., Mercer, C.D., & Miller, M.D. (2003). Teaching algebra to students with learning difficulties: An investigation of an explicit instruction model. *Learning Disabilities Research and Practice, 18*, 121–131.

Woodward, J. (2006). Developing automaticity in multiplication facts: Integrating strategy instruction with timed practice drills. *Learning Disability Quarterly, 29*, 269–289.

Xin, Y.P., Jitendra, A.K., & Deatline-Buchman, A. (2005). Effects of mathematical word problem-solving instruction on middle school students with learning problems. *The Journal of Special Education, 39*, 181–192.

8 Middle School Students' Thinking About Ratios and Proportions

Asha K. Jitendra, John Woodward, and Jon R. Star

Over the past decade, one of the most dramatic policy shifts in middle school math instruction has been the call for all students to learn more complex content in greater depth and frequently at earlier grade levels. A common rationale for introducing more challenging content at earlier grade levels is to keep students on track and prepare them for high-school courses such as Algebra II and beyond (Achieve, 2009; Loveless, 2008). An emphasis on teaching topics such as rational numbers in much greater depth in the middle grades is consistent with the agenda to teach content that is foundational for more advanced mathematics (e.g., algebra, geometry, trigonometry, and calculus) developed in high school and college (National Mathematics Advisory Panel, 2008).

Ratios and proportions, which are an extension of rational numbers, are central to mathematical development during the middle-school years. This topic exemplifies the kind of multiplicative thinking that is critical to further progress in secondary mathematics and algebra readiness (Hiebert & Behr, 1988; National Research Council, 2001; National Mathematics Advisory Panel, 2008). For example, understanding of ratios plays a fundamental role in the study of linear functions in algebra, particularly the concept of slope (Cheng, 2010). The difficulties that students exhibit in learning rational numbers as well as ratios and proportions are evident on a range of state, national, and international assessments (Wearne & Kouba, 2000). For example, on the 2003 Trends in International Mathematics and Science Study (TIMSS 2003 Assessment, 2005), only 44% of U.S. eighth-grade students could successfully complete the following ratio or

The research reported here was supported by the Institute of Education Sciences, U.S. Department of Education, through Grant R305K060002. The opinions expressed are those of the authors and do not represent views of the U.S. Department of Education. We thank the project coordinator, Kristin Starosta, and the research assistants at Lehigh University: Cheyenne Hughes, Jayne Leh, Sheetal Sood, and Toshi Mack. We gratefully acknowledge the administrators, faculty, and students at Shawnee Middle School. Without their cooperation and effort, this study would not have been possible.

proportion problem: "John sold 60 magazines and Mark sold 80 magazines. The magazines were all sold for the same price. The total amount of money received for the magazines was $700. How much money did Mark receive?" Even fewer students (35%) correctly answered the following problem[1]: "A painter had 25 L of paint. He used 2.5 L of paint every hour. He finished the job in 5.5 hours. How much paint did he have left?" Math educators have suggested that an adequate understanding of proportions takes years, and it is an area where even a significant portion of adults struggle (Ahl, Moore, & Dixon, 1992; Fujimura, 2001; Lamon, 2007).

One reason that proportional reasoning is challenging is that it requires the analysis of quantities in order to identify underlying mathematical relationships. For example, a problem might involve two situations that appear to have different quantities (e.g., $3 for 6 apples, $6 for 12 apples) but where the relationships between the quantities remain constant (e.g., each apple costs $0.50). As such, essential to solving problems in this mathematical domain is understanding how relationships between quantities covary, identifying relevant information to create an adequate mental representation of the problem followed by generating, executing, and monitoring a solution strategy (Desoete, Roeyers, & De Clercq, 2003; Lamon, 1999; Mayer, 1999). The specific nature of that mental representation is important. Hegarty and Kozhevnikov (1999) argued that schematic representations, in particular, are highly correlated with success in mathematical problem solving.

Schematic representations emphasize the underlying mathematical problem structure that is critical for problem comprehension and ultimately for problem solution. Such representations highlight the relations between the different elements described in the text (e.g., Hegarty & Kozhevnikov, 1999; Willis & Fuson, 1988). Unlike pictorial representations of problems that include concrete, but irrelevant details that "are superfluous to solution of the math problem" (Edens & Potter, 2006, p. 186), a schematic diagram depicts the spatial relations between objects in the problem text (Hegarty & Kozhevnikov, 1999, p. 685). Therefore, schematic representations that allow students to look beyond surface features of word problems to identify and analyze underlying mathematical relationships would appear to be especially important for ratio and proportion problems (Marshall, 1995). A particular challenge with ratio or proportion word problems is the many different ways that mathematically similar problems can be devised. For example, consider the following problem, also from TIMSS: "If there are 300 calories in 100 g of a certain food, how many calories are there in a 30 g portion of this food?" Although 69% of U.S. eighth graders correctly answered this problem, this problem is mathematically quite similar to the previously mentioned proportion problem in which students had relatively less success (44%). Although the surface features of these problems differ, they both entail the same underlying mathematical structure.

Figure 8.1 presents a variety of ratio and proportion word problems along with schematic and symbolic representations. Ratios, mixtures, and percent increase or decrease problems all vary in the way in which related quantities are

---

1. There are 20 red marbles and 10 green marbles in a bag. What is the ratio of the number of red to the number of green marbles? What is the ratio of the number of red marbles to the total number of marbles in the bag?

   Ratio of the number of red marbles to the number of green marbles: 20:10 or 2:1
   Ratio of the number of red marbles to the total number of marbles: 20:30 or 2:3

2. Light purple paint is made by mixing 3 parts red paint with 1 part blue paint. If I want to make 40 tins of light purple paint, how many tins of red and blue paint do I need?

Red paint	3	
Blue paint	1	
Total	4	40

   Because you multiplied the total, 4, by 10 to get 40, you multiply 3 by 10 and multiply 1 by 10. You need 30 ounces of red paint and 10 ounces of blue paint.

3. One dozen eggs cost $1.90. What would 4 dozen eggs cost?

   $$\frac{Eggs:\ 1\ dozen}{Cost:\ \$1.90} = \frac{4\ dozen}{\$x}$$

   4 dozen eggs would cost $7.60 ($1.90 × 4).

4. Two dozen eggs at SaveCo cost $2.70. Six dozen eggs at Merrimart cost $8.25. Which store has the better deal on eggs?

	SaveCo	Merrimart
Eggs	2 dozen	6 dozen
Cost	$2.70	$8.25
Eggs	6 dozen	6 dozen
Cost	$ 8.10	$8.25

   The eggs at SaveCo are a better deal.

5. Last year was unusually dry in Colorado. Denver usually gets 60 inches of snow per year. Vail, which is up in the mountains, usually gets 350 inches of snow per year. Both places had 10 inches less of snow than the year before. The weather announcer for KCRK said that the decline in snowfall was the same for both places. Can you think of a way to describe the decline in snow in both places so that it is not the same?

   Denver: $\dfrac{10}{60}$ = 0.167 or 16.67%   Vail: $\dfrac{10}{350}$ = 0.029 or 2.9%

   The decline in snow for Denver was much greater (16.7%) than for Vail (2.9%).

Figure 8.1. Schematic and symbolic representations of varied ratio and proportion problems.

represented. In the case of mixture problems, a table can be a useful way of representing the proportional relations between known quantities and as a means of identifying and then computing unknown quantities. Percent increase or decrease problems, on the other hand, require students to see that, although the absolute increase (or decrease) in two conditions may be the same, the relative proportional change may vary. Proportional reasoning extends in late middle school to other topics such as functions and the concept of slope (Van de Walle, 2007).

The challenge of developing accurate representations for proportion problems is compounded by the fact that different strategies (e.g., equivalent fraction, cross-multiplication, unit rate) can be used to solve these problems. For this reason, students need considerable practice discriminating between the superficial features of a problem and their underlying structure. This is evident in problems 3 and 4 in Figure 8.1. Problem 3 is a traditional proportion problem, where the student might use an equivalent fraction to find the cost of 4 dozen eggs. In contrast, a student would use number sense and equivalent fractions to find a common numerator or common denominator to compare which store had the better deal on eggs.

The importance of instruction that emphasizes an understanding of the underlying structure of word problems is even evident in the response to intervention (RTI) literature. The Institute of Education Sciences (Gersten et al., 2009) research synthesis for struggling students suggests that Tier 2 and Tier 3 interventions should focus on problem types and structures. Graphic aids such as diagrams, tables, or maps can assist learners as they move from the superficial features of a problem to understanding its type or underlying structure.

Unfortunately, research to date on proportions involving academically low-achieving students who would likely receive Tier 2 or Tier 3 services is scant. Moore and Carnine's (1989) study focused on low-achieving high-school students, and their results indicated that students could be successful on a limited range of proportion problems by using a direct translation strategy (i.e., read the problem to identify the units and related numbers) and an equivalent fractions algorithm for solving proportion problems. Viewed in a wider context, their findings represent a first step in understanding how low-achieving students develop proportional reasoning, even though direct translation strategies have been criticized in the problem-solving literature because they do not emphasize the mathematical relations (e.g., 300 c to 100 g is the same as x c to 30 g) between objects in the problem text needed to set up the mathematical equation (e.g., $\dfrac{300c}{100g} = \dfrac{xc}{30g}$; see Hegarty, Mayer, & Monk, 1995; Reed, 1999).

The literature on instruction in complex topics such as ratios and proportions is limited; therefore, the remainder of this chapter is devoted to a recent attempt to teach the topic to middle-school students, especially those students at risk for mathematics failure. We provide a detailed description of the class-wide Tier 1 instructional intervention and its effect on student thinking. Rather than using a direct translation strategy, we drew on schema theory and principles from cognitive psychology as the basis for our intervention.

Another important aspect of this research was the assessment of student thinking on three proportional tasks. We interviewed students as they solved each task, asking questions such as the following: How did you figure this problem out? How did you find the answer? Explain your diagram to me. Show me how you would represent this problem mathematically. Was this problem like any other you have solved before? How did you check your answer to see if it was correct?

As will be shown, assessing student thinking through structured interviews to complement their computational work can provide a clearer picture of what it means to make progress in a complex topic such as ratios and proportions—more so than traditional paper-and-pencil measures alone. This technique has important implications in light of common RTI recommendations to monitor progress frequently using instruments that assess computation skills and basic concepts or math vocabulary (see Foegen, Jiban, & Deno, 2007). We surmise that, although this type of assessment is time intensive, it could be used as a follow-up to typical formative assessment often used to identify students who are not responding to the Tier 1 curriculum. The assessment of student thinking is likely to yield in-depth information for designing Tier 2 and Tier 3 interventions for those students who are not responding to the Tier 1 curriculum in ratio and proportion. For example, the Tier 2 and 3 interventions may consider ad hoc tutoring (Woodward, Monroe, & Baxter, 2001) or interventions validated for at-risk learners (e.g., Xin, Jitendra, & Deatline-Buchman, 2005).

RECENT RESEARCH ON PROPORTIONAL THINKING

Jitendra et al. (2009) examined the impact of a 10-day intervention that taught seventh-grade students multiple strategies for solving proportion problems that emphasized the underlying structure of these problems as well as metacognitive strategy knowledge. This research extended earlier work on the use of visual models (i.e., schematic representations) for teaching capable as well as academically low-achieving students to solve word problems (e.g., Fuchs, Seethaler, Powell, Fuchs, Hamlett, Fletcher, 2008; Fuson & Willis, 1989; Jitendra, Griffin, Haria, Leh, Adams, & Kaduvetoor, 2007; Xin et al., 2005).

Jitendra et al.'s study (2009) involved 148 seventh-grade students and their teachers from eight classrooms. Students were already grouped into three different ability-level classes—academic (high), applied (average), and essential (low)—on the basis of their grades in mathematics from the previous school year (i.e., sixth grade). After matching classrooms in pairs on the basis of ability level, one classroom from each pair was randomly assigned to the intervention or "business-as-usual" groups.

The core curriculum in the middle school was the district-adopted textbook, *Glencoe Mathematics: Applications and Concepts, Course 2* (Bailey et al., 2004). However, materials were modified for the intervention students' unit on ratios and proportions so that there was greater emphasis on schematic representations of ratio and proportion problems as well as specific strategies for solving these problems. The unit was also modified so that the teacher was able to contrast different types of ratio and proportion problems for students.

For example, the first four lessons of the intervention unit focused on the meaning of ratios and equivalent ratios (i.e., comparing ratios to determine their equivalence or nonequivalence), as well as solving ratio word problems. Two of the lessons focused on expressing ratios in different ways (e.g., a:b; a is to b; a to b; a per b); part-to-part ratios as one part of a whole to another part of the same whole (e.g., the ratio of girls to boys in the class); and part-to-whole ratios as comparisons of a part to a whole (e.g., the ratio of girls to all students in the class). These lessons targeted ratio word problems in which students learned how to use schematic diagrams and students were shown different solution strategies (e.g., cross-multiplication, equivalent fractions, and unit rate).

The next five lessons extended the understanding of ratios to the topic of rates, which involve comparison of two quantities with different units (e.g., miles to gallons, computers to students). They also showed students how scale drawings and scale models require the use of proportional reasoning. Table 8.1 presents the scope and sequence of instruction for the intervention group.

Table 8.1.   Scope and sequence of ratio and proportion unit

Lessons	Content and unit objectives	Vocabulary
1	Ratios • *Define ratio as a multiplicative relationship.* • Identify the base quantity for comparison of quantities involving part-to-part and part-to-whole.	Base quantity; back term; compared quantity; front term; part-to-part ratio; part-to-whole ratio; ratio; value of the ratio/ratio value
2	Equivalent ratios; simplifying ratios • *Use visual diagrams to understand the meaning of equivalent ratios.* • *Identify integer ratios in their lowest or simplest form.* • Determine if ratios are in simplest form by using division of common factors.	Equivalent ratios; simplifying ratios
3 and 4	Ratio word problem solving • Apply ratio concepts to solve word problems. • Represent information in the problems using a ratio schematic diagram(s). • Plan to solve the problem using cross-multiplication and equivalent fraction strategies.	Cross-multiplication using ratios strategy; equivalent fraction strategy; multiplicative relationship
5	Rates and quiz • Define rate as a comparison of two quantities with different units. • Understand and learn how to calculate unit rates. • Learn to solve problems in which two rates are compared.	Rate; unit rate; equivalent rate
6 and 7	Proportion word problem solving • Apply ratio or rate concepts to solve proportion problems. • Represent information in the problems using a proportion schematic diagram(s). • Plan to solve the problem using a unit rate strategy as well as cross-multiplication and equivalent fraction strategies.	*If–then* statement of equality; proportion; unit rate strategy
8 and 9	Scale drawing word problem solving • Identify a proportional relationship in scale drawings and calculate dimensions in a scale drawing using a scale factor. • Represent information in the scale drawing problems using a proportion diagram. • Plan to solve the problem.	Scale drawing/scale model; scale factor

All of the students in the intervention condition were introduced to the same topics (i.e., ratios, rates, solving proportions, scale drawings) during the regularly scheduled mathematics instructional period for 40 minutes daily for 2 consecutive weeks (i.e., 10 school days). Their classroom teachers delivered instruction to their intact math classes. The structure of the lesson was as follows:

1. Students working individually to complete a review problem followed by the teacher reviewing it in a whole class format
2. The teacher introducing the key concepts or skills using a series of examples
3. The teacher assigning homework

Furthermore, students were allowed to use calculators to solve problems.

Students were taught to identify the problem type (*ratio* or *proportion*) and represent the features of the problem situation by using diagrams (see Figure 8.2 for a sample proportion diagram). Frequently, the teacher modeled the four-step process using "think alouds" to foster metacognition. Consider the following problem: "Carlos is on the school's track team. He takes 54 minutes to run 6 miles. How long did it take him to run 2 miles?" Using Step 1 of the strategy, the teacher described how to identify the problem type by examining the relevant information in the problem as a way of determining whether it was a ratio or a proportion problem. Students were taught to ask themselves questions such as "Why is this a *proportion* problem?" by focusing on both similarities and differences between the new problem and previously learned problems. Students were led to reason that this is a proportion problem because it involves a statement of equality between two ratios or rates $\left(\dfrac{54 \text{ minutes}}{6 \text{ miles}} = \dfrac{x \text{ minutes}}{2 \text{ miles}} \right)$ that allows

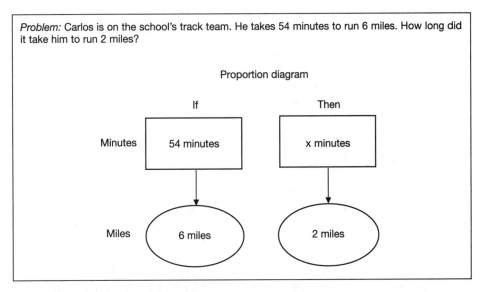

Figure 8.2.   Schematic proportion diagram.

one to think about the ways that two situations are the same. This differs from previously learned ratio problems that describe a multiplicative relationship between two quantities in a single situation.

The second step involved the teacher demonstrating how to organize information in the problem by using the schematic diagram (e.g., ratio). In short, these two steps required not only interpreting but also representing the main features of the problem as a diagram. In Step 3 of the plan, students learned to select the most appropriate solution method (e.g., cross-multiplication, equivalent fractions, unit rate strategies) to solve the problem. See Figure 8.3 for application of these solution strategies. Students discussed which solution strategy could be used to solve the problem and why this strategy would be appropriate. In the final step, students solved the problem by using the solution strategy

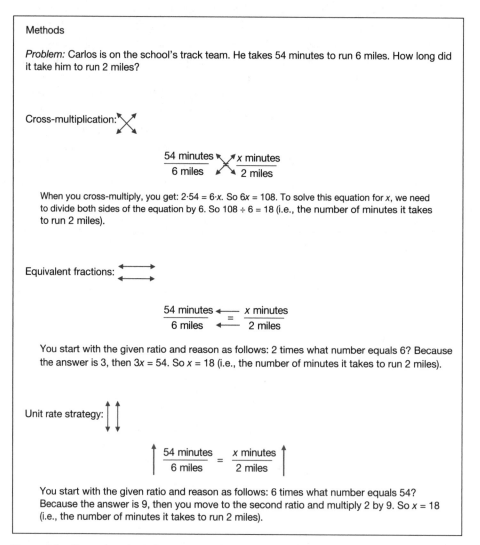

Figure 8.3. Examples of solution methods: Cross-multiplication, equivalent fraction, and unit rate solution.

identified in Step 3. They were encouraged to justify their solutions by using the schematic representation of the problem as anchors for explanations and elaborations, and to check the accuracy of not only the computation but also the representation. Students discussed the solution process by asking evaluation questions (e.g., "Does it make sense? How can I verify the solution?"). It must be noted that instructional support (e.g., schematic diagrams) in the intervention group was gradually faded within and across lessons.

The results indicated significant differences (d = .45) at both posttest and a 4-month delayed posttest (d = .52) favoring the intervention group on an 18-item multiple-choice test. However, the performance of low-achieving students in the intervention group was not significantly different from that of the low-achieving students in the control condition.

UNDERSTANDING INTERVENTION GROUP
PERFORMANCE THROUGH INDIVIDUAL PROPORTION TASKS

The major purpose of this chapter is to evaluate the diversity of students' proportional thinking to gain insight into their progress in learning ratios and proportions. As such, we administered three proportion tasks to a representative sample of students from the three different ability group classrooms that participated in the intervention in an effort to understand the differential effects of the schematic representations and strategies on student ability levels in the intervention group. Six students were selected from each of four classrooms, yielding a final sample of 24 out of the 75 students who participated in the larger study. Two classrooms of average-ability students participated, thus making a total of 6 high-achieving, 12 average-achieving, and 6 low-achieving students. Table 8.2 provides student demographic data by ability level status.

The three proportion tasks were unlike the multiple-choice test used in the larger study. Each task was administered at pretest and posttest, and they were recorded and transcribed. We felt that a detailed analysis of student performance on these measures might result in an understanding of why the academically low-achieving students in the intervention group did not do well and offer a richer picture of what makes proportional thinking difficult for all students at the middle grades, particularly when the topic is reviewed in a compressed manner as it was in this study. Students were administered all three performance assessments during the individual interview.

The three tasks employed in the study to assess student understanding of proportional reasoning were drawn from the mathematics literature on ratios and proportions (e.g., Lamon, 1999; Van de Walle, 2007). The examiner read each problem aloud and instructed the student to solve the problem and show all work. Following student solving of each problem, examiners used both open-ended and specific questions to probe students' proportional thinking that focused on processes and strategies (e.g., How did you figure out the problem?), conceptual understanding (e.g., Show how you would represent this problem

Table 8.2. Student demographics by ability level status

Variable	Total				High achieving				Average achieving				Low achieving			
	M	SD	n	%	M	SD	n	%	M	SD	n	%	M	SD	n	%
Age (in years)	12.77	4.36			12.55	3.32			12.78	2.50			13.02	7.01		
Gender:																
Male			7	29.20			2	33.33			5	41.70			0	0.00
Race/ethnicity																
American Indian			1	4.20			0	0.00			1	8.30			0	0.00
African American			4	16.70			1	16.70			2	16.70			1	16.70
Hispanic			7	29.20			2	33.33			3	25.00			2	33.33
White			12	50.00			3	50.00			6	50.00			3	50.00
Free/subsidized lunch			15	62.50			4	66.70			7	58.30			4	66.70
Special education status			2	8.30			0	0.00			1	8.30			1	16.70
English language learner			1	4.20			0	0.00			0	0.00			1	16.70

mathematically.), connections (e.g., Was this problem like any other you have solved before?), and communication (e.g., How did you check your answer to see if it was correct?) standards articulated in Buschman (2003).

Students were asked to complete the following problems:

- The first depicted two plants of different heights and their new heights after 2 months of growth. Both plants grew the same amount in those 2 months; however, the plants were of different heights at the start. This task required students to identify which plant grew more and to provide a reason for their response.
- The second was a picture-matching task in which six squares were arranged in two columns of three. Within each square was an arrangement of clip art pictures of soccer balls and skateboards. Students had to identify which cards represented the same ratio of number of soccer balls to number of skateboards.
- The final task involved a recipe for making 40 cookies using two eggs. Students were asked to calculate how many cookies could be made with one egg and with three eggs.

The same three proportion tasks were used as pretests and posttests.

A 5-point rubric was used to score each assessment (see Figure 8.4). The rubric was based on previous analyses of student thinking in proportions (e.g., Lamon, 1993), math performance assessment involving students with learning disabilities (Woodward, Monroe, & Baxter, 2001), and the common features of the three performance assessment tasks. The student protocols were also analyzed for other patterns based on interview questions. In particular, the final set of questions for each task asked students if they had seen a problem like this before in their math classes and how it related to other problems or math topics (Jitendra, Woodward, et al., 2009).

4	Student shows formal understanding of the question, demonstrates knowledge of relationships between objects, uses multiplicative thinking, clarifies what the problem is asking for, and gives the correct answer.
3	Student uses a combination of additive and multiplicative thinking, and gives the correct answer or makes a clerical error. Student shows partial use of proportional representations or describes systematic relations between objects in the problem.
2	Student only uses an additive relationship in solving the problem. The answer may be correct or incorrect. A complete answer is inhibited by attention to the superficial dimensions of the problem.
1	Student has some strategy for solving the problem and demonstrates some awareness of a relationship between the objects, though this is based on superficial features of the problem. The answer is incorrect.
0	The student offers no clear response (i.e., the response is incoherent, the student just guesses, or the remarks are unintelligible).

Figure 8.4.   General rubric for the three performance assessments.

ANALYSIS OF STUDENT THINKING
ON THE THREE PROPORTION TASKS

To investigate the influence of the intervention on students' proportional thinking, a one-way repeated measures analysis of variance (ANOVA) was conducted with time of testing (pretest versus posttest) as the within-subject factor on the three proportion tasks' scores separately as well as the cumulative total score for the tasks. Cohen's d was also used as a measure of effect size for the pretest–posttest comparisons that were statistically significant. Table 8.3 presents the mean scores and standard deviations for the pretest and posttest on individual and total performance assessments.

Results revealed a statistically significant effect for time, $F(1, 23) = 30.61$; $p < .001$, on the total score for the three tasks combined. A large effect size ($d = 1.18$) was found for posttest scores compared with pretest scores. In addition, statistically significant effects were found for the picture-matching task, $F(1, 23) = 14.62$; $p < .01$, and the recipe task, $F(1, 23) = 33.89$; $p < .001$. Again, posttest scores when compared with pretest scores revealed large effects for both the picture matching ($d = 0.91$) and recipe ($d = 1.49$) tasks. In contrast, pretest–posttest differences on the plant growth task were not statistically significant, $F(1, 23) = 1.33$; $p = 0.26$.

Because of the small sample size, we used effect sizes as descriptive statistics to determine whether student ability level status mediated problem-solving performance. Results indicated a similar pattern as the main analyses, with large effect sizes for posttest scores compared with pretest scores on the three tasks combined and on the picture-matching and recipe tasks for high- and average-achieving students (see Table 8.4). In contrast, low-achieving students showed improvement from pretest to posttest ($d > 0.90$) on all three tasks. However, we found a consistent pattern of decreasing mean performance from high- to average- to low-achieving students.

It is important to note that each of the three performance measures required a different kind of generalization. For example, the plant growth problem required the highest level of generalization. Although instructions required students to determine the proportional growth for the two plants (Which plant

Table 8.3. Means and standard deviations for the pretest and posttest on individual and total proportion tasks

	N	Pretest		Posttest		F(1, 23)	d
		M	SD	M	SD		
Plant growth	24	1.54	0.83	1.75	0.74	1.33	0.26
Picture matching	24	1.88	1.23	2.92	1.06	14.62*	0.91
Recipe	24	2.38	0.58	3.33	0.70	33.89**	1.49
Total	24	5.79	1.86	8.00	1.89	30.61***	1.18

Note: Scores ranged from 0 to 4 on each of the individual performance assessments. Effect sizes (Cohen's d) were calculated by dividing the difference between the posttest and pretest means by the pooled standard deviation.

*$p < .05$; **$p < .01$, ***$p < .001$.

Table 8.4.   Means and standard deviations on individual and total proportion tasks by time of testing and students' achievement level status

	n	Pretest		Posttest		
		M	SD	M	SD	d
Plant growth						
High	6	2.00	0.00	1.83	0.98	−0.25
Average	12	1.67	0.78	1.75	0.62	0.11
Low	6	0.83	0.98	1.67	0.82	0.93
Picture matching						
High	6	2.33	1.63	3.50	0.84	0.90
Average	12	1.92	1.24	2.92	1.08	0.80
Low	6	1.33	0.52	2.33	1.03	1.23
Recipe						
High	6	2.67	0.52	3.67	0.52	1.92
Average	12	2.50	0.52	3.33	0.65	1.41
Low	6	1.83	0.41	3.00	0.89	1.69
Total						
High	6	7.00	2.10	9.00	1.41	1.12
Average	12	6.08	1.51	8.00	1.81	1.15
Low	6	4.00	0.89	7.00	2.19	1.80

Note: Scores ranged from 0 to 4 on each of the individual performance assessments. Effect sizes (Cohen's d) were calculated by dividing the difference between the posttest and pretest means by the pooled standard deviation.

grew more?), the interviewers probed to make sure that students considered the distinction between absolute growth, which was identical for the two plants, and proportional growth, which was different. The picture-matching task required less generalization because of the extensive visual support embedded in the task. It also drew on instruction in Lessons 3 and 4 of the intervention. Students could look for proportional relations just by matching soccer balls and skateboards. The recipe problem drew on a common context or model for thinking about proportions. These kinds of problems commonly appear when ratios and proportions are introduced to students (see Van de Walle, 2007). Instruction throughout the intervention supported this task.

Of particular interest in this study were the ways students tried to solve the three proportion tasks before and after instruction. The picture-matching task was a moderately difficult task, as confirmed by the pretest and posttest data. Students' written work and transcriptions of their thinking revealed distinct differences in the ways students of different ability levels answered the picture-matching task during the pretest and posttest. Figures 8.5, 8.6, and 8.7 present the typical ways in which high-, average-, and low-achieving students solved the task. Although students at each ability level showed change, the high-achieving students were much more competent in representing the task formally and demonstrated evidence of multiplicative thinking than were low-achieving students, who tended to be distracted by the superficial features of the problem.

The contrast in solution strategies on the posttest makes it evident that high-achieving students like Charlene (Figure 8.5) see the multiplicative

Charlene (high-achieving student)

Pretest

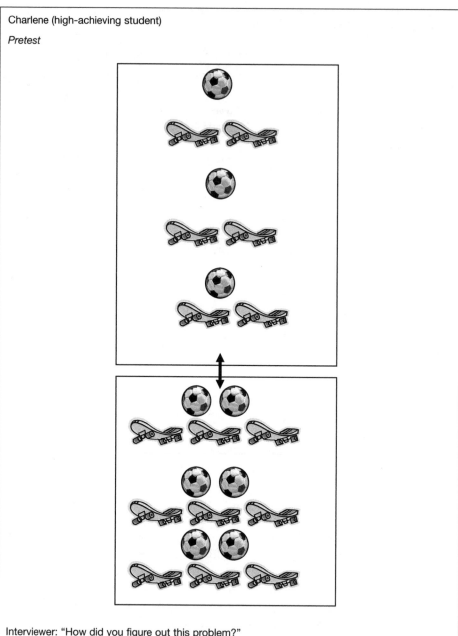

Interviewer: "How did you figure out this problem?"

Charlene: "I counted up the skateboards and went to the boxes and counted them up in their boxes and the amount of skateboards were each 3 apart and the amount of soccer balls were 3 apart."

Interviewer: "Can you explain how you represented the problem in numbers?"

Charlene: "Um, one of them has 9 skateboards and the other one has 6 so they are 3 apart and the 6 so this one is just like multiply the amount by 2."

Figure 8.5. High-achieving student's performance on the picture-matching task.

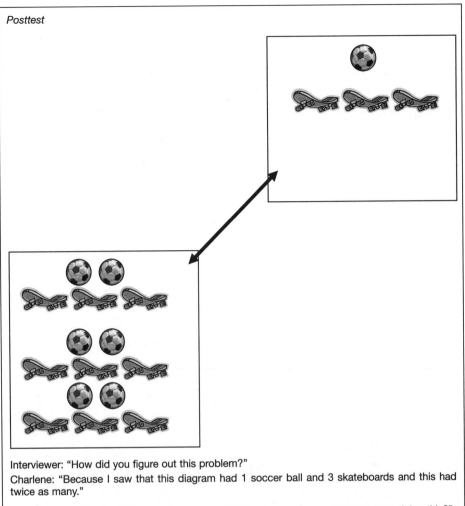

Posttest

Interviewer: "How did you figure out this problem?"
Charlene: "Because I saw that this diagram had 1 soccer ball and 3 skateboards and this had twice as many."

Interviewer: "And what kind of math were you thinking in your head when you were doing this?"
Charlene: "Multiplication."

Interviewer: "What were you multiplying?"
Charlene: "By 2."

Interviewer: "By 2? And the soccer balls and skateboards or ...?"
Charlene: "Both."

foundation for proportion problems like this one. Other high-achieving and even average-achieving students wrote ratio symbols for each picture to facilitate comparisons (e.g., 4:8, 1:3, 2:3; Figure 8.6). This kind of formal representation was virtually nonexistent among the low-achieving students. Instead, they tended to be distracted by the superficial features of the problem or to make comparisons between either skateboards or soccer balls only rather than compare both sets in the pictures (Figure 8.7).

Eva (average-achieving student)

Pretest

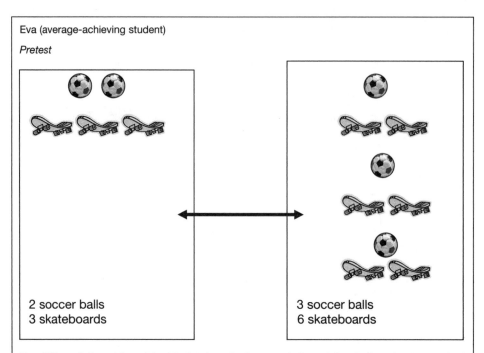

	2 soccer balls	3 soccer balls
	3 skateboards	6 skateboards

Eva: "Uh, well, I would say it had 3 skateboards, 2 soccer balls and then in the other box we had 3 skateboards and 6 soccer balls."

Interviewer: "Can you tell me how it might be the same or how it is different?"

Eva: "Well there definitely, it is kind of the same because we have been dealing with ratios and we been [unintelligible]."

Posttest

Eva writes this table above the pictures

	#					
Balls	4	1	2	3	2	6
SB	8	3	3	6	6	6

Interviewer: "Okay, can you tell me how you figured this problem out? What made you decide that none of them had the same ratio?"

Eva: "I counted the balls and the skateboards."

Interviewer: "Okay, so the ratio that you were finding—you were just adding the soccer balls and skateboards together, or… …?"

Eva: "I added up the soccer balls and I tried to see if any of them had the same number of soccer balls…. For each picture, I would put the number of soccer balls and the number of skateboards and compared each one to the other ones."

Figure 8.6.   Average-achieving student's performance on the picture-matching task.

All students were more successful on the recipe problem during the posttest phase than the two other problems. Many high- and average-achieving students represented the problem formally as fractions and then used the cross-multiplication strategy to determine the appropriate number of cookies that could be made with three eggs. In fact, one clear shift in thinking on the part of

Tyree (low-achieving student)

Pretest

Tyree: "I'm going to say these two, but this one has 1 more soccer ball than this one. These, I don't think any of them have them."

Interviewer: "Okay, do you want to write down your answer? Okay, now I'm going to ask you some more questions about this problem. How did you figure this problem out?"

Tyree: "Because like I went back and counted how many soccer balls were like in each, and none of them seemed to be equal to any of them. Except like those one, the soccer balls they are equal in this one, but if you look at the skateboards this one, the skateboards weren't like the same as like the one that actually was equal. Like this one has 2 soccer balls and this one has 2 soccer balls, but this one has 6 skateboards and this one has 3. And the other ones...this one had 9 and this one had 8 and then 6, and 6 right here too but his one has 3 soccer balls and this one has 2."

Posttest

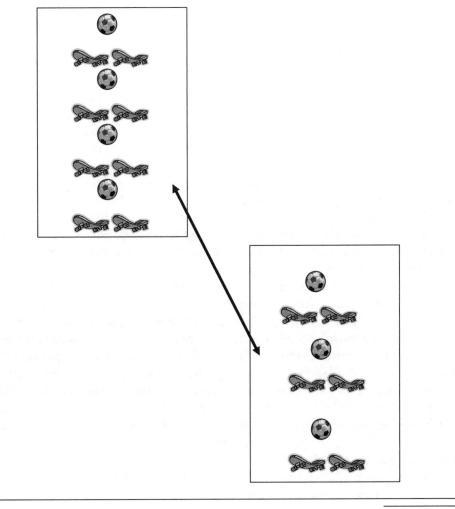

(continued)

Figure 8.7. Low-achieving student's performance on the picture-matching task.

Figure 8.7. *(continued)*

Tyree: "There are 4 skateboards and 4 more skateboards and it's all equal."

Interviewer: "OK, can you draw a line between the two of them to show your answer? Now can you tell me how you figured this problem out?"

Tyree: "Because the skateboards—there's 4 and the soccer balls there's 4 and then there's 4 more skateboards."

Interviewer: "So there's 4 skateboards and 4 soccer balls, and then 4 more skateboards, you said. Okay, then about this one, what made you decide that this was the same?"

Tyree: "There's 3 skateboards, 3 soccer balls, and then 3 more skateboards."

Interviewer: "Okay. Now can you show me mathematically what you were thinking when you did this?"

Tyree: "I did count it, and the row I counted and then I counted the soccer balls and I got the same and then this one I did the same thing."

Interviewer: "And were there numbers that helped you decide the answer?"

Tyree: "Yeah, 4 and 3."

---

the average- and high-achieving students was far less reliance on the "count by 20" strategy that so many of them used on the pretest (i.e., "If 1 egg makes 20, then 2 eggs make 40, so 3 eggs make 60"). This count-by strategy, however, was still evident in many of the low-achieving students' responses on the posttest.

The plant growth problem unquestionably lends itself to an answer that involves the same absolute difference (e.g., "they grew the same," "they both grew 3 inches"). Yet, the interviewer probed each student on this, asking if there was another way to think about the plant growth. Although only one of the students was able to answer this problem correctly on the posttest, note that the intervention did not include instruction on percent of change.

In addition to the analysis of student responses to the three proportion tasks, the transcripts of student interviews were examined for other patterns. Of particular interest was the questioning that followed the administration of each task. Before moving to the next task, students were asked if they had seen a problem like this before and how it related to other kinds of problems they were doing in math class. We analyzed student statements by using the categories for student responses shown in Table 8.5. The table presents the number and percentage of occasions for each kind of statement. There were some instances when students were asked whether they had seen the problem before, and the answers were ambiguous or unclear. In these cases, the answers were not included as part of this categorical analysis.

Several patterns emerged from Table 8.5. First, even though many students recognized the plant growth problem, even at the pretest phase, most students thought about it in a way that did not pertain to ratios and proportions. In most cases, students perceived this problem to be a measurement task, one that involved a tool such as a ruler. Their explanations were often confusing or ones

Table 8.5. How students conceptualized each proportion task

	Proportion task		
	Plant	Picture matching	Recipe
Had seen the problem before			
Pretest	16 (67%)	5 (21%)	15 (63%)
Posttest	15 (63%)	17 (71%)	21 (88%)
Had not seen the problem before			
Pretest	8 (33%)	18 (75%)	8 (33%)
Posttest	4 (17%)	6 (25%)	2 (8%)
Used confusing or additive explanation			
Pretest	10 (42%)	4 (17%)	5 (21%)
Posttest	10 (42%)	0 (0%)	4 (25%)
Used proportions vocabulary			
Pretest	1 (4%)	2 (8%)	0 (0%)
Posttest	2 (8%)	11 (46%)	2 (8%)
Described task through quantitative relationships			
Pretest	4 (17%)	1 (4%)	3 (13%)
Posttest	0 (0%)	0 (0%)	4 (17%)

that involved additive relationships. Some students related the plant problem to an addition or subtraction problem so that it was consistent with the absolute difference (e.g., "A driver drove 12 miles; how many more miles before he drove 53 miles?"). Although many students also seemed to recognize the recipe problem at the pretest phase, fewer of them tended to provide irrelevant explanations of how the recipe problem related to other math problems or topics than the plant problem.

Students tended to be unfamiliar with the picture-matching task during the pretest phase. Of note, on this task students were most likely to use some kind of proportion vocabulary (e.g., ratio, proportion, rate) as a way of relating it to other problems that they had seen before in other classes.

One other general pattern had to do with the way students thought about each task. Only on the recipe problem were a small number of students able to describe the covarying relationship between eggs and number of cookies as part of the pretest as well as the posttest. Whereas students may have attempted to use a quantitative relationship to explain the plant problem on the pretest, this mode of reasoning disappeared on the posttest. More generally, students tended to describe the way they thought about the three proportion tasks through operations (e.g., "I added and then I divided").

IMPLICATIONS FOR TEACHING RATIOS AND PROPORTIONS TO AT-RISK STUDENTS IN TIER 2 INTERVENTIONS

By selecting high-, average-, and low-achieving students, we were able to capture representative changes on three different commonly taught types of proportion problems. The most challenging of the three proportion problems—percent change—proved to be difficult for all of the students before and after the intervention. One plausible explanation for the overall low level of success on this task was that students had been presented with percent change problems in the previous year's instruction, but it was not part of the current study. Nonetheless, it is still worth noting that none of the students reconsidered their "absolute" answers on this task (e.g., "they grew the same") in spite of probing on the part of the interviewer. This consistent response across 24 students helps corroborate Lamon's (2007) observation that proportional thinking is complex and develops over a long period of time. It also suggests that some review of various problem types each year is critical for students at all ability levels.

There were clear and significant shifts in thinking on the two other proportion tasks. Changes in thinking reflected the content of the 10-day intervention. High- and average-achieving students tended to use formal ratio notation to solve the picture-matching task. Many of these students also used fractional notation and the cross-multiplication strategy to solve the recipe task. Low-achieving students showed mean improvement on their rubric scores for each of the three tasks. However, cases of complete multiplicative thinking on the picture-matching or recipe tasks were rare among these students. For example, these students often referred to ratio notation to describe the relationship between soccer balls and skateboards for an individual card, but they would mix division and addition to describe the relationship between cards.

The way students thought about proportion problems in a general sense—how it related to other kinds of math topics, the degree to which it was similar to other problems—was also instructive. Many students were prone to look at the most difficult performance task (i.e., the plant problem) as a measurement task or one involving an additive relationship. In contrast, the picture-sorting task seemed to provoke the clearest sense of proportional relationships as indicated by a much higher use of terms such as ratio, proportion, and rate. The recipe task tended to be much more familiar to students. There was a greater tendency to describe the relationship between eggs and cookies in a relational manner, particularly on the posttest. For example, low-achieving students might tend to find the unit rate first (i.e., 20 cookies for one egg) and then multiply each quantity by three to derive the correct answer.

This research adds to the growing literature on schematic representations in mathematical problem solving as well as the importance of teaching students the underlying structure of problems. This latter point is a key recommendation in the practitioner literature of RTI in mathematics (Gersten et al., 2009). The emphasis on schematic representations, metacognition, can enable a range of students to develop deeper understanding of the mathematical problem structure and foster flexible solution strategies. The influence of these features of the intervention was apparent in student performance on the picture-matching and recipe tasks.

A broader issue also related to RTI policies merits attention. In order for us to obtain district cooperation for students and teachers to participate in the study, all students in each of the academic tracks (i.e., high, average, and low) were given the same Tier 1 instruction over the same period of time. In other words, the intensity of the intervention was the same for all students. However, the very nature of the tracked classrooms left students at different "starting places." Although all students in this study were taught rational numbers and proportions in sixth grade, it is possible that the amount of instruction provided was sufficient for students in the high- and average-track classes to learn the content. Consequently, the intervention functioned as a review of previously taught material for these students. In contrast, the content of the intervention may have appeared to be relatively new for the low-achieving students, who did not learn the content well enough to exit the low-track class. As a result, the instruction in proportions for these students was cognitively demanding.

Given these natural conditions, it seems unreasonable for all students to learn a new and relatively complex topic such as ratios and proportions in the same amount of time. Furthermore, the well-documented difficulty of rational numbers as a mathematical topic would suggest that, by middle grades, different tiers of instructional interventions would merit serious consideration. Students who have yet to consolidate their understanding of whole numbers and operations on whole numbers need to have this issue resolved before moving on to in-depth instruction in a topic such as fractions. It is also likely that struggling students may need more time to make connections among fractions, decimals, and percents before studying proportions. All of this implies that Tier 2 students may need more time to make adequate progress in topics such as rational numbers and proportions.

In this respect, the move to put more students irrespective of their ability into heterogeneous, "on track" secondary math courses has had questionable effects for the lowest achieving students. Loveless's (2008) analysis of a national sample of eighth-grade students indicated that, since 2000, many low-achieving students have been placed in "dead-end" tracks that lead to general math in high school in favor of ones that build toward Algebra I and II. However, a careful examination of the performance of the bottom 10th percentile of students—those who are like to qualify for Tier 2 or 3 interventions—suggests that many eighth graders are performing five or six grade levels behind in their understanding of mathematics.

Clearly, there are many reasons for continued low performance in mathematics across the late elementary- and middle-grade years. In all likelihood, the low expectations found in so many low-track classrooms are a contributing factor. However, a rapid move to raise standards for all students without providing critical support services as suggested in the RTI framework is likely to be counterproductive. A central problem in this dilemma of where to place low-achieving students is the fundamental issue of rate of learning (Smith, 2002).

Finally, the nature of student thinking evidenced through the individual proportion tasks should be considered in light of a common call in special education to do frequent and "easy-to-administer" formative assessments such as curriculum-based measurement. This perspective is nicely summarized in the recent literature on RTI in the area of mathematics (Gersten et al., 2009), and, of interest, the empirical support for this type of practice is low. One reason for this can be found in the results of this study. Student responses on the more difficult plant task were not only incorrect but also reflected an inability to move beyond an absolute framework for thinking about the problem even when probed. This problem also provoked a relatively high number of confusing explanations, which was in contrast to the other two tasks. Furthermore, student explanations revealed the persistent difficulty they experienced after the 10-day intervention in terms of using appropriate vocabulary when describing the proportional relationship as well as demonstrating a clear understanding of the quantitative relationships in the problem. Put simply, success in topics such as ratios and proportions depends heavily on how one represents the problem as much as the numbers used to compute the answer. Understanding how students think about these kinds of problems by having them verbalize as well as compute answers is an important way to determine what kind of progress they are making on the topic.

For example, Tier 2 students learning about proportions through activities such as the picture-matching task used in this study are likely to evidence various types of additive thinking in their initial stages of learning. These students may match picture cards based on the same number of soccer balls irrespective of differences in the number of skateboards. They may also match cards based on an "add on" strategy (e.g., match a card with 3 soccer balls and 6 skateboards with one that has 4 soccer balls and 7 skateboards because there is one more of each item). Individual assessments that identify the way these students set up and make comparisons can be helpful to teachers as they remedy initial stages of understanding or serious misconceptions about the nature of proportions.

The implications of the individualized interview assessment are considerable, because they entail a very different kind of assessment than the practices commonly associated with progress monitoring in math (see Foegen, Jiban, & Deno, 2007). That is, progress monitoring strategies in special education rely heavily on timed, paper-and-pencil computational tasks. In many instances, student responses are scored based on the number of correct digits or percent correct. This kind of framework for assessing student understanding would seem ill-suited to understanding how students are learning proportions as they were taught in this intervention and, more generally, how students understand complex mathematical ideas.

Capturing student thinking, particularly the way an individual represents a proportion problem, requires a considerable level of expertise on the part of the individual conducting the assessment. As was often the case in this study, the background knowledge (or lack of it) that students drew on as they solved each problem was illuminating. Furthermore, it is often the representation of the problem and the strategies used (e.g., additive versus multiplicative) that gives educators a better insight into how much a student understands a complex topic. Although this type of individualized interview assessment may be impractical for general education classrooms in which the pressure is for teachers to cover more grade-level material in a limited amount of time, Tier 2 and Tier 3 students have the benefit of extended time for such individualized assessments. With increased demands for mathematics proficiency, using assessment methods that inform Tier 2 and Tier 3 instructional practices such as the individualized interview assessment using think alouds is critical.

REFERENCES

Achieve. (2009). *Math works*. Achieve.org: Retrieved from http://www.achieve.org/mathworks

Ahl, V.A., Moore, C.F., & Dixon, J.A. (1992). Development of intuitive and numerical proportional reasoning. *Cognitive Development, 7*, 81–108.

Bailey, R., Day, R., Frey, P., Howard, A.C., Hutchens, D.T., McClain, K., et al. (2004). *Glencoe Mathematics: Applications and Concepts: Course 2*. New York: McGraw-Hill.

Buschman, L. (2003). *Share and compare: A teacher's story about helping children become problem solvers in mathematics*. Reston, VA: National Council of Teachers of Mathematics.

Cheng, D. (2010). *Connecting proportionality and slope: Middle school students' reasoning about steepness* (Unpublished doctoral dissertation). MA: Boston University.

Desoete, A., Roeyers, H., & De Clercq, A. (2003). Can off-line metacognition enhance mathematical problem solving? *Journal of Educational Psychology, 95*, 188–200.

Edens, K., & Potter, E. (2006). How students "unpack" the structure of a word problem: Graphic representations and problem solving. *School Science and Mathematics, 108*, 184–196.

Foegen, A., Jiban, C., & Deno, S. (2007). Progress monitoring measures in mathematics: A review of the literature. *The Journal of Special Education, 41*(2), 121–139.

Fuchs, L.S., Seethaler, P.M., Powell, S.R., Fuchs, D., Hamlett, C.L., & Fletcher, J.M. (2008). Effects of preventative tutoring on the mathematical problem solving of third-grade students with math and reading difficulties. *Exceptional Children, 74*, 155–173.

Fujmura, N. (2001). Facilitating children's proportional reasoning: A model of reasoning processes and effects of intervention on strategy change. *Journal of Educational Psychology, 93*, 589–603.

Fuson, K.C., & Willis, G.B. (1989). Second graders' use of schematic drawings in solving addition and subtraction word problems. *Journal of Educational Psychology, 81*, 514–520.

Gersten, R., Beckman, S., Clarke, B., Foegen, A., Marsh. L., Star, J.R., et al. (2009). Assisting students struggling with mathematics: Response to intervention (RtI) for elementary and middle grades. National Center for Education Statistics. Retrieved from http://ies.ed.gov/ncee/wwc/pdf/practiceguides/rti_math_pg_042109.pdf

Hegarty, M., & Kozhevnikov, M. (1999). Types of visual-spatial representations and mathematical problem solving. *Journal of Educational Psychology, 91*, 684–689.

Hegarty, M., Mayer, R., & Monk, C. (1995). Comprehension of arithmetic word problems: A comparison of successful and unsuccessful problem solvers. *Journal of Educational Psychology, 87*, 18–32.

Hiebert, J., & Behr, J. (1988). *Number concepts and operations in the middle grades*. Reston, VA: National Council of Teachers of Mathematics.

Jitendra, A.K., Griffin, C., Haria, P., Leh, J., Adams, A., & Kaduvetoor, A. (2007). A comparison of single and multiple strategy instruction on third grade students' mathematical problem solving. *Journal of Educational Psychology, 99*, 115–127.

Jitendra, A.K., Star, J., Starosta, K., Leh, J., Sood, S., Caskie, G., et al. (2009). Improving students' learning of ratio and proportion problem solving: The role of schema-based instruction. *Contemporary Educational Psychology, 34*, 250–264.

Jitendra, A.K., Woodward, J., Star, J.R., & Starosta, K. (2009, April). *Does schema-based instruction and self-monitoring influence seventh grade students' proportional thinking?* Paper presented at the American Educational Research Association (AERA) annual convention, San Diego, CA.

Lamon, S.J. (1993). Ratio and proportion: Connecting content and children's thinking. *Journal for Research in Mathematics Education, 24*, 41–61.

Lamon, S. (1999). *Teaching fractions and ratios for understanding: Essential content knowledge and instructional strategies for teachers*. Mahwah, NJ: Lawrence Erlbaum Associates.

Lamon, S.J. (2007). Rational numbers and proportional reasoning: Toward a theoretical framework for research. In F.K. Lester Jr (Ed.), *Second handbook of research on mathematics teaching and learning* (pp. 629–668). National Council of Teachers of Mathematics. Charlotte, NC: Information Age Publishing.

Loveless, T. (2008). *The misplaced math student: Lost in eighth-grade algebra.* Washington, DC: Brookings Institution Press.

Marshall, S.P. (1995). Schemas in problem solving. New York: Cambridge University Press.

Mayer, R.E. (1999). *The promise of educational psychology: Vol. I. Learning in the content areas.* Upper Saddle River, NJ: Merrill Prentice Hall.

Moore, L.J., & Carnine, D. (1989). Evaluating curriculum design in the content of active teaching. *Remedial and Special Education, 10,* 28–37.

National Mathematics Advisory Panel (2008). *Foundations for Success: The Final Report of the National Mathematics Advisory Panel.* Washington, DC: U.S. Department of Education.

National Research Council (2001). Adding it up: Helping children learn mathematics. J. Kilpatrick, J. Swafford, and B. Findell (Eds.), *Mathematics Learning Study Committee, Center for Education, Division of Behavioral and Social Sciences and Education.* Washington, DC: National Academies Press.

Reed, S. (1999). *Word problems: Research and curriculum reform.* Mahwah, NJ: Lawrence Erlbaum Associates.

Smith, F. (2002). *The glass wall: Why mathematics can seem difficult.* New York: Teachers College Press.

TIMSS 2003 Assessment. (2005). MA: TIMSS & PIRLS International Study Center, Lynch School of Education, Boston College. Retrieved from http://timss.bc.edu/timss2003i/released.html

Van de Walle, J.A. (2007). *Elementary and middle school mathematics: Teaching developmentally* (6th ed.). Boston: Pearson Education.

Wearne, D., & Kouba, V.L. (2000). Rational numbers. In E.A. Silver & P.A. Kenney (Eds.), *Results from the seventh mathematics assessment of the National Assessment of Educational Progress* (pp. 163–191). Reston, VA: National Council of Teachers of Mathematics.

Willis, G.B., & Fuson, K.C. (1988). Teaching children to use schematic drawings to solve addition and subtraction word problems. *Journal of Educational Psychology, 80,* 191–201.

Woodward, J., Monroe, K., & Baxter, J. (2001). Enhancing student achievement on performance assessments in mathematics. *Learning Disabilities Quarterly 24,* 33–46.

Xin, Y.P., Jitendra, A.K., & Deatline-Buchman, A. (2005). Effects of mathematical word problem solving instruction on students with learning problems. *Journal of Special Education, 39,* 181–192.

9 Using Visual Representations to Instruct and Intervene with Secondary Mathematics

Bradley S. Witzel, Deborah V. Mink, and Paul J. Riccomini

The National Mathematics Advisory Panel's (NMAP's) final report, *Foundations for Success* (NMAP, 2008) and the Institute for Educational Sciences' (IES's) practice guide, *Assisting Students Struggling with Mathematics* (Gersten et al., 2009), agree: teaching students to use visual representations when solving math problems can assist the students who struggle to learn mathematics. Gersten and his colleagues (2009) found support for use of visual and concrete representations in 13 rigorous and well-designed studies. However, because the representations were usually part of a multicomponent intervention, the exact effect of specific representations was uncertain. Thus, the panel concluded that use of representations has a moderate level of evidence.

Witzel, Riccomini, and Schneider (2008) also summarized the research using less-stringent criteria. They concluded that instruction using a range of visual representations:

1. Provides multiple opportunities to memorize and retrieve by encoding through visual, auditory, kinesthetic, and tactile means (Engelkamp & Zimmer, 1990; Nilsson, 2000)
2. Increases engagement and improves attitudes toward content (Oberer, 2003)
3. Provides meaningful manipulations of materials so that students may better understand abstract mathematics (Demby, 1997; Noice & Noice, 2001)
4. Allows meaningful alternatives to shallow memorization of algorithms and rules taught in isolation of the purpose of computation
5. Increases problem-solving options when one is confronted with mathematics questions on tests, homework, and work-related situations

Visual representations can help students who struggle to learn mathematics, but representations are also useful and important for all students. In fact, Stylianou and Silver (2004) found that expert mathematicians use visual representations more frequently and more efficiently than undergraduate math

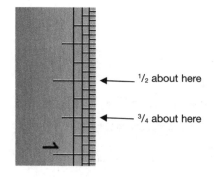

Figure 9.1.   Recognizing fraction magnitude on a number line.

majors when solving novel complex mathematics problems. For students who struggle with learning mathematics at a pace commensurate with their peers, using visual representations is not sufficient to ensure success. Use of one alternate representation improves learning, but empirical studies show that when taught using multiple, sequential representations, "students reached criterion performance, maintained the skills over time, and generalized to more difficult problem types" (Maccini, Strickland, Gagnon, & Malmgren, 2008, p. 22). Note that the authors stressed that alternate representations were used in a systematic, sequential fashion.

One of the most crucial visual representations is the number line (see Figure 9.1). There is a small but important evidence base suggesting that learning to use a number line can help students learn mathematics. In a study of 105 first-grade students, Booth and Siegler (2008) found that children who learn through accurate, precreated, visual representations of numerical magnitude (number lines) improved their learning of arithmetic. Woodward (2006) found that using a number line visual not only helped fourth-grade students improve fluency in multiplication facts, but they were also better able to estimate. Geary and his colleagues (2007, 2008) found that low-achieving students and students with disabilities are delayed in their development of linear mathematics on a number line. Without learning foundational skills, such as linear number understanding, students are likely to find difficulty with more advanced mathematics coursework, such as fractions and even algebra (NMAP, 2008). In the IES practice guide on fractions instruction, Siegler and his colleagues (2010) stated that there is a moderate level of evidence in the use of number lines when one is teaching fractions: "The panel believes that given the applicability of number lines to fractions as well as whole numbers, these findings indicate that number lines can improve the learning of fractions in elementary and middle school" (p. 20).

Although one could easily envision a chapter on the importance of teaching students to use a

> "Intervention materials should include opportunities for students to work with visual representations of mathematical ideas and interventionists should be proficient in the use of visual representations of mathematical ideas." (Gersten et al., 2009, p. 30).

number line, that is not the focus of this chapter. Rather, we discuss why and how a wide array of visual representations can be used as part of the instructional or intervention process and how their use can potentially help students who have a history of low achievement in mathematics. The central focus of this chapter is the use of *graduated representations* or CRA (concrete to representational to abstract), one strategy for teaching mathematics to low-achieving students. We provide a brief review of the research supporting CRA in instruction and intervention settings, and provide examples of how visual representations can be used to teach students important concepts, principles, and operations involving fractions, decimals, and algebra, with answers both positive and negative. We also point out some of the pitfalls in using representations during instruction and how to avoid those pitfalls.

To begin, we present a vignette of a struggling student who receives a fractions intervention by a teacher who implements systematic and multiple representations.

Vonda was a ninth grader who struggled in math throughout middle school, scoring below basic in sixth, seventh, and eighth grades. She could add and subtract numbers up to 100 with some proficiency, but was inconsistent with multiplication and division facts. In elementary school, teachers reported that she performed poorly but at least attempted her work and participated in class, asking questions frequently. In middle school, however, teachers began to report that Vonda's math performance had suffered even more. She was now becoming noncompliant during math class. One teacher noted that she felt Vonda believed it was easier to look noncompliant than to look incompetent. Vonda not only acted like an academic failure, but she had also become a behavior problem.

The following year, Vonda entered algebra, as mandated by district policy. In algebra she was asked to complete more complex problems. Thus, her anxiety increased. However, what happened in her new high school was unexpected, especially to Vonda.

Her schedule included two math classes, one in algebra and another 30-minute block every day that simply read "math." She must have thought that if one math class was awful, having two was a nightmare. Vonda entered the "extra math class" and met Mrs. Hunt, a teacher who used different strategies than those in which Vonda had previous experience. Mrs. Hunt incorporated organizational charts and diagrams into the lessons to explain what was happening and why. She used a variety of instructional strategies including hands-on activities, pictures, and extra practice.

Vonda seemed reluctant to use the hands-on materials at first, but after watching her classmates participating and succeeding, she increased her effort and improved her attitude. Vonda soon learned content that had once frustrated her. She learned and practiced decimals, fractions, and even proportions. Not surprisingly, Vonda performed much better in both math classes. She improved her multiplication and division accuracy as well as her computation of fractions. She even understood enough of the algebra coursework to pass. Vonda eventually tested well enough to leave the math intervention class and achieved a C in algebra, scoring basic on the statewide achievement test.

Vonda's improvement in mathematics and the strategies her teacher incorporated are not unique. Using the extra time allotted for an intervention, the teacher systematically used multiple representations aimed at helping her improve her accuracy of operational skills and fractions.

CONCRETE–REPRESENTATIONAL–ABSTRACT

Concrete–representational–abstract involves each major form of representation as a means to develop abstract understanding. Each level of CRA is designed to build on the previous one to promote overall improved mathematical performance. Once a student has achieved understanding at the concrete stage, that student must now be challenged at the representational stage. Once successful there, the student must be challenged at the abstract stage. Successful performance at the abstract level is the goal of CRA. Thus, these interventions should be designed to move from concrete objects (manipulatives) to visual representations in an expeditious fashion.

The three levels of CRA are sequentially interrelated activities. They should not be treated as three separate activities (Witzel, Riccomini, & Schneider, 2008). The connections between the levels of learning are critical to mathematical understanding. Students need to be taught how to easily move back and forth between visual representations and abstract symbolic reasoning (see Figure 9.2). For example, if algebra blocks or tiles are used to teach simple equations, then students must be able to connect the reasoning of each manipulation to the reasoning of each abstract problem-solving step.

A concrete lesson on a given skill, concept, or idea must be designed so that students can easily represent the lesson pictorially. It also needs to logically move toward the use of abstract notation. Thus, the representation used for intervention must accurately represent the abstract problem and allow the student to reason from it.

When levels are not connected or designed in sequence, the lack of consistency may leave a student with a vague and incomplete understanding of how to solve the problem. For example, if students learn about fractions using fraction strips, then strip diagrams would serve as an effective pictorial representation.

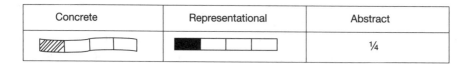

Concrete	Representational	Abstract
		¼

Figure 9.2.   Fraction strip example of the connection from Concrete to Representational to Abstract.

Table 9.1.   Representation options: Examples of ways to help students understand and compute trigonometric ratios

Concrete representations		Visual representations		Abstract representations	
Physical	Manipulative	Pictorial	Graphical/ diagrammatic	Symbolic	Descriptive
Students use measuring tape and protractors to determine the height of a flag pole or the school gym.	Students use premeasured sticks and a protractor to work different ratios.	Students draw trigonomet- ric problems on white- boards.	Students use tables that list angle/ adjacent/ opposite/ hypotenuse to determine what right angle ratio to use to solve the problem.	Students find angles and ratios in problem sets according to the demands of each prob- lem.	Students explain the reasoning to solving for different trigonomet- ric ratios.

To use pie charts would provide an alternate representation *inconsistent* with the reasoning and procedures used with the fraction strips. Although such multiple representations provide multiple vantages of fractions, they do not necessarily lead sequentially to abstract understanding. Thus, the journey might appear disjointed and incongruent to students. Table 9.1 shows the difference between details within the three levels of learning.

Support for CRA

This graduated CRA approach has been shown to be effective in interventions with students with math disabilities and difficulties in the following areas: computation (Mercer & Miller, 1992), place value (Peterson, Mercer, & O'Shea, 1988), fractions (Butler, Miller, Crehan, Babbit, & Pierce, 2003; Jordan, Miller, & Mercer, 1999), algebra and algebraic equations (Maccini & Hughes, 2000; Witzel, 2005; Witzel, Mercer, & Miller, 2003; Witzel, Smith, & Brownell, 2001), and geometry (Cass, Cates, Smith, & Jackson, 2003). Clearly, the use of the graduated CRA approach has positive implications for students with and without disabilities across a variety of mathematical content.

Witzel, Mercer, and Miller (2003) found that secondary students with learning disabilities who learned to solve equations using a sequenced set of representations that advances students from the concrete to representational to abstract level outperformed students who received repeated instruction at the abstract level.

In a study comparing 231 sixth- and seventh-grade students across two instructional conditions, Witzel (2005) grouped students by stanine ranges on the previous years' statewide examination and tested pre- and postinstruction of multiple-step transformational equations (e.g., $3X - 4 = 5X + 6$, solve for X). One group's instructional condition was a graduated multiple-step CRA sequence of instruction, whereas the other group received multiple abstract lessons. Both groups received explicit instruction and equal time for instruction. He found that not only did students who struggled in mathematics benefit from

Table 9.2. CRA fractions action research findings

	Gains per student									
	CRA						Abstract			
Pretest score	1	3	10	0	6	3	8	0	2	3
Posttest score	18	20*	19	20*	20*	13	15	11	14	15
Score increase	17	17	9	20	14	10	7	11	12	12

Note: *Denotes maximum score on the assessment. (From Witzel, B.S., Riccomini, P.J., & Tiberghien, T. [2010]. A fractions intervention in high school. *MathMate, 34*[1], p. 18; reprinted by permission.)
Key: CRA = concrete to representational to abstract.

graduated multiple representations, but also students who were typically achieving and high-achieving. These positive findings for the use of the graduated CRA approach with secondary students with disabilities are of particular importance because evidence-based strategies for secondary students are limited.

One ninth-grade interventionist compared her CRA fractions intervention (Witzel & Riccomini, 2009) to an intervention that only used repeated abstract instruction and found very different results with her students. Both groups of students participated in the intervention for a 30-day period, received the same problems to answer, received explicit instruction, and were taught by the same Masters-plus-30 special education teacher. The students who received CRA instruction outperformed their abstract-only peers in the posttest score (Witzel, Riccomini & Tiberghien, 2010; see Table 9.2). The teacher concluded that not only was focused intervention on fractions necessary, but also CRA allowed students to relearn computational skills, such as multiplication and division, that had previously interfered with their learning of more advanced computational concepts.

Although this research is an action research project and not a clinical analysis, it provides insight into the potential of CRA-based interventions for improving math performance. For more details on district reported successes of implementing CRA and visual-based math interventions, visit the Algebra Success Keys (http://rtitlc.ucf.edu/ask/index.html) and Doing What Works (http://dww.ed.gov/practice/?t_id=28&p_id=71).

Potential Pitfalls of Using Visual Representations

Although it might be obvious from the research and rationale stated previously that all educators should use CRA whenever possible to teach mathematics, many cautions exist. One critique of concrete and pictorial methods is that they do not work as easily as mathematics advances in complexity. That is absolutely correct. However, the purpose of providing CRA as an intervention is to teach the process that sets up more advanced practice. Once the process is understood abstractly, then these procedures may work more easily with larger and more complex numbers.

Another critique is that preparing and enacting representations such as CRA is difficult to do well. Stylianou and Silver, in their work on using representations for complex mathematics stated, that "It is precisely because visual representations can carry so much information that they can be difficult to interpret, construct, or use" (2004, p. 356). Teachers need help understanding the reasoning of mathematics processes and learning how to clearly explain this reasoning to students while modeling manipulations.

Selecting the right representation to teach is also difficult. Some manipulatives are more appropriate than others for explaining certain mathematical content. For example, base-10 blocks may be an excellent manipulative for teaching place value of decimals (see Figure 9.3). It is important for teachers to carefully consider the targeted mathematical content when selecting the manipulatives used in the CRA instructional sequence.

In some cases, following CRA is important in helping students accurately answer problems, whereas in other cases, starting with a pictorial representation is more appropriate. What is important is to use a sequence of representations that best helps the students succeed. Maccini and her colleagues (2008) found that even teachers who agree with using multiple and sequential representations use them infrequently in their classrooms. Gersten and his colleagues stated that "occasional and unsystematic exposure (the norm in many classrooms) is insufficient and does not facilitate understanding of the relationship between the abstract symbols of mathematics and various visual representations" (2009, p. 30). It is important to find what works for students who struggle, and then continue to use the same instructional strategies throughout instruction

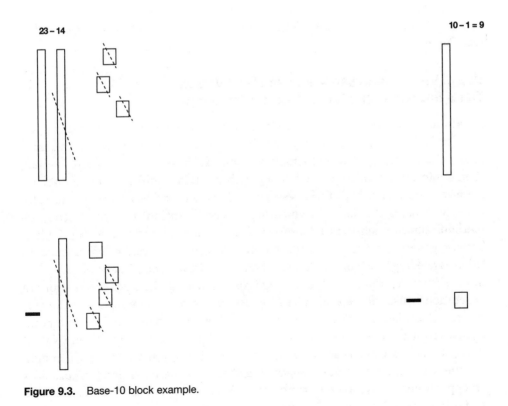

Figure 9.3. Base-10 block example.

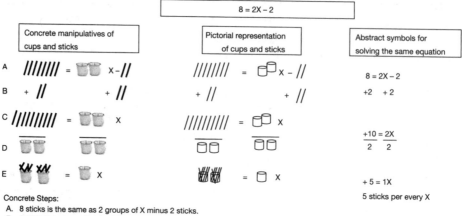

Concrete Steps:
A. 8 sticks is the same as 2 groups of X minus 2 sticks.
B. Add 2 sticks to each side of the equation.
C. The equation now reads as 10 sticks is the same as 2 groups of X.
D. Divide each side of the equation by two groups.
E. Each cup of X contains 5 sticks per cup (1X/group = 5 sticks/group; 1X = 5 sticks).

Figure 9.4. CRA algebra example. (From Gersten, R., Beckmann, S., Clarke, B., Foegen, A., Marsh, L., Star, J. R., et al. [2009]. *Assisting students struggling with mathematics: Response to intervention (RtI) for elementary and middle schools* [NCEE 2009-4060]. Washington, DC: National Center for Education Evaluation and Regional Assistance, Institute of Education Sciences, U.S. Department of Education. Retrieved from http://ies.ed.gov/ncee/wwc/publications/practiceguides/ [p. 35]; adapted by permission.) *Key:* CRA = concrete to representational to abstract.

in the difficult areas. This helps to circumvent student difficulties and possible misconceptions that can arise from the use of multiple visual representations (see Figure 9.4).

Use of Visual Representations in Tier 2 Versus Tier 3 Interventions: Some Critical Distinctions

To differentiate Tier 2 and 3 interventions when using visual representations, we must consider student knowledge and time of instruction. If students have minimal understanding of a mathematical topic, such as proportional reasoning, then the interventionist may consider starting with a significant number of concrete and subsequently pictorial lessons to show why and how to solve the problems. Also, using the table shown earlier, the interventionist may proceed more methodically through the CRA process to teach accuracy and reasoning. This is because generally more time is allotted in Tier 3, and the student has been identified as needing much more intensive help. If, however, the student who requires intervention in proportional reasoning is only in Tier 2, the teacher can afford to expeditiously use concrete and pictorial instruction to provide sufficient time for practice. Also, because of the more individualized design of Tier 3, an interventionist can use more student think alouds, an NMAP recommendation (NMAP, 2008), to facilitate and coach more abstract terminology and reasoning throughout the representational work. Regardless of the instructional tier, CRA provides an opportunity for teachers to facilitate understanding and learning of essential and often difficult mathematical areas for students who are struggling.

IMPLEMENTING CRA

Visual representations are often more efficient instructionally than merely writing procedures on the board or a large adhesive note pad. The following section displays some of the ways that CRA might be used to teach secondary content. We then explain multiple representations for integers, fractions, and decimals, and basic inverse operations. One rule to keep in mind is that manipulatives should be easy and obvious for users. The point of their use is to ease learning, not to complicate it.

Integer Examples

It is important to introduce students early to the idea that numbers exist on the right *and* left side of the zero on a number. In fact, Witzel, Mercer, and Miller (2003) found lack of ability to compute integers to be a frequent problem for students who struggle with solving equations in a secondary-level intervention. Often students who struggle to learn mathematics in middle and high school need to develop a better understanding of negative numbers to succeed in algebra.

Reviewing our curricular approach with several elementary school teachers revealed that oftentimes students do not learn math on a number line, but instead learn using a number ray. For students who work with metric units, the concept of numbers on both sides of the zero is not difficult when representing cold weather. However, for those who are not used to seeing or hearing about negative numbers, introduction must be explicit. Temperature and altitude are common ways to introduce the concepts of negative numbers because these concepts may be represented by using a number line. It might appear obvious to use money to explain negative numbers. However, using money to explain negative number values to young children will not always be easily understood. Unless children have used money and have owed money to another person, using money to teach negative numbers will prove difficult.

To compute negative numbers, ask students to label a line segment with markings that increase in absolute value as they travel to the left. For this example, instruction starts with a pictorial representation. As mentioned earlier, instruction does not always need to start with a concrete representation to improve student performance. In this example, the first number is negative 6, so the teacher places her finger on that point. Then, the student goes seven in the positive direction (to the right; see Figure 9.5). After seven jumps, the student places her finger on positive 1. This procedure can be repeated to show the action. Have students practice this several times until they master the principle.

When students are asked to compute numbers with mixed signs, such as adding or subtracting negatives, the movement of the second addend is not as clear. Using a visual or even physical representation of the field model may help students simplify the expression to aid computation. Although the example uses tallies per digit, using Arabic numbers works well for students who are more proficient with calculations. No matter the approach, maintaining consistent language across levels of representation helps transition students' learning. In this example, the student is asked to answer, +3 – −5 (see Figure 9.6). The language

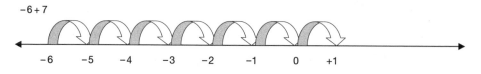

Figure 9.5.   Integer line. A student using a number line which visually includes integer markings to solve the problem –6+7.

that the student uses here is to start with positive 3 and then determine the computation applied to the next addend. Because it reads subtraction of a negative, the student is taught to interpret the computation as the opposite of subtraction, or addition. So, the student crosses out the subtraction option and keeps the addition option. The final problem reads, +3 + 5 or +8. This strategy can also work along a number line like in the previous problem.

Fractions and Decimals

Many educators are concerned with how well students understand and use fractions and decimals. The use of fractions and decimals as rational numbers is highly important for accurate problem solving in secondary mathematics. Although many teachers use manipulatives, such as pattern blocks (shown above) or fraction strips, the use of these objects does not always translate to successful computational procedures and problem solving. Thus, in this section, we show two additional strategies to teach computation of fractions and decimals (concrete objects and arrays). In this first example of the multiplication of fractions, $1/3 \times 2/4$, we describe the multiplication process similarly to show how multiplication is represented for students in elementary school as "groups of" objects (Figure 9.7). In this example, the multiplication is visualized as one group of two objects in the numerator and three groups of four objects in the denominator, $(1/3) (2/4)$.

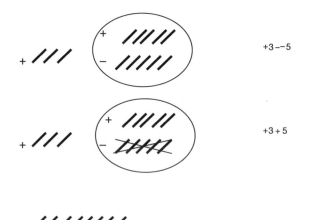

Figure 9.6.   Integer field model. A student uses verbal and visual clues to solve integer computation problems such as +3–5.

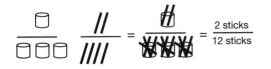   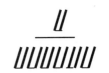

Figure 9.7. Fractions part 1. In this example, the student uses a visual of cups and sticks to solve the fractions multiplication problem ($^1/_3$) ($^2/_4$).

Figure 9.8. Fractions part 2.

With an answer of 2 objects over 12 objects (2 sticks over 12 sticks above), it is important to show how to simplify the answer. By grouping the objects of similar number, students compute the common factors in both the numerator and denominator. In this example, the student shows one set of two objects in the numerator and six sets of two objects in the denominator (Figure 9.8). The simplified answer may be interpreted as 1 set over 6 sets or $^1/_6$.

To transition from manipulative objects to pictorial representations, the teacher should teach students the same steps, but use tally marks instead of sticks. The use of tally marks helps to make the transition to paper simpler and is less traumatic than moving from concrete objects directly to abstract symbols. Finally, to provide students with as seamless a transition as possible to the abstract notation, they must be shown the procedures that occurred concretely and pictorially in abstract notation. Using the same language and steps allows students to see the connections. Using each of these levels of learning allows the students a better opportunity to learn and memorize the steps.

$$\left(\tfrac{1}{3}\right)\left(\tfrac{2}{4}\right) = {}^{(1)(2)}/_{(3)(4)} = {}^{2}/_{12} \quad {}^{(2)(\div2)}/_{(12)(\div2)} = {}^{1}/_{6}$$

Whereas concrete objects provide one way to multiply fractions, visual–graphical array models also provide effective means to visualize the computation. If students are accustomed to working with fraction strips and fractional points on a number line, then arrays can be a logical intervention representation to help teach multiplication of fractions. To start, fraction strips help show the fractional point on a number line. Fraction strips can be created to provide a physical and visual depiction of a fraction. In the example below, the fraction of $^2/_3$ is represented by two shaded parts of a strip of paper out of three equal sized parts. When this strip is aligned with a number line, the fraction shows more obviously as a number rather than a display (see Figure 9.9).

Fraction strips physically show multiplication when overlapped by the first shaded number line. However, most teachers use an array to show the visual–graphical representation of multiplication of fractions. In the example of ($^2/_5$) ($^2/_3$), the first fraction is represented on the top row and the second on

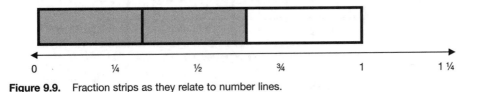

Figure 9.9. Fraction strips as they relate to number lines.

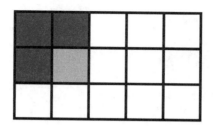

Figure 9.10. Array with fractions.

the left column (see Figure 9.10). They overlap in their first shaded numerator. To multiply the fractions, students must first form a numerator rectangle by shading in one more square for the numerator as shown below. Then, students must form a denominator rectangle by boxing in the ends of each of the denominator representations. What are now formed are four shaded areas out of 15, or $^4/_{15}$.

The steps of this should be made explicit to students. We first set up the equation by aligning the fractions together. We then calculated the numerators two by two. We then calculated the denominators five by three.

$$(^2/_5)\,(^2/_3) = {}^{(2\times2)}/_{(5\times3)} = {}^4/_{15}$$

The more directly the calculations are designed, the more seamless the transition to abstract symbols for the students.

The same method for multiplying fraction arrays works for decimal arrays (Figure 9.11). In this example, we represent the multiplication problem 0.8 × 0.3. On the top row we shade eight out of 10 squares for eight tenths. On the left

24 out of 100 tiles are filled. Decimal answer = 0.24

Figure 9.11. Array with decimals.

column we shade three out of 10 squares for three tenths. To form the answer, we multiply the shaded areas by shading in the remaining squares to form a rectangle of 24. We then box in the total area of the place value of 100 for decimal placement. The answer is $^{24}/_{100}$ or 0.24. This method requires students to be able to recognize decimal place value as well as to mirror the abstract problem-solving steps.

In Figure 9.12, one and two tenths is multiplied by four tenths. The problem is set up similarly to the ones before. However, to represent the first decimal, another 100 × 100 grid is required (see Figure 9.12). In this example, the 1.0 is multiplied by 0.4 separately from the 0.2 by 0.4. The answer is the addition of these two. The reason for this additional step is because when one is multiplying decimals using a traditional algorithm, these two problems are completed separately and then added for the answer.

The multiple steps of a multiplication algorithm work here like they do when the factors are whole numbers. With rational numbers, the steps work similarly.

Algebra

Clearly, the knowledge of advanced mathematics is bound by procedural rules (Glaser, 1988), so it is important to help students learn these rules and procedures. However, many students who struggle academically have weaknesses in working memory (Alloway & Alloway, 2010). The limits in working memory exhibited by struggling students are often overlooked and underestimated by math teachers as a barrier to learning more advanced mathematics, especially problems involving multiple steps. Numerous studies have demonstrated that students who struggle, and specifically those with learning disabilities, have clear impairments in their working memory (see Henry, 2001; McNamara & Wong, 2003; Maehler & Schuchardt, 2009). Limitations in working memory will have an impact on the learning of multiple-step problems involving rules and

1.2 × 0.4 is decomposed to (1.0 × 0.4) + (0.2 × 0.4)

1.0 × 0.4

0.2 × 0.4

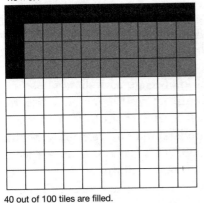
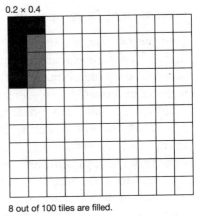

40 out of 100 tiles are filled.

8 out of 100 tiles are filled.

Total = 48 of 100 tiles are filled. Decimal answer = 0.48 or 48 hundredths.

Figure 9.12. Another array with decimals.

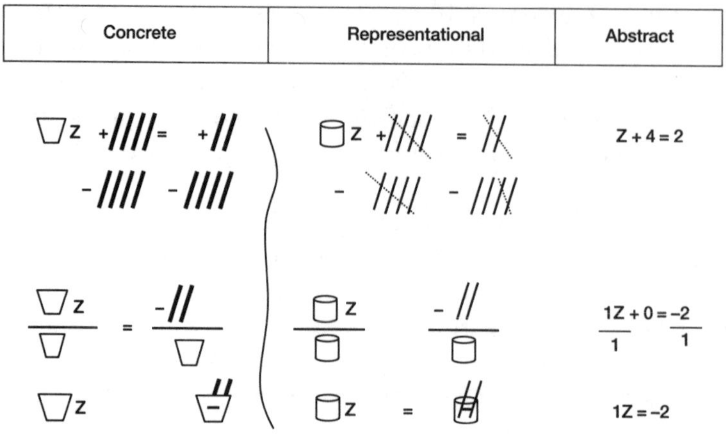

Concrete	Representational	Abstract

$$Z + 4 = 2$$

$$\frac{1Z + 0}{1} = \frac{-2}{1}$$

$$1Z = -2$$

Figure 9.13. CRA algebra example of 1Z + 4 = 2. (*Key:* CRA = concrete to representational to abstract.)

procedures; therefore, these two phases are important instructional considerations by those teaching advanced mathematics to struggling students and students with disabilities.

The NMAP's (2008) final report recognized the learning challenges of students who have limitations in working memory and put forth instructional recommendations for teachers to consider when teaching students who struggle. First, appropriate practice combined with explicit instructional methods can help students overcome working memory limitations. Second, fostering conceptual understanding through the use of visual representations (concretely and/or pictorial; see Figure 9.13) makes possible the transfer of learning to new problems and increases retention. It is important to note that mass practice is not appropriate for students who struggle, but rather, a combination of explicit instruction on concepts and guided practice with distributed independent practice will better help students overcome memory limitations (Riccomini & Witzel, 2010).

Professional Development

Using visuals and, in particular, CRA, may require more material management, a higher level of mathematical understanding, and more preparation. Selecting and delivering high-quality math instruction and intervention using visual representations requires excellent mathematical knowledge as well as classroom motivational skills. The better the interventionist knows the mathematics, the more likely the representational instruction will be used to scaffold abstract reasoning and understanding. Students must understand the reasoning behind what they are computing and why (NCTM, 2009). This is because knowledge of mathematics helps with the explanations behind representations.

Thus, not all teachers will expertly deliver the representations. In a recent study by the lead authors, two of the four intervention teachers who participated did not accurately deliver the intervention despite having a script and attending the same training.

Designing instructional lessons that effectively utilize visual representa-tions requires content understanding and technical expertise in the use of numerous manipulatives. Application of the principles of visual representation to existing curriculum is not necessarily easy and will likely require high-quality, ongoing professional development. Focusing professional development opportu-nities on both mathematical content and visual representation instructional components is essential. The willingness to continue to infuse visual representa-tions systematically will depend heavily on teachers' content knowledge and comfort level with manipulatives. Professional development is a necessity if teachers are to successfully implement visual representations as a standard part of their instructional program.

Mathematics instruction and intervention strategies are a must for profes-sional development, and teaching skills in behavior management and motiva-tional strategies are particularly important for this aspect of instruction. Many students may misuse the concrete manipulatives or visual representations or may simply refuse to try. It is important to motivate students to try them.

Materials

Inherent in the use of visual representations are the hands-on interactions by teachers and students with either concrete objects or visual representations. As seen in the examples presented in this chapter, there is no specific set of manip-ulatives required; however, it is necessary to have sufficient manipulatives for all students to participate in the activities. The many benefits of using visual repre-sentations (e.g., improved math outcomes, motivated students) will only be real-ized when each student has the opportunity to interact with the manipulatives in purposeful and engaging activities. Manipulatives take many different forms and are available for purchase through various education supply companies, but are also available at many local stores.

Curricular Programs and Interventions

Generally, secondary mathematics textbooks do not necessarily contain the care-ful sequencing that would allow easy adaptation of visual representations, espe-cially the CRA instructional sequence. Because few commercial programs exist that are designed and/or founded on the use of visual representations, imple-mentation requires significant planning and modification on the part of the teacher. Careful consideration is needed in the selection of curricular and inter-vention materials and the instructional sequence of visual representations should be reviewed closely.

A PERSONAL PERSPECTIVE ON THE TOPIC

As a high-school freshman at a magnet school for math and science, I (Brad) was led to believe that the best way for me to learn was through open dialogue. However, I often struggled with the fast pace and abstractness of discussions held in class. It was not until a biology lesson that I learned of my need for instructional support. The teacher, well versed in science but not so well versed in how to promote student learning, spent more than a half hour covering aspects of DNA and how dominant and recessive genes made each person who they are. The conversation was replete with words such as *haploid* and *heterozygote* and, for me, was one-sided.

Curt, a student more astute than me, asserted his confusion. He did not understand the terms, nor could he keep track of the various aspects of dominant and recessive genetic influences. Annoyed, the teacher turned to the board and drew a chart asking about our mothers' and fathers' traits and our features as a result. Using us as examples, she demonstrated the reason why we look like we do, and then tied in the vocabulary.

What we, the students, learned from this lesson was not just the content, but also what helped us learn. It was not because we had high potential that we did not need sound instruction. We were now empowered and began a year-long bombardment on our teachers asking for reasoning and visual support. From biology to geometry to English 9, we asked our teachers to come up with diagrams, charts, graphs, and hands-on activities that helped us relate to the information being taught.

REFERENCES

Alloway T.P., & Alloway, R.G. (2010). Investigating the predictive roles of working memory and IQ in academic attainment. *Journal of Experimental Child Psychology, 106*(1), 20–29.

Booth, J.L., & Siegler, R.S. (2008). Numerical magnitude representations influence arithmetic learning. *Child Development, 79*, 1016–1031.

Butler, F.M., Miller, S.P., Crehan, K., Babbit, B., & Pierce, T. (2003). Fraction instruction for students with mathematics disabilities: Comparing two teaching sequences. *Learning Disabilities Research & Practice, 18*(2), 99–111.

Cass, M., Cates, D., Smith, M., & Jackson, C. (2003). Effects of manipulative instruction on solving area and perimeter problems by students with learning disabilities. *Learning Disabilities Research and Practice, 18*(2), 112–120.

Demby, A. (1997). Algebraic procedures used by 13- to 15-year-olds. *Educational Studies in Mathematics, 33*, 45–70.

Engelkamp, J., & Zimmer, H.D. (1990). Memory for action events: A new field of research. *Psychological Research, 51*, 153–157.

Fuchs, L.S., Fuchs, D., Finelli, R., Courey, S.J., & Hamlett, C.L. (2004). Expanding schema based transfer instruction to help third graders solve real life mathematical problems. *American Educational Research Journal, 41*(2), 419–445.

Geary, D.C., Hoard, M.K., Byrd-Craven, J., Nugent, L., & Numtee, C. (2007). Cognitive mechanisms underlying achievement deficits in children with mathematical learning disability. *Child Development, 78*, 1343–1359.

Geary, D.C., Hoard, M.K., Nugent, L., & Byrd-Craven, J. (2008). Development of number line representations in children with mathematical learning disability. *Developmental Neuropsychology, 33*(3), 277-299.

Gersten, R., Beckmann, S., Clarke, B., Foegen, A., Marsh, L., Star, J.R., et al. (2009). *Assisting students struggling with mathematics: Response to intervention (RtI) for elementary and middle schools* (NCEE 2009-4060). Washington, DC: National Center for Education Evaluation and Regional Assistance, Institute of Education Sciences, U.S. Department of Education. Retrieved from http://ies.ed.gov/ncee/wwc/publications/practiceguides

Glaser, R. (1988). Expert knowledge and processes of thinking. In M. Chi, R. Glaser, & M. Farr (Eds.), *The nature of expertise* (pp. 63–75). Mahwah, NJ: Lawrence Erlbaum Associates.

Henry, L.A. (2001). How does the severity of a learning disability affect working memory perform-ance? *Memory, 9*(4/5/6), 233–247.

Jordan, L., Miller, M.D., & Mercer, C.D. (1999). The effects of concrete to semi-concrete to abstract instruction in the acquisition and retention of fraction concepts and skills. *Learning Disabilities: A Multidisciplinary Journal, 9*, 115–122.

Maccini, P., & Hughes, C.A. (2000). Effects of a problem-solving strategy on the introductory alge-bra performance of secondary students with learning disabilities. *Learning Disabilities Research & Practice, 15*, 10–21.

Maccini, P., Strickland, T., Gagnon, J.C., & Malmgren, K. (2008). Accessing the general education math curriculum for secondary students with high-incidence disabilities. *Focus on Exceptional Children, 40*(8), 1–32.

Maehler, C., & Schuchardt, K. (2009). Working memory functioning in children with learning dis-abilities: Does intelligence make a difference? *Journal of Intellectual Disability Research, 53*, 3–10.

McNamara, J.K., & Wong, B. (2003). Memory for everyday information in students with learning disabilities. *Journal of Learning Disabilities, 36*(5), 394–406.

Mercer, C.D., & Miller, S.P. (1992). Teaching students with learning problems in math to acquire, understand, and apply basic math facts. *Remedial and Special Education, 13*(3), 19–35.

National Council of Teachers of Mathematics. (2009). *Focus in high school mathematics: reasoning and sense making.* Reston, VA: Author.

National Mathematics Advisory Panel. (2008). *Foundation for Success: The Final Report of the National Mathematics Advisory Panel.* Washington DC: U.S. Department of Education. Nilsson, L.G. (2000). Remembering actions and words. In E. Tulving & F.I.M. Craik (Eds.), *The Oxford handbook of memory* (pp. 137–148). New York: Oxford University Press.

Noice, H., & Noice, T. (2001). Learning dialogue with and without movement. *Memory and Cognition, 29*, 820–828.

Oberer, J.J. (2003). Effects of learning-style teaching on elementary students' behaviors, achieve-ment, and attitudes. *Academic Exchange Quarterly, 7*, 193–200.

Peterson, S.K., Mercer, C.D., & O'Shea, L. (1988). Teaching learning disabilities students place value using the concrete to abstract sequence. *Learning Disabilities Research, 4*(1), 52–56.

Riccomini, P.J., & Witzel, B.S. (2010). *Response to intervention in math.* Thousand Oaks, CA: Corwin Press.

Siegler, R., Carpenter, T., Fennell, F., Geary, D., Lewis, J., Okamoto, Y., et al. (2010). *Developing effective fractions instruction for kindergarten through 8th grade: A practice guide* (NCEE #2010-4039). Washington, DC: National Center for Education Evaluation and Regional Assistance, Institute of Education Sciences, U.S. Department of Education. Retrieved from what-works.ed.gov/publications/practiceguides

Stylianou D.A., & Silver, E.A. (2004). The role of visual representations in advanced mathematical problem solving: An examination of expert-novice similarities and differences. *Mathematical Thinking and Learning, 6*(4), 353–387.

Witzel, B.S. (2005). Using CRA to teach algebra to students with math difficulties in inclusive set-tings. *Learning Disabilities: A Contemporary Journal, 3*(2), 49–60.

Witzel, B.S., Mercer, C.D., & Miller, M.D. (2003). Teaching algebra to students with learning diffi-culties: An investigation of an explicit instruction model. *Learning Disabilities Research & Practice, 18*(2), 121–131.

Witzel, B.S., & Riccomini, P.J. (2009). *The CRA mathematics intervention series book 1: Fractions.* Boston: Pearson.

Witzel, B.S., & Riccomini, P.J. (2011). *The CRA mathematics intervention series: Solving equations.* Boston: Pearson.

Witzel, B.S., Riccomini, P.J., & Schneider, E. (2008). Implementing CRA math instruction with sec-ondary students with learning disabilities. *Intervention in School and Clinic, 43*(5), 270–276.

Witzel, B.S., Riccomini, P.J., & Tiberghien, T. (2010). A fractions intervention in high school. *MathMate, 34*(1), 15–19.

Witzel, B.S., Smith, S.W., & Brownell, M. (2001). How can I help students with learning disabilities in algebra? *Intervention in School and Clinic, 37*, 101–104.

Woodward, J. (2006). Developing automaticity in multiplication facts: Integrating strategy instruc-tion with timed practice drills. *Learning Disability Quarterly, 29*(4), 269–289.

10 Double-Dose Algebra as a Strategy for Improving Mathematics Achievement of Struggling Students

Evidence from Chicago Public Schools

Takako Nomi and Elaine Allensworth

There is a nationwide push to increase the rigor of high-school coursework so that all students graduate with the skills required for college and the workforce. As part of this challenge, policy makers have been calling on states and districts to abandon low-level coursework and require college-preparatory curriculum for all students, including 3 to 4 years of mathematics starting with algebra in the ninth grade or earlier (National Governor's Association, 2005).

However, it is also widely recognized that many students enter high school with weak math skills—on the 2005 National Assessment of Educational Progress (NAEP) 30% of eighth graders scored below basic level, and only 30% were at or above the proficient level (U.S. Department of Education, 2007). Requiring algebra for students with weak math skills also raises a concern about "mismatch" between students' skills and the courses they take. For example, some students scoring at the bottom 10th percentile or below on NAEP took algebra in eighth grade, even though the majority of them lacked a basic understanding of the number system (e.g., rounding simple decimals to the nearest whole number) and failed to solve problems involving multiplication (Loveless, 2008). From the perspective of teachers, it is challenging to instruct a class where some students perform well below grade level, whereas others have more advanced skills.

In Chicago, where we based this study, all students are now required to enroll in algebra in ninth grade. However, many students enter high school with weak math skills. Each year, about a quarter of ninth-grade students fail their ninth-grade algebra course, and failure rates are higher for those with weaker math skills (Allensworth & Easton, 2005; Roderick & Camburn, 1999).

High failure rates in ninth grade are particularly concerning because freshman year course failure is directly tied to dropping out in later grades, as failures prevent students from accumulating the credits that they need to graduate (Allensworth & Easton, 2007; Bottoms, 2008). Thus, reducing failure rates in ninth grade is crucial in urban high schools, where nearly 40% of students eventually drop out of high school.

Under the current policy climate, educators are caught in a dilemma. Requiring college preparatory coursework for all students makes sense in an age when the vast majority of students aspire to attain a 4-year college degree.[1] At the same time, raising requirements without sufficient support mechanisms could also lead more students to fail and drop out (Darling-Hammond, 2004). This presents a challenge for educators who are charged with teaching students entering high school with academic abilities that are well below grade level.

To help struggling students succeed in mathematics, an increasingly popular strategy is to require algebra instead of remedial math but offer extended instructional time, in which students receive an extra period of algebra instruction each day. At some schools this is achieved through a second "shadow" or "support" algebra course, sometimes called *algebra foundations*; other schools use blocked scheduling in which algebra takes up two periods in the day instead of one (Chait, Muller, Goldware, & Housman, 2007). We refer to both of these as a "double-dose" strategy—where students with weak math skills receive twice the algebra instruction that they otherwise would receive.

The double-dose algebra strategy is a Tier 2[2] intervention as it attempts to prevent future failure by offering preventative, proactive support for struggling students who are identified as needing additional supports based on their incoming skill levels. It was put in place in the Chicago Public Schools in 2003, when the district required all students entering high school with below-average math skills to take two periods of algebra—a regular algebra class and a support algebra class.

In this chapter, we examine the effectiveness and consequences of this approach in Chicago Public Schools, paying particular attention to its effects on students with identified disabilities and students entering high school with math skills well below grade level. We begin by describing the policy context in Chicago. We then look at how instruction and classroom learning environment changed as a result of the policy. Next, we look at the extent to which students' academic outcomes, including algebra failure and performance on the standardized tests, improved as a result of taking double-dose algebra. We then focus our discussions on students with the lowest math skills who receive special education services. Last, we look at some unintended consequences of the policy on students with above-average math skills who were not targeted by the policy.

---

[1] Seventy percent of 12th graders in the United States wanted to obtain a bachelor's degree in 2006 (National Center for Education Statistics, 2006).

[2] While double-dose strategies are used as a Tier 2 intervention in many districts, Chicago Public Schools officials did not conceive of the strategy as RTI.

THE DOUBLE-DOSE ALGEBRA POLICY IN CHICAGO PUBLIC SCHOOLS

The Chicago Public Schools (CPS) is the third-largest school district in the nation and predominantly serves low-income and minority children; approximately 85% of students are eligible for free or reduced-price lunch programs, and the racial/ethnic composition is 54% African American, 34% Latino, 9% White, and 4% Asian. There were 71 high schools in 2003 with more than 17,000 students entering ninth grade each year.[3] Nearly 20% of incoming ninth-grade students were identified as eligible for special education services. Although Chicago struggles with high dropout rates—only about half of students who enter ninth grade graduate in 4 years—the district was at the forefront of the current curricular policy movement in the nation to require a college-preparatory curriculum for all students. In 1997, CPS decided that all students should graduate ready for college. The double-dose algebra policy of 2003 built on that earlier policy.

The 1997 policy intended to provide all students with a curriculum that would prepare them for college. However, many CPS students entered high school with math skills well below grade level, and failure rates were particularly high in ninth-grade algebra (Roderick & Camburn, 1999).[4] The double-dose algebra policy was intended to improve failure rates in algebra by providing students with weak math extra instructional time. All first-time ninth graders with eighth-grade math scores below the national median (i.e., the 50th percentile) on the Iowa Tests of Basic Skills (ITBS) were required to enroll in an algebra support course, in addition to their regular algebra course. The cutoff score for eligibility at the national median was arbitrary; CPS researchers examined the distribution of ITBS test scores, and the relationship between test scores and algebra failure, to see if there was a point at which incoming achievement levels were associated with a much higher failure rate. However, they found the relationship to be fairly linear, so they simply targeted students for intervention based on the national median. This meant that some of the students who received the intervention had incoming math abilities close to the national average, whereas others were entering high school with skills several years below grade level.

Almost all schools complied with the policy immediately and began offering double-dose algebra for the target students in 2003. Figure 10.1 displays the double-dose algebra enrollment rates by students' ITBS percentile scores. Overall, most students below the 50th percentile enrolled in double-dose algebra the first year of the policy, whereas students above the national median did not. However, school compliance varied considerably with regard to the course enrollment for students receiving special education services. Some schools did not enroll their special education students in double-dose algebra. As Figure 10.1 shows, students with ITBS scores below the 20th percentile had lower double-dose algebra enrollment rates than students with slightly

---

[3]Districtwide statistics derived from analysis of administrative data sources.
[4]Forty-two percent of students failed at least one core course (Roderick & Camburn, 1999).

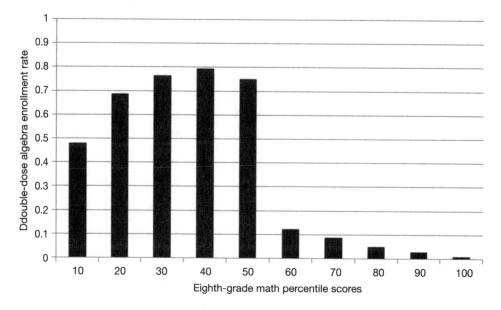

Figure10.1. The percentage of students taking double-dose algebra by eighth-grade ITBS math percentile score. This figure is based on first-time ninth-grade students who entered regular high school in 2003. *Key:* ITBS = Iowa Tests of Basic Skills.

higher achievement; about half of students with the lowest entering test scores took double-dose algebra, and almost 80% of other students eligible for double-dose algebra took double-dose algebra. Most students with eighth-grade test scores below the 20th percentile were receiving special education services.

In addition to doubled instructional time, the policy provided curricular resources and lesson plans for double-dose teachers. The district offered two curricular options—*Agile Mind* (Agile Mind, Inc.) and *Cognitive Tutor* (Carnegie Learning, Inc.)—and stand-alone lesson plans that teachers could use. By providing these curricular options for the double-dose algebra classes, the district hoped to bring greater coherence in algebra curricula across the district, particularly for students entering high school with below-average math skills. They were concerned about the wide variation in algebra curricula across the district and used this policy as a means to increase consistency. The district also ran professional development workshops three times a year to provide training on how to use the two periods of instructional time effectively.

According to internal evaluations by the district, teachers who taught support classes reported that, with additional instructional time, they were able to focus on foundational prealgebra skills, such as fractions, decimals, and positive and negative numbers. Also, additional time allowed flexibility in terms of the instructional content; double-dose algebra teachers reported that they were able to cover materials in a different order than the textbook as stipulated (Starkel,

Martinez, & Price, 2006; Wenzel, Lawal, Conway, Fendt, & Stoelinga, 2005). Some teachers were also concerned that students would be disengaged from class if they were required to take two periods of math. Thus, to facilitate students' engagement, teachers tried to minimize time for lectures and use more interactive instructional activities, such as working in small groups, asking probing and open-ended questions, and using board work. External observers also reported that support course teachers spent more time in these interactive activities than regular algebra teachers, who spent more time giving lectures and individual seat work (Starkel, Martinez, and Price, 2006).

In addition to the instructional supports, the district provided guidelines for the structure of the support courses. The guidelines strongly suggested that schools program their algebra support courses in three specific ways:

1. Double-dose algebra students should have the same teacher in algebra and algebra support.
2. The two courses should be offered sequentially in the day.
3. Students should take their algebra support course with the same students that were in their regular algebra course.

Most schools responded to these guidelines by tracking students into double-dose classes for those with low skills and single-period classes for those with high skills. For example, in a typical algebra course taken by "double-dose" students, nearly 90% of their classmates were also double-dose students. As a result, algebra classes became much more homogenous in students' ability, compared with algebra classrooms prepolicy. Peer ability levels declined considerably for students with below-average math skills, while students with above-average math skills were more likely to have higher ability peers postpolicy.

The changes in peer composition were likely to affect classroom instructional environment and students' academic outcomes, and this brought particular concern for students with low academic skills—the very students the policy intended to support. Much research on tracking is critical of the practice because grouping low-achieving students together often leads to poor instructional environments (i.e., see Oakes, 2005; Rosenbaum, 1976). For example, teachers often do not provide academically challenging material and engaging instruction in low-track classrooms. Low-track classrooms are more likely to have disruptive environments with less student attentiveness. Teachers tend to have lower expectations, and often spend more time on giving simple drills and dealing with behavior problems in low-track classrooms, whereas they spend more time on critical thinking and less time on classroom management issues in high-track classrooms.

However, Chicago's double-dose algebra approach differed from traditional tracking in a number of ways. Whereas tracking typically offers different curricula and expectations for students with differing skill levels (e.g., algebra versus remedial math), under the double-dose policy all students were expected to master algebra. As a Tier 2 intervention, the double-dose algebra provided supports for struggling students to help them succeed in algebra classes while using homogenous settings to target the intervention. It provided extended instructional time for students who were likely to struggle in algebra. It also provided professional development and curricular resources with lesson plans for double-dose algebra teachers. These supports were intended to help teachers improve instructional practices with extended time, potentially countering adverse effects of grouping together more students with behavioral issues. Thus, the structure of the double-dose policy might have countered many of the adverse effects of traditional tracking for low-achieving students. Furthermore, grouping students by ability had the potential to allow teachers to better target instruction to students at their skill levels, as it is often challenging for teachers to provide effective instruction to meet the needs of all students in heterogeneous classrooms.

POLICY EFFECTS ON INSTRUCTION AND CLASSROOM LEARNING ENVIRONMENTS FOR LOW-ACHIEVING STUDENTS IN DOUBLE-DOSE ALGEBRA CLASSES

In this section, we look at three elements of classroom learning environments: the degree to which teachers used interactive pedagogy, students' perceptions of academic demand, and the concentration of students with behavior problems. Interactive pedagogy captures the extent to which students themselves are involved in instructional activities, such as explaining and discussing how to solve a math problem to the class, discussing multiple solutions to a problem, writing sentences explaining how to solve a problem, applying math to situations outside school, and writing math problems for other students to solve, compared with listening to a lecture.

Academic demand captures how difficult or challenging students find their algebra class, based on how often the student feels challenged, feels their teacher asks hard questions, feels the class really makes them think, and feels she or he has to work hard to do well. These two indicators of instruction—interactive pedagogy and academic demand—were based on students' responses to questions about their math classes on biannual surveys conducted by the Consortium on Chicago School Research.[5] Two other indicators—the concentration of students with disciplinary problems and absentee problems—capture classroom behavioral climate. Disciplinary problems were derived from students' responses to the survey questionnaires about how often they "got in trouble" at schools, such as fighting, being sent to the office, and receiving suspension. Classroom absentee problems were constructed by calculating each student's total number of days absent, across all of their courses, and then calculating a classroom average.[6]

---

[5]Response rates were 50% for the 2002–2003 cohort and 67.5% for the 2004–2005 cohort. (Also see Nomi and Allensworth [2010] for discussions about response rates.)

[6]We were concerned about potentially confounding instructional effects of the algebra class on attendance with the effects of concentrating students with attendance problems together on the instructional environment of the algebra class. We wanted our attendance indicator to capture whether students generally had attendance problems, not just whether they missed algebra. This is why we calculated their absences across all of their classes.

To study policy effects, we compared two cohorts of students—those who began high school in 2002 and 2004—one prepolicy cohort and one postpolicy cohort. The Consortium on Chicago School Research conducts surveys of all schools every 2 years, and these cohorts of students participated in the spring 2003 and spring 2005 surveys. Although the survey was given to all students in the spring semester, questionnaires about math classes were administered to a subset of students. Thus, only students who responded to math questions were included in our analysis. Students were also excluded from the analysis if they attended magnet schools with selective enrollment criteria. These schools did not implement the policy because most of their students scored above the 50th percentile. The total number of students in the analysis of classroom environment was 3,278 in 2002 and 3,501 in 2004. Analysis of the concentration of students with absentee problems and student outcomes used all first-time ninth-grade students in each cohort who were not attending selective enrollment schools (about 17,000 students in each year).

To understand how the policy affected classroom learning environments, we compared interactive pedagogy, academic demand, and behavior problems in algebra classes between cohorts of students who attended the same schools before and after the policy. Pre- and postpolicy students were similar in terms of background characteristics, including incoming academic skills and sociodemographic characteristics, and the type of schools they attended. However, postpolicy students were the only students who took double-dose algebra because of the policy. Thus, prepolicy students served as our "comparison" students, informing us of what the classroom environment would look like if postpolicy students did not enroll in double-dose algebra in the absence of the policy (see Nomi & Allensworth, 2010, for more detail about the data and analytic procedures).

Instructional Practices Improved, but Students with Behavior Problems Were More Concentrated in Double-Dose Algebra Classes

Pedagogy improved substantially in double-dose algebra classrooms, compared with the instruction that students with below-average achievement had received before the policy. Postpolicy students who took double-dose algebra reported much more frequent use of interactive instructional activities than did similar students prepolicy, all of whom took single-period algebra. Furthermore, teachers were more likely to use interactive pedagogy the more that the students in their double-dose algebra classes had very low entering math skills. This suggests that teachers were most likely to attempt to change their pedagogical practices if they were teaching particularly struggling students. As shown in Figure 10.2, interactive pedagogy in algebra classes improved dramatically for students entering high school with below-norm skills, so that the typical postpolicy class had a much more interactive pedagogy than a class that was half a standard deviation above average, or at about the 75th percentile prepolicy.

Although there is concern that concentrating low-achieving students in the same classroom would create unchallenging learning environments, academic

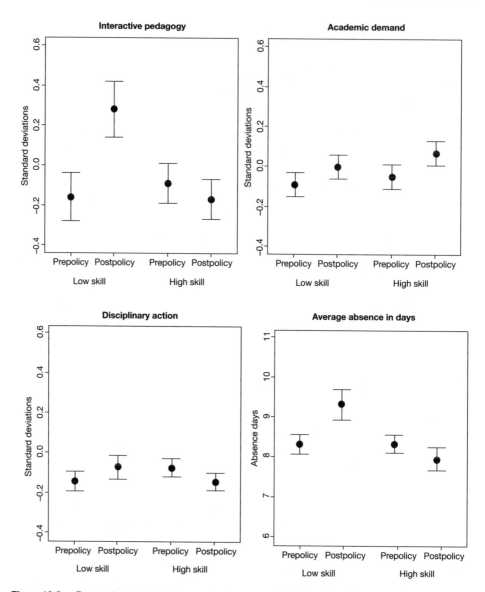

Figure10.2. Pre- and postpolicy changes in classroom instructional environments: interactive pedagogy, academic demand, concentration of students with discipline and absentee problems. *Note:* Dots represent the average classroom environment for each group with 95% percent confidence intervals, based on students' responses. Low-skill students represent students who enrolled in double-dose algebra. High-skill students represent students who enrolled in single-period algebra.

demand also *improved* for low-achieving students; students in double-dose algebra classes reported that their math classes were more challenging than similar students who took single-period algebra classes reported prepolicy. The improvements in instructional practices and academic demand were likely attributable to instructional supports provided by the policy; extended instructional time allowed greater content coverage and more flexible time use, and professional development helped improve instructional practices.

However, although the policy was successful in providing more challenging instruction for low-skilled students, grouping low-ability students in the same classes did result in concentrations of students with behavior problems; peers in double-dose algebra were more likely to have disciplinary problems and high absentee problems than classmates in prepolicy algebra classes. This presented additional challenges for teachers teaching double-dose algebra because they had more students who could potentially disrupt instruction and hold back the entire class.

Understanding changes in classroom environments helps us understand the effects of this policy on improving students' academic outcomes. In the next section, we show how the policy affected students' academic outcomes in terms of algebra course failure and algebra test scores, and how classroom instructional environments are related to students' academic outcomes.

Policy Effects on Academic Outcomes of Low-Achieving Students in Double-Dose Algebra Classes

Improving algebra failure rates was the primary goal of the double-dose algebra policy in Chicago. Thus, we first show whether the policy was successful in reducing algebra failure. We then show the extent to which the policy improved students' algebra skills, measured by a standardized test. Standardized test scores are based on the algebra subset of the math portion of the PLAN examination, a test that is part of the Educational Planning and Assessment System (EPAS) developed by American College Testing (ACT, Inc.). The EPAS system was introduced in 2001 and all students are required to take the PLAN examination in the fall of 10th grade.

We also examined whether taking double-dose algebra was beneficial for all low-skilled students, or whether the benefit depended on their initial skill levels. The double-dose algebra cutoff score was arbitrarily chosen at the national median; thus, it is possible that students close to the national median did not need much support to pass algebra. Alternatively, these students may have more easily responded to increased support and instruction than students with very low skill levels or students who were identified as needing special education services. Students with the weakest math skills may still have struggled the most, even when they received extended instructional time.

To understand the policy effects on students' academic outcomes for students targeted by the policy (i.e., those with below-average math skills), we compared the academic outcomes of first-time ninth graders entering high school after the policy was enacted to students with the same entering skills and backgrounds who began ninth grade in the same schools before the policy.[7] For the analysis of student achievement, we examined the population of first-time ninth-grade students, not just those who participated in the survey. We also

---

[7]Students' background control variables included age, gender, race/ethnicity, poverty levels, social status, and residential mobility. See Nomi and Allensworth (2009) for statistical models and details of our analyses.

Table 10.1.   Descriptive statistics on cohorts of students used for analysis of policy effects on math achievement

Student characteristics	Cohort				
	2000	2001	2002	2003	2004
% Below norm	57.8	59.5	50.0	53.5	54.3
% Special education	18.8	20.1	19.1	18.6	19.2
% Black	55.7	55.5	54.0	58.3	56.4
% White	7.7	8.0	7.9	7.1	6.9
% Hispanic	33.8	33.9	35.3	32.1	34.3
% Asian	2.76	2.6	2.8	2.5	2.4
Number of students	*17,276*	*17,681*	*17,623*	*19,512*	*20,055*

Source: Nomi & Allensworth (2009).

divided students into three groups based on their incoming test scores to see whether the policy effects were different by student incoming skills:

1.   Students scoring between the national median and the 35th percentile
2.   Students scoring between the 34th and 20th percentile
3.   Students scoring below the 20th percentile, most of whom receive special education services

We used five cohorts of students—three prepolicy cohorts (2000–2001, 2001–2002, and 2002–2003 cohorts) and two postpolicy cohorts (2003–2004 and 2004–2005 cohorts) for the analyses of algebra course failure. For the test score analyses, we used four cohorts of students from 2001–2002 to 2004–2005 because the test score data are not available in 2000. In general, the five cohorts have similar demographic compositions, although academic composition differs slightly (see Table 10.1). The percentage of students entering high school with math scores below national norms varied from 59% in 2001 to 50% in 2002. The 2002–2003 cohort had slightly higher initial math abilities than other cohorts. Statistical models controlled for any differences across cohorts in initial skills and sociodemographic characteristics (see Nomi & Allensworth, 2009, for more detail about the data and analytic methods used in this study).

Double-Dose Algebra Improved Test Scores, but Not Failure Rates

The double-dose algebra policy in Chicago attempted to address the problem of high failure rates in algebra. However, the policy was not very successful at reducing course failure. Algebra failure rates had been declining slightly in the years immediately before the policy, but they remained fairly stable among students eligible for double-dose algebra when the policy was implemented (see Figure 10.3). If we separate out students eligible for double-dose algebra by their incoming skills, though, there are some noticeable differences. Failure rates continued to decline very slightly among students whose eighth-grade scores were between the 20th and 50th percentile, by about 5 percentage points between 2000 and 2005. However, because the trend in declining failure rates for

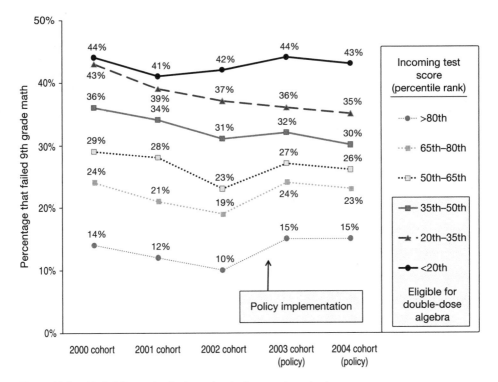

Figure 10.3.   Math failure rates by incoming test scores by cohort.

these groups of students began before the policy, and did not change markedly with the policy, we cannot say that the policy had any substantial benefit on failure rates for this group of students. Furthermore, if we look at failure rates among the students with the weakest math skills—those whose incoming ITBS scores were below the 20th percentile, their failure rates actually *increased* in the first year of the policy. When compared with failure rates in 2002, just 1 year before the policy, failure rates increased by 6% in 2003 and by 4% in 2004 among the lowest achieving students.

Lack of improvements in failure rates was disappointing. However, when we looked at students' performance on the standardized test, the policy looked quite successful. Whereas algebra test scores did not change from 2001 to 2002 (the prepolicy period), test scores rose sharply in 2003 with the implementation of the policy (see Figure 10.4). Students between the 20th and 50th percentiles made the largest improvements, particularly in the first year, where scores rose at a rate that was 30% to 40% higher than was typical (by .56 to .76 of a point more, compared with an average improvement of 1.97 points on the compressed scale). Students who entered ninth grade with the lowest ability levels—those with test scores below the 20th percentile—also showed higher scores under the double-dose algebra policy than similar students in previous cohorts (26% higher than average in 2003 and 10% in 2004). However, the improvements were more modest than among students with somewhat higher entering skills.

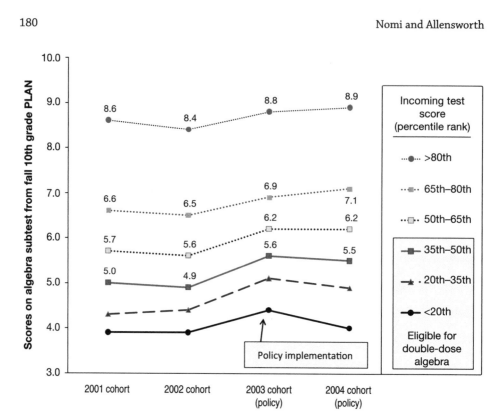

Figure 10.4. Algebra scores by incoming test scores by cohort.

One may wonder why students who took double-dose algebra did not show lower failure rates even though they demonstrated greater content mastery, suggested by higher algebra scores. We offer several possible explanations. First, course grades reflect more than content mastery. Teachers consider multiple factors when assigning grades, such as attendance, assignment completion, engagement, and performance relative to other students. Other research has shown that the primary reason that students fail their courses is poor attendance (Allensworth & Easton, 2007), and this policy did not address high rates of absence in schools.

In fact, this policy resulted in concentrating students with behavior problems in double-dose algebra classes. Even though double-dose algebra classes did not show low-level content or poor instructional practices that often characterize low-track classrooms, they had more students with absentee and disciplinary problems. Absenteeism is not merely a problem for an individual student, but it also could affect other students' behaviors and engagement, making them more likely to fail.

In addition, as we showed earlier, double-dose algebra classes provided more challenging instruction than the typical single-period algebra classes that low-ability students took prepolicy. This is partly why test scores improved—students are more likely to have higher test scores when they are taught more demanding material with more engaging pedagogical practices.[8] However, greater demand can make students less likely to complete their assignments or to do less well on their assignments. In fact, grades are typically lower in more demanding classes.[9] This also explains why students with the weakest math skills had higher failure rates than other students taking double-dose algebra; their algebra class was more demanding while their skill improvements were more modest than students with higher incoming math skills.

Why Did the Policy Not Provide More Benefit for Students with the Weakest Math Skills?

Double-dose algebra was least effective for students entering high school with the weakest math abilities. Yet, this is often the group that is seen as most in need of academic support to be able to handle algebra. The students with the lowest math skills showed higher failure rates as a result of taking double-dose algebra, and their test scores did not improve as much as other low-ability students. Why did these students not benefit as much from taking double-dose algebra? One reason seems to stem from the fact that so many of the students with the lowest math skills had identified learning disabilities, and schools were unclear how to apply the policy to students receiving special education services.

Special education students, in general, benefited less from double-dose algebra than did regular education students. The improvement in test scores for special education students eligible for double-dose algebra was only 60% of the improvement observed among students without disabilities in 2003, and less than half in 2004. Furthermore, failure rates rose sharply among special education students who enrolled in double-dose algebra; their failure rates increased by 8 percentage points postpolicy, whereas students with similar incoming test scores without disabilities did not have higher failure rates postpolicy.

The policy affected the classroom experiences of special education students differently than those of students without identified disabilities. Before the policy, many special education students took algebra in small, self-contained special education classrooms. Because the policy did not offer guidelines about how to accommodate students with disabilities within the policy, schools were unclear about how to respond to this policy for special education students. Thus, school responses varied considerably: Many schools enrolled their special education students in double-dose algebra classes together with other students who did not have identified disabilities; other schools kept the self-contained special education classes without providing double-dose algebra.

For many special education students, the policy caused them to receive algebra instruction in large classes with other students who were not eligible for

---

[8]Increases in classroom academic demand and pedagogy by 1 standard deviation unit are associated with increases in students' test scores by two tenths of a standard deviation unit.

[9]For a typical student, attending a class with greater demand by 1 standard deviation unit is associated with an increase in failure rates by 8%.

special education services, instead of small, self-contained classes. Although double-dose algebra increased academic demand for special education students, their teachers may have lacked strategies to reach students with disabilities. In fact, conversations with the district personnel suggest that many double-dose algebra classes contained large percentages of students with disabilities, and that algebra teachers felt unprepared to teach them. Consequently, some special education students may have been less well-served than they would have been with teachers who had more experience teaching students with disabilities.

All of this suggests that schools and teachers need to better monitor students with disabilities and provide a more intense intervention (Tier 2 or Tier 3 intervention) for those who are not responding to the Tier 1 intervention. In particular, there is a need to pay attention to course attendance, as well as skill development. The primary reason that students with disabilities fail their ninth-grade courses at higher rates than other students is because they miss more days of school (Gwynne, Lesnick, Hart, & Allensworth, 2009). By concentrating together students with high absence and behavior problems, without teachers trained to work with students with behavioral issues, problems with absenteeism were aggravated. In recent years, the district has put monitoring reports into place that alert teachers and counselors to students with high absence rates or failing grades in their ninth-grade classes. Such reports may help schools target more intense interventions to those students who continue to struggle with the Tier 1 support.

Unintended Consequences for High-Skilled Students

In the last section of this chapter, we show how the double-dose policy unintentionally affected students with high academic skills who were not targeted by the policy. This illustrates how a reform or intervention for one group of students can introduce other changes within school, such as reallocating resources and restructuring classrooms (e.g., tracking), which affect all students, even those who are not targeted by that reform.

Under the double-dose algebra policy in Chicago, students who scored above the national median on the ITBS were not required to take double-dose algebra. However, the policy affected these students because schools separated algebra classes based on students' incoming test scores; thus, higher achieving students enrolled in more homogenous algebra classrooms. This allowed teachers to cover more difficult material to meet the higher skill levels of their students. In addition, single-period algebra classes had less disruption and better attendance because classes with higher average skills had fewer students with behavior problems. This created a better learning environment for high-achieving students.

In fact, student surveys showed that academic demand in algebra classes increased postpolicy for students scoring above the national median on ITBS (see Figure 10.2), even though they were not targeted by the policy, and this improvement was largely attributable to improvements in peer ability levels.

Classroom behavior problems also declined for higher ability students: Post-policy algebra classes had fewer students with absenteeism and disciplinary problems than prepolicy algebra classes attended by higher ability students. At the same time, pedagogical practices did not change. Teachers in single-period algebra classes used similar instructional practices both before and after the policy. This suggests that improvements in pedagogy in the double-dose algebra were a result of the resources provided by the policy—extended time and instructional supports.

Test Scores Improved, but Failure Rates Rose for High-Skilled Students

As a result of improved peer ability levels, high-skilled students received more demanding course material in a less disruptive environment. Consequently, their performance on the standardized tests improved. Among students who were near the cutoff score (the 50th percentile), test scores improved by about half a point in 2003, compared with the 2002 cohort, which is about 28% higher on the condensed scale. There is also evidence of spillover effects of double-dose algebra: high-skilled students' scores improved more in classes that also enrolled students who took double-dose algebra. Although most single-period algebra classes did not have any students who took double-dose algebra, some classes enrolled a small group of students who took support coursework—either because of scheduling difficulties or insufficient availability of double-dose classes. Our evidence suggests that having "double-dose" students in single-period algebra classes helped raise test scores of single-period algebra students because "double-dose" students were learning at a faster pace than they would have without receiving additional supports. In other words, students with weaker math skills were less likely to hold back instruction because they were receiving supplemental instruction.

However, despite improvements in test scores, course grades did not improve for high-skilled students. Particularly among students whose incoming test scores were close to the national median, failure rates increased by as much as 5 percentage points from 2002 to 2003. Other research also has shown that students tend to receive lower course grades in classrooms with high-ability peers (Farkas, Sheehan, & Grobe, 1990; Kelly, 2008). Increased failure rates in postpolicy algebra classes are partly attributable to the fact that teachers assign lower grades to students who look worse in their classes relative to their peers; students at the national median became among the lowest ability students in their algebra classes postpolicy. Also, increased course demand made it more difficult for students to pass.

CONCLUSION

The double-dose algebra policy was designed to address a clear problem in Chicago's high schools—high failure rates in ninth-grade algebra. Research had shown a strong link between ninth-grade failure and eventual dropout, and district officials felt it was crucial to fix this problem. Yet, the strategy they developed—double-dose algebra—did not reduce failure rates. For some students, failure rates even increased in ninth-grade algebra with the policy. Thus, many people in the district viewed the policy as a failure, and conversations with district personnel suggest that the policy was widely criticized.

However, it seems that math failure was the wrong outcome on which to judge this policy. This was a policy that sought to improve failure rates by giving students more and better algebra instruction, that is, by improving their algebra skills. It succeeded at doing this. Algebra test scores increased substantially—by almost a third of a standard deviation—among students who received double-dose algebra classes. Improvements in test scores occurred despite the fact that double-dose algebra classes concentrated students with low math skills together. Double-dose algebra classes did not suffer from poor instructional practices, which often characterize low-track classrooms. This is most likely because the policy provided a number of instructional supports, including extended instructional time, curricular resources, and professional development around instruction. Classroom instruction—both academic demand and pedagogy—improved as a result of the policy, leading to higher test scores. It is also likely that homogenous classes allowed teachers to focus more effectively on skills that students were lacking.

However, the policy did not address how to improve students' motivation and behavior, including their attendance and classroom engagement. Even though double-dose algebra classes provided better and more challenging instruction, they also concentrated together students with behavior problems. Teachers in low-ability classrooms often struggle with classroom management and attendance problems (Oakes, 1985; Page, 1991), but they rarely get extra support in this area. In fact, in Chicago, support for classroom management is often overlooked in favor of curricular and instructional support—that is, how to teach the curriculum rather than how to manage the classroom (Sporte, Correa, Hart, & Wechsler, 2009). For schools considering double-dose algebra, it is important to make an effort to improve students' motivation and engagement—factors that are crucial for improving students' course grades. For example, teachers need to make sure that students come to the class regularly and actively participate in instructional activities. Teachers also need to make students turn in homework and provide feedback on the assignments on a regular basis. Any reform efforts that address low skills will have limited effects on grades unless they address problems of students' behavior, motivation, and classroom engagement.

Another implication of the Chicago double-dose algebra policy, and possibly other Tier 2 support interventions in mathematics, is that a large-scale intervention targeting low-ability students can affect students who are not targeted by the policy. The double-dose policy led schools to reorganize all math classrooms, and, as a result, classroom academic composition changed considerably for all students. The effects of changing classroom composition are not small. In fact, their effects on algebra scores for high-skilled students appear to be almost as large as the effects of doubling instructional time for low-skilled students. Furthermore, the policy had larger consequences on algebra failure for high-skilled students than for low-skilled students, making them more likely to fail. Thus, the details of how curricular policies are implemented and programmed may matter as much as the changes in the content of curriculum to which students are being exposed.

As states and districts increasingly mandate all students to take algebra in the ninth or eighth grade, schools should be concerned about the potential effects this could have on the way that students are programmed together into classes, creating more heterogeneous classes. For students with weak skills, who will be grouped with much higher skilled peers, increased academic demand has the potential to encourage students to struggle and withdraw from instruction. Schools might consider closely monitoring students who enter these classes with weak skills, and plan Tier 2 interventions for those who show weak grades or multiple course absences.

Last, large-scale curricular reforms that are targeted to students with low academic abilities particularly need to pay attention to their effects on students with learning disabilities. We found only modest benefit and some detriments of double-dose algebra for students entering high school with very low math skills. Given that ninth-grade course failure is the most significant factor of high-school graduation, increases in failure rates among special education students are particularly troubling because they already are the least likely to graduate from high school of any subgroup of students. In many cases, schools substituted small, separate classrooms for students with disabilities with large, heterogeneous, double-dose algebra classes. This does not seem to have substantially benefited students' achievement or helped their grades. To better assist students with disabilities, schools or teachers need to monitor students' progress throughout a year to see whether they are responding to double-dose algebra in large, heterogeneous classes. If students do not show improvements in double-dose algebra classes, schools need to provide a more intense intervention.

REFERENCES

Allensworth, E., & Easton, J.Q. (2005). *The on-track indicator as a predictor of high school graduation.* Chicago: Consortium on Chicago School Research.

Allensworth, E., & Easton, J.Q. (2007). *What matters for staying on-track and graduating in Chicago Public Schools.* Chicago: Consortium on Chicago School Research.

Bottoms, G. (2008). *Redesigning the ninth-grade experience: Reduce failure, improve achievement and increase high school graduation rates.* Atlanta: Southern Regional Education Board.

Chait, R., Muller, R.D., Goldware, S., & Housman, N.G. (2007). *Academic interventions to help students meet rigorous standards: State policy options.* Washington, DC: The National High School Alliance at the Institute for Educational Leadership.

Darling-Hammond, L. (2004). Standards, accountability, and school reform. *Teachers College Record, 106,* 1047–1085.

Farkas, G., Sheehan, D., & Grobe, R.P. (1990). Coursework mastery and school success: Gender, ethnicity, and poverty groups within an urban school district. *American Educational Research Journal, 27,* 807–827.

Gwynne, J., Lesnick, J., Hart, H.M., & Allensworth, E.M. (2009). *What matters for staying on-track and graduating in Chicago public schools: A focus on students with disabilities.* Chicago: Consortium on Chicago School Research.

Kelly, S. (2008). What types of students' effort are rewarded with high marks? *Sociology of Education, 81,* 32–52.

Loveless, T. (2008). *The Misplaced Math Student: Lost in Eighth-Grade Algebra.* Washington DC: Brown Center on Education Policy, the Brookings Institution.

National Center for Education Statistics. (2006). *The condition of education 2006.* Washington, DC: U.S. Department of Education.

National Governors Association Center for Best Practices. (2005). *Getting it done: Ten steps to a state action agenda.* Retrieved from http://www.nga.org/files/pdf/05warnerguide.pdf

Nomi, T., & Allensworth, E. (2009). "Double-dose" algebra as an alternative strategy to remediation: Effects on students' academic outcomes. *Journal on Research on Educational Effectiveness, 2,* 111–148.

Nomi, T., & Allensworth, E. (2010). The effects of tracking with supports on instructional climate and student outcomes in high school algebra. Retrieved from http://ccsr.uchicago.edu/downloads/5347effects_of_tracking_working_paper.pdf

Oakes, J. (1985). *Keeping track: How schools structure inequality.* New Haven, CT: Yale University Press.

Oakes, J. (2005). *Keeping track: How schools structure inequality* (2nd ed.). New Haven, CT: Yale University Press.

Page, R. (1991). *Lower track classroom: A curricular and cultural perspective.* New York: Teachers College Press.

Roderick, M., & Camburn, E. (1999). Risk and recovery from course failure in the early years of high school. *American Educational Research Journal, 36,* 303–343.

Rosenbaum, J.E. (1976). *Making inequality: The hidden curriculum of high school.* New York: Wiley.

Sporte, S.E., Correa, M., Hart, H.M., & Wechsler, M.E. (2009). *High school reform in Chicago public schools: Instructional development systems.* Menlo Park, CA: SRI International. Retrieved from http://policyweb.sri.com/cep/publications/IDS_final.pdf

Starkel, R., Martinez, J., & Price, K. (2006). Two-period algebra in the 05–06 school year: Implementation report. Retrieved from https://research.cps.k12.il.us/resweb/DownLoaderAdv?dir=program_evaluation&file=Two_Period_Algebra_final_report1.pdf

Wenzel, S., Lawal, K., Conway, B., Fendt, C., & Stoelinga, S. (2005). *Algebra problem solving: Teachers talk about their experiences, December 2004.* Retrieved from https://research.cps.k12.il.us/resweb/DownLoaderAdv?dir=program_evaluation&file=APS_external_evaluation_focus_group_report_010405.pdf

U.S. Department of Education, National Center for Education Statistics, National Assessment of Educational Progress (NAEP). (2007). *The condition of education 2000-2007.* Retrieved from http://nces.ed.gov/programs/coe/

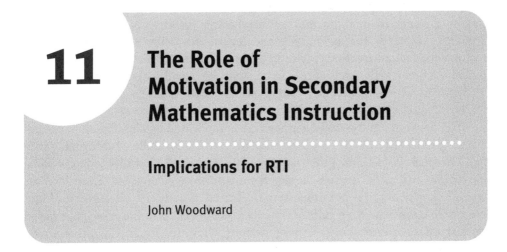

11

The Role of Motivation in Secondary Mathematics Instruction

Implications for RTI

John Woodward

The recent Institute of Education Sciences publication, *Assisting Students Struggling with Mathematics: Response to Intervention (RtI) for Elementary and Middle Grades* (Gersten et al., 2009), makes an important contribution to an emerging area of policy and research. The report, written for practitioners, largely focuses on instructional techniques such as visual diagrams, developing fact fluency, and teaching the underlying structure of word problems to improve the academic performance of Tier 2 and 3 students. It is also noteworthy that this practitioner's guide recommends motivational strategies such as verbal praise and having students chart progress as methods that teachers can use to reinforce the effort a student employs in learning, even though the panel could not find specific support for the effect of motivational techniques in the context of mathematics interventions in its review of the literature. Nonetheless, including motivation as an intervention technique, particularly in the nascent response to intervention (RTI) literature, is a significant step forward in our thinking about how to help students who struggle in a difficult academic discipline such as mathematics. Too often, the field of special education emphasizes instructional techniques, methods for designing curriculum, and ways to assess academic progress at the expense of motivational issues.

Recommending that teachers contingently praise student effort is an essential practice at the elementary grades, and it is consistent with a wide body of correlational and intervention research (Heller & Fantuzzo, 1993; Schunk & Cox, 1986). An emphasis on effort can enhance a student's self-efficacy (i.e., belief in one's ability to succeed on a task) and, in turn, the student's choice of tasks, task persistence, and long-term achievement (Schunk & Pajares, 2002, 2005). Detailed accounts of Japanese classrooms suggest that an emphasis on effort over ability is one of the hallmarks of its educational system, leading to much greater task persistence and increased academic performance (Lewis, 1995; Stevenson, Lee, & Nerison-Low, 1998; Tsuneyoshi, 2001). Finally, stressing effort is an important counterbalance to the natural tendency for students—even in the primary grade levels—to make social comparisons. An unavoidable awareness of who finishes tasks early, who answers questions quickly and correctly, and who is in a particular small instructional group are all ways in which ability can trump effort in a student's self-concept as a learner (Dweck, 1999).

RTI concerns in the middle grades are complicated by significant structural issues, particularly in the way students are tracked formally or informally into mathematics classes. Some districts try to serve almost all students in the same heterogeneous track of math classes from sixth to eighth grade. Even in cases where this is policy, it is not unusual to find an advanced track of classes for high-ly capable students. Other middle schools make placements more formally based on test scores and teacher recommendations, thus creating in this process a de facto "low track" of what would be called in today's RTI vernacular Tier 2 and/or 3 students (see Loveless, 1999). Efforts to provide additional support for strug-gling Tier 2 students through remediation classes (a.k.a., "double dipping") adds further to the different scenarios for addressing the range of math abilities in the middle grades.

Motivational issues are also more complex by the middle grades, and this is documented in a wealth of descriptive and intervention research, particularly in the area of mathematics. As students move from elementary to middle school, there are general declines in academic motivation and self-efficacy (Anderman & Maehr, 1994; Wigfield, Eccles, Mac Iver, Reuman, & Midgley, 1991; Wigfield & Wagner, 2005). These changes are related to the shift from a strong association with one teacher to more superficial contacts with multiple teachers. Grades also take on much greater importance as a form of evaluation and feedback, and they are typically distributed unevenly among students within classrooms or between academic tracks of instruction (i.e., the traditional tendency to award high grades to only a minority of students). A consistent stream of low grades helps reinforce in low-achieving students that ability rather than effort explains academic performance. Recent research indicates that declining motivation in mathematics persists through high school, particularly with boys (Chouinard & Roy, 2008).

Low achievement for some middle-school students can also reflect the culmination of an unsuccessful learning history and the varied efforts to avoid failure in eyes of teachers and peers. Covington and his colleagues (Covington, 1992; Covington & Dray, 2002) have described how evasive behaviors such as "losing homework," being sick, acting out, and passivity are all attempts to maintain a high level of contingent self-worth by offering internal and external explanations of poor performance. These kinds of avoidance behaviors erode a student's sense of competence, and they are negatively associated with a mas-tery orientation toward learning (Turner et al., 2002).

A year-long, naturalistic study of low-achieving students in the intermediate grades captured several dimensions that likely lead to the development of contingent self-worth (Baxter, Woodward, & Olson, 2001). Over the course of the year, the low-achieving children in the class generally did not participate in whole class discussions, and they adopted passive roles as they worked in small groups. Frequently, they discreetly copied answers from neighbors when completing independent practice workbook activities. Interviews with these students conducted throughout the year indicated that the complexity of the tasks as well as the manifest superior performance of peers in whole class discussions and small group work were central reasons for their reluctance to participate in class.

This pattern was even more evident in a subsequent study of middle-grade students (Baxter, Woodward, & Olson, 2005). In this setting, unwillingness to discuss mathematics in class led the teacher and researchers to use journals as the central form of classroom communication, thus allowing students to present their thinking privately to the teacher and thus insulating the student from possible peer comparisons and/or criticisms.

Consequently, how students *think about* their ability to do mathematics by the middle grades seems to have a significant effect on performance. Weiner (1986, 2005) theorized that, over time, a student's academic experience is linked to causal beliefs framed by three dichotomous variables. The extent to which a student believes his or her performance is internal or external, changeable or unchangeable, and controllable or uncontrollable can have a dramatic effect on effort and academic outcomes. A failing student comes to believe that his or her math ability will not change, even with extra effort. This internal sense of low ability is thought to be unchanging and beyond the individual's control. Thus, a struggling student will accept failure in a subject such as math as part of a consistent set of causal beliefs that focuses on ability over effort. Dweck and colleagues (Dweck, 1999; Elliot, 2005) presented similar observations for how a belief in a fixed ability over an incremental or effort orientation comes to dominate a student's thinking in academic subjects such as mathematics.

A complementary and crucial factor that can also reinforce low academic performance is the extent to which a student values or has interest in a subject such as mathematics. Much has been made in mathematics education and, for that matter, recent educational reform, over the past 2 decades in respect to getting students "engaged" in the subject matter and increasing students' "productive dispositions" (Chazan, 2000; Cohen, McLaughlin, & Talbert, 1993; National Research Council, 2001). Some argue that by making mathematics more relevant, a student's interest in the subject will increase.

Thus, real-world applications such as racing cars on ramps (Bottge, Rueda, Laroque, Serlin, & Kwon, 2007) or developing business plans for school fundraisers (Vye, Goldman, & Voss, 1997) are thought to not only improve mathematical understanding, but also to make math more meaningful and engaging. Most certainly these kinds of application-oriented activities may be preferable to a constant routine of drill on computational procedures for many low-achieving students. However, the extent to which real-world problems are a superior alternative is unclear. What researchers or curriculum developers believe are real world problems may not be the case for many students, who simply find them one more abstract exercise or simply irrelevant to their lives (Woodward, 2004).

Whether it is through real-world problems or in-depth discussions of mathematical ideas (see Lampert, 2001), some students may simply lack interest—and, hence, be unmotivated—in math as a subject because it does not have any perceived *usefulness* at this point in their lives. Motivation researchers (Eccles, 2005; Ryan & Deci, 2000) highlighted the concepts of cost and utility as a way of explaining how some students think about demanding academic tasks such as mathematics. When math is perceived as not having some future payoff, particularly in the form of an occupation or long-term success in school, then students do not see that the cost or effort associated with doing well in the subject is worth it. Students disengage not because of a lack of ability necessarily, but because they do not perceive the longer term rewards associated with learning mathematics (see Chouinard & Roy, 2008).

Social context and peer influences also can shape a student's sense of ability in ways that present considerable dilemmas for secondary educators. Tracking in middle and high school has long been the subject of severe criticism, particularly the way an inferior quality of instruction often permeates remedial education tracks as well as the way mutually held beliefs among low-ability students can lead to low levels of effort and, in turn, can have a reciprocal effect on teacher expectations (Boaler & Staples, 2008; National Research Council, 2004; Oakes, 2008). Yet detracking students can also raise a set of issues that are both academic and motivational in nature. (See chapter by Nomi and Allensworth in this volume for further exploration of this phenomenon.)

Recently, researchers have looked at policies that place many students who would have normally been in remedial tracks in the more challenging regular track classes. The achievement results are mixed, at best, and in some studies it is unclear exactly how low-achieving students were supported as they move through increasingly difficult secondary math classes.

For example, Burris, Wiley, Welner, & Murphy (2008) suggested that detracking in the middle grades can lead to students having a much higher probability of obtaining a New York State Regents Diploma when they controlled for aptitude in their analyses. Their study was limited to students from a relatively high socioeconomic setting, and it included only those who were continuously enrolled in the school district from ninth grade to the end of high school. It also excluded special education students who appeared to have severe disabilities, though the specific criteria for what constituted severe disabilities was not explicated.

Yet perhaps the greatest problem with the study is that it did little to explain what accounted for the performance improvement other than putting students in accelerated, heterogeneous classrooms. As will be noted shortly, this finding contradicts broader analyses of detracking.

In contrast, Boaler and Staples (2008), offered a much more detailed account of detracking in a comparative study of high schools. Math teachers in the detracked high school of interest tended to pose challenging, conceptual problems that combined student presentations with teacher questioning. It is important to notice that the same challenging problems were presented in an undifferentiated manner. Teachers lectured only a small portion of the period and, instead, spent the vast majority of the time (72%) having students work in small groups with the teacher circulating the room providing input and assistance. Although the comparative results for the three schools in the study favored the detracked school, 30% of students in this school scored at the basic level on the California Standards Algebra test (California Department of Education, 2006), and another 60% scored at below or far below basic level. Thus, the majority of students in all three schools failed to learn algebra, at least as measured by state grade-level examinations.

At the same time, Loveless (2008) offered a disturbing picture of the way many low-achieving students, particularly those in the lowest 10th percentile and who are likely to qualify for special education services, are moved through the middle grades in a simple effort to keep these students on track for high-school courses such as Algebra II rather than traditional dead-end courses such as Consumer Math. Using the National Assessment of Educational Progress as an index for academic performance, Loveless found that a surprising number of low-achieving students floundered in the detracked middle-school courses and had performance levels more akin to third or fourth grade by the time they were in the eighth grade.

Gamoran and his colleagues (Gamoran, Porter, Smithson, & White, 1997; Gamoran & Weinstein, 1998) also reported that efforts to eliminate general track math classes and replace them with transition courses (i.e., courses that allow students to keep up with students who enroll in college prep classes) have been only partially successful. Students' achievement tended to be somewhere between those in low-track, skills-based classrooms and students in college prep courses.

These studies present a mixed picture of the effects of detracking on academic performance, but research also raises concerns about the impact of heterogeneous classrooms on student motivation. As mentioned earlier, the issue of social comparisons among peers in an academic context is a significant issue in a middle-school environment. Marsh and his colleagues (Marsh, 1991; Marsh, Kong, & Hau, 2000) have carefully documented the effects of placing students of the same ability in classrooms that vary in their level of challenge. On the whole, students who are relatively low achieving in higher achieving classrooms—the very type of students Loveless (2008) described in his research—tend to have lower academic self-concepts than students of the same ability in classrooms that more closely match their academic levels. They also tend to have a lower interest in mathematics than students who are more homogeneously grouped (Ludke, Marsh, Koller, & Baumert, 2006).

Qualitative research corroborates in much greater detail the effects of being overwhelmed in math classes that are too challenging and where students frequently make negative comparisons with more capable peers (Usher, 2009). Over time, research has indicated that low levels of past academic achievement affect subsequent achievement and self-concept, though not necessarily in a unidirectional manner (e.g., from achievement to self-concept only; Bandura, 1997; Guay, Marsh, & Boivin, 2003).

In addition, peer groups take on added importance, and one's reference group—particularly in tracked classes—can have a significant impact on academic performance. Socially competent students tend to achieve classroom goals—either task-related or ones involving a specific standard of proficiency—by establishing productive working relationships with teachers and peers. They do so by clarifying and interpreting a teacher's instructions, modeling strategies, giving advice, and working cooperatively with others (Schunk & Pajares, 2005; Wentzel, 2005). By contrast, socially troublesome students tend to be less compliant, as well as more aggressive and disruptive in the classroom (Rubin, Bukowski, & Parker, 1998). These kinds of conditions often lead to negative classroom environments and relatively ineffective classroom instruction. The added consequence of this kind of an academic experience is that many students, particularly those marginalized by their peers, become increasingly uninterested in school (Wentzel, 2005; Wentzel & Asher, 1995).

Consequently, the effects of tracking or detracking students create dilemmas for educators that go well beyond academic outcomes, and the impact of such practices on motivation appear to vary. Many of these motivation themes were apparent in a study of low-track, middle-school mathematics classrooms (Woodward, Baxter, Robinson, & Bush, 2006). The researchers used multiple sources of data to document the experience of remedial and special education students over 2 academic years of instruction. Some of the key findings from their first year of research are summarized in the following paragraphs.

A STUDY OF MOTIVATION AND LOW ACHIEVERS IN THE MIDDLE GRADES

Woodward et al.'s study (2006) involved 62 junior-high students and their teachers from three classrooms in one school in a medium-sized, suburban district. There were 33 eighth graders and 29 ninth graders, 37 (or 60%) of whom had individualized education programs (IEPs) in mathematics. The rest were considered at least two grade levels behind in their academic skills. All of these students were enrolled in the lowest math track (a.k.a., "Math Apps") classes in the school.

The three teachers in the study used a mix of curricular materials, which included a core prealgebra text (Collins et al., 1998), daily problem-solving tasks created by the district, and teacher-developed skills worksheets. The district had created or encouraged many of these materials in an effort to raise the problem-solving and computational performance of low-achieving students on annual standardized tests.

Researchers used multiple methods to document student behavior and motivation, including observations in each classroom at least once per week. They took extensive notes of classroom practices and interviewed students informally before, during, and after class. The researchers coded observation notes and interviews for themes and periodically transformed their notes into memos as another method of thematic analysis (see Merriam, 1998; Miles & Huberman, 1994).

Researchers collected school record data on grade point average; enrollment in a remedial class for teaching study skills and completing homework; the amount of absenteeism, in-school suspension, and out-of-school suspensions. In addition, all of the low-achieving students in the three Math Apps classrooms as well as a random selection of 33 eighth graders and 29 ninth graders from four on-track classes (i.e., average achieving) were given the Piers-Harris self-concept measure (Piers, 1994) as well as a researcher-developed Attitudes Toward Math survey (Woodward, Baxter, & Monroe, 2001). The Piers-Harris self-concept measure contained six cluster scales, and the Attitudes Toward Math survey was constructed around three basic themes. The latter measure also asked questions about future plans, including plans for postsecondary education. As well, the measure asked whether the student had an older sibling(s) who had attended some kind of postsecondary education.

Statistical analyses of the self-concept and attitude data revealed significant differences between the random selection of average-ability students and those in the low-track classes. School record data showed significant differences in terms of math subtest on the Comprehensive Tests of Basic Skills (CTBS; CTB, 2001) ($F[1, 123] = 228.71$; $p < .001$; $d = 2.72$), total score on the CTBS ($F[1, 123] = 279.34$; $p < .001$; $d = 3.00$), and grade point average ($F[1, 123] = 111.44$; $p < .001$; $d = 1.89$) favoring the comparison students in on-track classes.

Differences in amounts of in-school ($F[1, 123] = 11.33$; $p < .001$; $d = .60$) and out-of-school suspensions ($F[1, 123] = 10.25$; $p < .01$; $d = .59$) favored the Math Apps students. The suspension rates were particularly striking among the Math Apps students. Thirty-nine percent of the Math Apps students accounted for all of the in-school suspensions. Thirty percent of the Math Apps students accounted for all of the out-of-school suspensions.

Differences in self-concept and attitudes toward mathematics were also telling. Overall scores on the Piers-Harris scale were significantly different ($F[1, 123] = 8.68$; $p < .01$; $d = .53$), indicating much higher levels of self-concept for the average-track students. Specific cluster subscales were even more revealing. Students in the Math Apps classroom tended to have significantly lower scores in the area of behavior ($F[1, 123] = 5.28$; $p < .05$; $d = .52$), intellectual and school status ($F[1, 123] = 4.69$; $p < .05$; $d = .39$), anxiety ($F[1, 123] = 7.54$; $p < .01$; $d = .50$), and happiness ($F[1, 123] = 8.81$; $p < .01$; $d = .53$).

The 50-item Attitudes Toward Math survey probed

1. The extent to which students disliked or liked mathematics
2. Their conception of mathematics (e.g., skills practice, problem solving, use of manipulatives, or representations)
3. The social nature of mathematics (e.g., willingness to participate in class, attitudes toward group work)

Overall scores on the Attitudes Toward Math survey were significantly lower for Math Apps students ($F[1, 123] = 11.27$; $p < .001$; $d = .60$) as well as the subscales of dislike or like ($F[1, 123] = 7.21$; $p < .01$; $d = .48$), and conceptions of mathematics ($F[1, 123] = 5.42$; $p = .02$; $d = .42$). In particular, the Math Apps students tended to not like the subject and believed that they could not get a good grade in the class. They did not perceive how mathematics was or could be used outside the classroom, and they saw math as skills practice in which one worked problems very quickly with little or no problem solving. Most important, the Math Apps students did not see additional practice as a means of improving their math ability.

Finally, Math Apps students tended to be significantly more unlikely to have plans for some form of postsecondary education ($\chi^2 = 5.31$; $p < .05$). This was also reflected in significant differences between the groups in terms of the number of siblings who had attended some form of postsecondary schooling ($\chi^2 = 23.36$; $p < .001$).

Qualitative analyses of observations and interview data provided a vivid picture of many of the findings from the school record data and attitude surveys. Classroom observations generally showed well-meaning teachers who struggled to engage students in the district's mix of curricular materials. Our observations also revealed a pattern of daily instruction that contributed to a general level of student disengagement. This was often accompanied by students interrupting the flow of instruction and task-irrelevant banter between the teacher and students.

For example, it was common to begin class with a daily word problem such as the ones shown in Figure 11.1. There was little or no pattern to the problems from day to day, and they were unrelated to the text materials or the practice worksheets. Typically, students worked on them individually for less than 5 minutes before the teacher discussed the answers. On most occasions, students were reluctant to offer their answers when called upon by the teacher, and many gave up in frustration almost immediately when the problems were presented on the overhead projector. Tareina, one of the students commonly interviewed before

---

A snail is at the bottom of a 30-foot well. It climbs up 3 feet but slides back 2 feet, each day. How many days does it take for the snail to climb out of the well?

What is the sum of the number of corners, the number of sides, and the number of edges on a cube?

The Sound of Music, one of the all-time favorite movies, won an Academy Award in what year? The sum of the digits of the year is 21, the tens digit is greater than the ones digit, and the product of the digits is 270.

As of 1984, the New York Yankees had been in 33 World Series. They had won twice as many Series as they had lost. How many World Series had they won?

You have a million dollars, and you are going to spend 100 dollars a day. How many days will it take you to spend it?

A chukker in polo is a period of play that is 7½ minutes long. There are 8 chukkers in a game of polo. How many chukkers are left in the game after 45 minutes of play?

Figure 11.1.   Sample daily word problems given in the Math Apps classrooms.

and during class, stated that she did not see the point of these exercises. "Who cares about these problems? It doesn't help me with math, and I'm no good at it [mathematics] anyway. It's just another waste of time. I'm never going to do anything with math anyway."

A significant number of other students echoed Tareina's comments in individual interviews over the course of the year. Some said that they started to fall behind in fourth or fifth grade and could not keep up. Others could not remember doing well in math, particularly those who had IEPs in the subject. A common thread through all of the conversations was the extent to which they perceived their failure to be rooted in a lack of ability, and this was something beyond their control and unchangeable.

Work in the textbook and worksheets, which varied in their relative emphasis from day to day, was equally unsatisfying to most students. Many students complied and worked on the assigned tasks individually at their desks, but the instructional flow in the classroom was interrupted frequently by off-task behavior or student questioning, which seemed designed to distract the teacher from explaining concepts or ensuring that the majority of class remained on task. Many students also engaged in low-level conversations throughout the period about topics that had nothing to do with mathematics. What they tended to say to each other varied from gossip about other students to dramatic and sometimes disturbing discussions of life at home or in the community.

Corey, another student commonly interviewed throughout the year, reflected a general sentiment about the text and the worksheets this way: "The stuff in the book can get really hard, and the teacher goes over it too quickly. I don't get it. But the worksheets are for babies. I've had this stuff before, like in third grade." Corey's comments about the text and related instruction were consistent with the observations. The district had designed a guide to ensure that Math Apps classes would complete the prealgebra text in a year, and topics such as operations on integers (e.g., $-4 - -3$), which can be confusing to average students, were baffling to most in the Math Apps classrooms. Students frequently confused the rules as well as the difference between the negative sign and the operation of subtraction.

In contrast, a large number of students interviewed throughout the year complained about the repetitive computational practice. A sample of worksheets collected at the end of class throughout the year indicated success rates between 60% and 70%. Lower success was found on multidigit multiplication and division problems as well as tasks in which one added more than two fractions with unlike denominators.

A final theme that emerged from the observations and student interviews was the way discordant relationships between students upstaged the flow of instruction. Some students, particularly the ones who sat closest to the walls, rarely said anything to either the teacher or other students throughout the year. Their goal, it appeared, was to remain somewhat "invisible" in the classroom. They were shy students and, in some cases, social isolates. Infrequently, they were targets of derisive commentary by the more vocal students in the class.

Many others were much more outgoing and even defiant. A small group of students refused to do homework or even classroom tasks in a constructive manner. A later check of school records indicated that these students were generally the ones who had the highest absentee rates as well as high levels of out-of-school suspension. When these students did come to class, they could be disruptive and subjected to repeated reprimands or private conversations between the teacher and the student around classroom behavior expectations. It is a credit to the teachers in each of these classrooms that these interactions rarely escalated or resulted in threats or expulsion.

The vast majority of students could interact with the teacher in a pleasant manner, but this did little to affect their overall disengagement in the lesson and lesson activities. As mentioned earlier, they passively completed tasks such as in-class problems from the text, skills worksheets, or the daily problem-solving exercise. These students often completed their work with little attention to detail or it had the functional effect of producing manifest frustrations.

A complex problem or textbook exercise often produced many hands in the air as soon as it was assigned. Students often needed to have the assignment reexplained or clarified immediately. Once engaged in the task, students tended to talk among themselves or make pejorative comments about others in the class.

Shyla, another student frequently interviewed throughout the year, typified the social relations in the classroom and the extent to which it affected class climate and low expectations. "I hate it when somebody makes fun of somebody else. The guys [a core group of four boys in the class] are always saying something mean. They're always calling other people dumb or weird. The teacher tries to do something about it, but he kind of gives up after a while. He just kind of lets it slide 'cause it's a hard class to teach. Everybody complains, but he really doesn't make us work that hard." Shyla was referring to her teacher's tendency to not assign homework and to fill time with worksheet practice as a way to appease students who "hate math."

The teachers' frustrations across all three classrooms with the students were manifest in repeated calls for "eyes and ears up here" to pleas of "just get through the problem(s)." At times, it seemed easier to engage in the student off-topic banter than to develop the lesson further. All three teachers were articulate about the challenges they faced with the low-achieving students in interviews conducted by the researchers. Tom Marshall, one of the Math Apps teachers, often contrasted his two low-achieving classes with the climate and expectations in his other on-track math classes. "They don't seem to care much about school, and certainly not much about math. I have a hard time adjusting to their lack of effort and how hard it is to keep their attention. I can joke with kids in my other classes, but I can start the lesson pretty quickly. It's not the case with my Math Apps kids. I just can't get them to do much work." Melanie Johnson characterized the attitude many of her students exhibited, particularly when it came to tasks requiring a good deal of effort, "Many of these students would rather fail than try and fail."

IMPLICATIONS FOR WORKING ON STUDENT MOTIVATION IN MIDDLE SCHOOL CLASSROOMS

The Woodward et al. study (2006) offers a glimpse into the many motivational problems that Tier 2 and 3 middle-school students face as they struggle with a complex subject such as mathematics. The themes from this research are commensurate with the broader findings from the National Research Council's (2004) report on motivation and secondary education, as well as recent qualitative research into resistant structures in eighth-grade math classes (see Hand, 2010). This report, cosponsored by the National Institute of Medicine, carefully articulates the nested conditions for improving the academic performance and long-term outcomes of the many disaffected secondary students. Put simply, changing instructional techniques or more clearly articulating standards or applying specific curriculum design principles are not enough to address this problem. That being said, high-quality instruction with interesting, engaging lesson content is likely to be an important beginning framework for tackling the problem of motivation in Tier 2 or 3 classrooms.

The research literature on secondary mathematics and motivation suggests that a well-structured curriculum that focuses on tasks presented at an appropriate challenge can yield higher levels of engagement and academic achievement (Meyer & Turner, 2006; Turner & Patrick, 2004). Instruction that intentionally attempts to deepen students' understanding of mathematical ideas is one way to create the right kind of academically challenging tasks (Donovan & Bransford, 2005; Turner et al., 1998). Furthermore, a class that presents an appropriate level of challenge is also one where students actively participate and explain their thinking, where they are given the opportunity to choose tasks (and determine the nature of their outcomes), and where errors are treated in a constructive manner (Boaler, 2002; Lampert, 2001; Stipek, 2002).

In contrast, a daily routine such as the one found in the Woodward et al. (2006) study, one that moves dramatically from overly difficult tasks for students to ones that are primarily procedural and not integrated, undermines student engagement and long-term interest. A subsequent, year-long study by Woodward and Brown (2006) indicated significant, positive attitudinal differences for Tier 2 and 3 students who had appropriately challenging material that emphasized understanding and linked procedures to problems and mathematical ideas.

A second key to motivating Tier 2 and 3 students involves managing classroom interactions. Conventional classroom management techniques are unquestionably important, and this kind of knowledge is common to preservice education and inservice training for teachers. However, managing interactions in math classrooms where students work challenging tasks at an appropriate level involves the development of a risk-taking environment where students feel free to discuss ideas or explain their thinking without fear of criticism. In fact, this kind of classroom discourse should limit reflexive, "right–wrong" judgments on the part of the teacher.

Research supports the view that risk taking around challenging tasks helps develop a mastery orientation as well as greater classroom attentiveness. It also promotes the use of strategies for monitoring progress toward goals (Lau, Liem, & Nie, 2008; Meyer & Turner, 2006). Finally, it is important that students develop productive working relationships with their teachers and their classroom peers. This facilitates greater levels of social competence, which is essential to higher academic motivation (Schunk & Pajares, 2005; Wentzel, 2005).

The importance of a cooperative classroom environment was evident in the second year of the Woodward et al. study (2006). Tom Marshall, one of the Math Apps teachers, employed techniques from the *Tribes* program (Gibbs & Ushijima, 2008) for building classroom community. The various techniques in *Tribes* for helping students learn more about each other and interact in positive ways took time away from mathematical tasks at the beginning of the year. However, the benefits throughout the remainder of the year in terms of a reduction in levels of derision and ridicule were demonstrable. Observation notes as well as classroom interviews with students and the teacher indicated a marked improvement in classroom climate.

Another sense of managing classroom interactions addresses the dilemma of tracking mentioned earlier in this chapter. Detracked classes may be a desirable policy, because, in theory at least, they keep students on track for the algebra classes in high school (Oakes, 2005). Yet the possible downsides of detracking are manifest when students are passed along with increasingly deficient knowledge of mathematics and lower self-concepts that result from peer comparisons. One response to this problem is for teachers in tracked classrooms (e.g., Tier 2 or 3 settings or double-dose algebra classes or algebra foundations classes) to maintain high expectations or "academic press" (Shouse, 1996; Lee & Smith, 1999). Teachers "press" students by holding students accountable for higher-quality work, by encouraging them, and by providing constructive feedback and assistance as needed (National Research Council, 2004). This disposition toward an ability track class, along with a coherent, challenging curriculum, can go a long way to helping Tier 2 and 3 students move in the direction of passing algebra in high school.

A final framework that is essential for improving motivation in Tier 2 and 3 classrooms has to do with teacher–student relations. Many of the students in the Woodward et al. (2006) study had come to believe in a fixed ability orientation where their low achievement was internal, stable, and beyond their control (see Weiner, 1986). In these circumstances, the importance of effort as it relates to academic outcomes needs to be stressed to students. This process once again involves the selection of tasks that have an appropriate level of challenge as well as opportunities to give specific feedback on the relationship between persistence and improved performance or outcomes. Teachers also need to model and then stress strategies for working challenging mathematical tasks. Blackwell, Trzesniewski, and Dweck (2007) demonstrated that coaching middle school students in math classrooms on an incremental or effort orientation led to higher levels of motivation and task outcomes.

Improved teacher–student relationships also entail a systematic effort to help students understand the *utility* of doing well in mathematics. If students are to exert higher effort in the subject, they need to fully understand what positive results will accrue from the cost of their efforts. As survey data and student interviews from the Woodward et al. (2006) study suggested, many of the low-achieving students did not plan to complete a postsecondary education nor did many of them have role models for this kind of accomplishment.

As the National Research Council's (2004) report on motivation in secondary schools indicated, far too many disengaged and/or low-achieving students have little idea what the long-term benefits are of success in a subject such as mathematics. Teachers and school counselors can help by showing active interest in a student's life and his or her future plans. Moreover, teachers and counselors are in a position to help students understand the role mathematics plays in obtaining a postsecondary education. The use of media, guest speakers, or structured contact with community members who apply mathematics on a regular basis are all ways to affect how students think about the subject.

This latter issue is especially important in an era where politicians, professional educators, and the wider media endorse the virtues of "college for all." Critics of this agenda argue that many family-wage jobs today and the near future do not require a 4-year college education. By only stressing this kind of long-term, educational outcome, we are setting unrealistic (and undifferentiated) expectations for all students (Grubb & Lazerson, 2004). Furthermore, estimates of employment growth through 2020 indicate almost as many jobs for individuals with specialized credentials or 2-year degrees as those with 4-year college educations (Holzer & Lerman, 2007). Tier 2 and 3 students in particular may be unsuited to a college trajectory for academic and/or financial reasons. Thus, it is essential that teachers and school counselors take the time to explain the utility of knowing mathematics either as it directly relates to occupations or because it is a necessary requirement for entering or exiting postsecondary degree programs. Counseling that is intentional and well informed can go a long way to helping many students find the right career paths and avoid repeated failure in math classes at the postsecondary level.

These three frameworks differ substantially from the kinds of recommendations found in much of the instructional literature for Tier 2 and 3 students, particularly in the area of mathematics. To be sure, they challenge what it means to be an effective teacher in these emerging instructional contexts. It is for this reason, if for no other, that the literature on motivation is central to understanding secondary interventions in mathematics.

REFERENCES

Anderman, E., & Maehr, M. (1994). Motivation and schooling in the middle grades. *Review of Educational Research, 64,* 287–209.

Bandura, A. (1997). *Self-efficacy: The exercise of self-control.* New York: W.H. Freeman.

Baxter, J., Woodward, J., & Olson, D. (2001). Effects of reform-based mathematics instruction in five third grade classrooms. *Elementary School Journal, 101*(5), 529–548.

Baxter, J., Woodward, J., & Olson, D. (2005). Writing in mathematics: An alternative form of discourse for academically low-achieving students. *Learning Disabilities Research & Practice, 20*(2), 119–135.

Blackwell, L., Trzesniewski, K., & Dweck, C. (2007). Implicit theories of intelligence predict achievement across an adolescent transition: A longitudinal study and an intervention. *Child Development, 78*(1), 246–263.

Boaler, J. (2002). *Experiencing school mathematics: Traditional and reform approaches to teaching and their impact on student learning.* Mahwah, NJ: Lawrence Erlbaum Associates.

Boaler, J., & Staples, M. (2008). Creating mathematical futures through an equitable teaching approach: The case of railside school. *Teachers College Record, 110*(3), 608–645.

Bottge, B., Rueda, E., Laroque, P., Serlin, R., & Kwon, J. (2007). *Learning Disabilities Research & Practice, 22*(2), 96–109.

Burris, C., Wiley, E., Welner, K., & Murphy, J. (2008). Accountability, rigor, and detracking: Achievement effects of embracing a challenging curriculum as a universal good for all students. *Teachers College Record, 110*(3), 700–712.

California Department of Education (2006). *California standards algebra test.* Sacramento, CA: California Department of Education.

Chazan, D. (2000). *Beyond formulas in mathematics and teaching: Dynamics of the high school algebra classroom.* New York: Teachers College Press.

Chouinard, R., & Roy, N. (2008). Changes in high-school students' competence beliefs, utility value and achievement goals in mathematics. *British Journal of Educational Psychology, 78,* 31–50.

Cohen, D., McLaughlin, M., & Talbert, J. (1993). *Teaching for understanding: Challenges for policy and practice.* San Francisco: Jossey-Bass.

Collins, W., Dritsas, L., Frey-Mason, P., Howard, A., McClain, K., Molina, D., et al. (1998). *Math/applications and connections.* New York: Glencoe/McGraw Hill.

Covington, M. (1992). *Making the grade: A self worth perspective on motivation and school reform.* Cambridge, UK: Cambridge University Press.

Covington, M., & Dray, E. (2002). The developmental course of achievement motivation: A need-based approach. In A. Wigfield & J. Eccles (Eds.), *The development of achievement motivation* (pp. 33–56). New York: Academic Press.

CTB/ McGraw-Hill (2001). *Comprehensive tests of basic skills.* Monterey, CA: CTB/ McGraw-Hill.

Donovan, M., & Bransford, J. (2005). *How students learn: Mathematics in the classroom.* Washington, DC: National Academies Press.

Dweck, C. (1999). *Self-theories: Their role in motivation, personality, and development.* Philadelphia: Psychology Press.

Eccles, J. (2005). Subjective task value and the Eccles et al. model of achievement-related choices. In A. Elliot & C. Dweck (Eds.), *Handbook of competence and motivation* (pp. 105–121). New York: Guilford Press.

Elliot, A. (2005). A conceptual history of the achievement goal construct. In A. Elliot & C. Dweck (Eds.), *Handbook of competence and motivation* (pp. 52–72). New York: Guilford Press.

Gamoran, A., Porter, A., Smithson, J., & White, P. (1997). Upgrading high school mathematics for low-achieving, low income youth. *Educational Evaluation and Policy Analysis, 19*(4), 325–338.

Gamoran, A., & Weinstein, M. (1998). Differentiation and opportunity in restructured schools. *American Journal of Education 106*(3), 385–415.

Gersten, R., Beckmann, S., Clarke, B., Foegen, A., Marsh, L., Star, J.R. et al. (2009). *Assisting students struggling with Mathematics: Response to intervention (RtI) for elementary and middle schools* (NCEE 2009–4060). Washington, DC: National Center for Education Evaluation and Regional Assistance, Institute of Education Sciences, U.S. Department of Education. Retrieved from http://ies.ed.gov/ncee/wwc/publications/practiceguides/

Gibbs, J., & Ushijima, T. (2008). *Engaging all by creating high school learning communities.* Windsor, Ontario: CenterSource Systems.

Grubb, W., & Lazerson, M. (2004). *The education gospel: The economic power of schooling.* Cambridge, MA: Harvard University Press.

Guay, F., Marsh, H., & Boivin, M. (2003). Academic self-concept and academic achievement: Developmental perspectives on their causal ordering. *Journal of Educational Psychology, 95,* 124–136.

Hand, V. (2010). The co-construction of opposition in a low-track mathematics classroom. *American Educational Research Journal, 47*(1), 97–132.

Heller, L.R., & Fantuzzo, J.W. (1993). Reciprocal peer tutoring and parent partnership: Does parent involvement make a difference? *School Psychology Review, 22*(3), 517–534.

Holzer, H., & Lerman, R. (2007). *America's forgotten middle-skill jobs: Education and training requirements in the next decade and beyond.* Washington, DC: The Workforce Alliance.

Lampert, M. (2001). *Teaching problems and the problems of teaching.* New Haven, CT: Yale University Press.

Lau, S., Liem, A., & Nie, Y. (2008). Task- and self-related pathways to deep learning: The mediating role of achievement goals, classroom attentiveness, and group participation. *British Journal of Educational Psychology, 78,* 639–662.

Lee, V., & Smith, J. (1999). Social support and achievement for young adolescents in Chicago: The role of school academic press. *American Educational Research Journal, 36,* 907–945.

Lewis, C. (1995). *Educating hearts and minds: Reflections on Japanese preschool and elementary education.* New York: Cambridge University Press.

Loveless, T. (2008). *The misplaced math student: Lost in eighth-grade algebra.* Washington, DC: The Brookings Institute.

Loveless, T. (1999). *The tracking wars: State reform meets school policy.* Washington, DC: The Brookings Institute.

Ludke, U., Marsh, H., Koller, O., & Baumert, J. (2006). Tracking, grading, and student motivation: Using group composition and status to predict self-concept and interest in ninth-grade mathematics. *Journal of Educational Psychology, 98*(4), 788–806.

Marsh, H. (1991). The failure of high-ability high schools to deliver academic benefits: The importance of academic self-concept and educational aspirations. *American Educational Research Journal, 28,* 445–480.

Marsh, H., Kong, C., & Hau, K. (2000). Longitudinal multilevel models of the big-fish-little-pond effect on academic self concept: Counterbalancing contrast and reflected glory-effects in Hong Kong schools. *Journal of Personality and Social Psychology, 47,* 213–231.

Merriam, S. (1998). *Qualitative research and case study applications in education.* San Francisco: Jossey-Bass.

Meyer, D., & Turner, J. (2006). Reconceptualizing emotion and motivation to learn in classroom contexts. *Educational Psychology Review, 18,* 377–390.

Miles, M., & Huberman, A. (1994). *Qualitative data analysis* (2nd ed.). Thousand Oaks, CA: Sage Publications.

National Research Council. (2001). *Adding it up: Helping children learn mathematics.* Washington, DC: National Academies Press.

National Research Council. (2004). *Engaging schools: Fostering high school students' motivation to learn.* Washington, DC: National Academies Press.

Oakes, J. (2005). *Keeping track: How schools structure inequality.* New Haven, CT: Yale University Press.

Oakes, J. (2008). Keeping track: Structuring equality and inequality in an era of accountability. *Teachers College Record, 110*(3), 700–712.

Parker, J., & Asher, S. (1987). Peer relations and later personal adjustment: Are low-accepted children at risk? *Psychological Bulletin, 102,* 357–389.

Piers, E. (1994). *Piers-Harris Children's Self-Concept Scale.* Los Angeles: Western Psychological Services.

Rubin, K., Bukowski, W., & Parker, J. (1998). Peer interactions, relationships, and groups. In W. Damon (Series Ed.) & N. Eisenberg (Vol. Ed.), *Handbook of child psychology: Vol. 3. Social, emotional, and personality development* (5th ed., pp. 619–700). New York: Wiley.

Ryan, R., & Deci, E. (2000). Intrinsic and extrinsic motivation: Classic definitions and new directions. *Contemporary Educational Journal, 25,* 54–67.

Schunk, D.H., & Cox, P.D. (1986). Strategy training and attributional feedback with learning disabled students. *Journal of Educational Psychology, 78*(3), 201–209.

Schunk, D., & Pajares, F. (2005). Competence perceptions and academic functioning. In A. Elliot & C. Dweck (Eds.), *Handbook of competence and motivation* (pp. 85–104). New York: Guilford Press.

Schunk, D., & Pajares, F. (2002). The development of academic self-efficacy. In A. Wigfield & J. Eccles (Eds.), *The development of achievement motivation* (pp. 16–32). New York: Academic Press.

Shouse, R. (1996). Academic press and sense of community: Conflict, congruence, and implications for student achievement. *School Psychology of Education, 1,* 47–68.

Stevenson, H., Lee, S., & Nerison-Low, R. (1998). *The educational system in Japan: Case study findings*. Washington, DC: National Institute on Student Achievement.

Stipek, D. (2002). Good instruction is motivating. In A. Wigfield & J. Eccles (Eds.), *The development of achievement motivation* (pp. 310–334). New York: Academic Press.

Turner, J., Meyer, D., Cox, K., Logan, C., DiCintio, M., & Thomas, C. (1998). Creating contexts for involvement in mathematics. *Journal of Educational Psychology, 90*(4), 730–745.

Turner, J., Midgley, C., Meyer, D., Gheen, M., Anderman, E., & Kang, J. (2002). The classroom environment and students' reports of avoidance strategies in mathematics: A multimethod study. *Journal of Educational Psychology, 94*, 88–106.

Turner, J., & Patrick, H. (2004). Motivational influences on student participation in classroom learning activities. *Teacher College Record, 106*, 1759–1785.

Tsuneyoshi, R. (2001). *The Japanese model of schooling*. New York: Routledge Falmer.

Usher, E. (2009). Sources of middle school students' self-efficacy in mathematics: A qualitative investigation. *American Educational Research Journal, 46*(1), 275–314.

Vye, N., Goldman, S., & Voss, J. (1997). Complex mathematical problem solving by individuals and dyads. *Cognition and Instruction, 15*(4), 435–84.

Wentzel, K. (2005). Peer relationships, motivation, and academic performance at school. A. Elliot & C. Dweck, Eds., *Handbook of competence and motivation* (pp. 279–317). New York: Guilford Press.

Wentzel, K., & Asher, S. (1995). Academic lives of neglected, rejected, popular, and controversial children. *Child Development, 66*, 754–763.

Weiner, B. (1986). *An attributional theory of motivation and emotion*. New York: Springer-Verlag.

Weiner, B. (2005). Motivation from an attributional perspective and the social psychology of perceived competence. In A. Elliot & C. Dweck (Eds.), *Handbook of competence and motivation* (pp. 52–72). New York: Guilford Press.

Wigfield, A., Eccles, J., Mac Iver, D., Reuman, D., & Midgley, C. (1991). Transitions at early adolescence: Changes in children's domain-specific self-perceptions and general self-esteem across the transition to junior high school. *Development Psychology, 27*, 552–565.

Wigfield, A., & Wagner, A. (2005). Compentence, motivation, and identity development during adolescence. In A. Elliot & C. Dweck (Eds.), *Handbook of competence and motivation* (pp. 222–239). New York: Guilford Press.

Woodward, J. (2004). Mathematics reform in the US: Past to present. *Journal of Learning Disabilities, 37*(1), 16–31.

Woodward, J., Baxter, J., & Monroe, K. (2001). *Attitudes toward math survey*. Unpublished attitude survey. Tacoma, WA: University of Puget Sound.

Woodward, J., Baxter, J., Robinson, R., & Bush, C. (November, 2006). *Meeting the needs of failing students in secondary mathematics*. International Dyslexia Association Conference, Indianapolis, IN.

Woodward, J., & Brown, C. (2006). Meeting the curricular needs of academically low achieving students in middle grade mathematics. *Journal of Special Education, 40*(3), 151–159.

12 Practical Considerations in the Implementation of RTI in Mathematics

Lauren Campsen, Alex Granzin, and Douglas Carnine

A broad variety of research studies supports many of the practices commonly associated with response to intervention (RTI), such as the use of screening measures to identify students at risk for failure (see Chapter 2), the use of progress monitoring to assess student response to intervention (see Chapter 3), and the use of evidence-based practices to improve the quality of general education instruction (see Chapters 4–10). In spite of the limited research available on the organizational variables surrounding RTI, the authors contend that the success of RTI is often the result of careful attention to practical factors, such as teacher buy-in, provision of adequate professional development and collaboration time, and the construction of class schedules that facilitate the provision of supplemental instruction. In this chapter, we flesh out the context of successful RTI implementation (defined by a significant increase in student achievement in mathematics) to illuminate the complexity of RTI in practice.

The adoption of a multitier RTI model carries with it certain assumptions that often present significant challenges during implementation. These assumptions include the notion that both rate and severity of academic failure can be reduced by the use of

1. Screening measures to identify students at risk for failure
2. Evidence-based instructional practices and curricula
3. Checks on the fidelity of implementation of those practices and curricula
4. Frequent assessment of progress combined with instructional adjustments

We discuss these assumptions in the context of exemplars provided by one of the coauthors (Campsen) who served as a principal in an elementary school that implemented RTI.

Ocean View Elementary School in urban Norfolk, Virginia, was both low performing and unaccredited entering the 21st century. In an effort to increase universal student proficiency and eliminate achievement gaps, a tiered intervention system (RTI) was initiated gradually beginning in 2002 and fully adopted in reading and math in the fall of 2005. Ocean View's success in improving student achievement with the combination of data-driven decision making and tiered intervention led to recognition as a National No Child Left Behind Blue Ribbon School in 2008 and a Virginia Distinguished Title I School in both 2009 and 2010. (Read Ocean View's story in *Data Teams: The Big Picture— Looking at Data Teams Through a Collaborative Lens* [Rose et al., 2010, Chapter 7]). In this chapter, we document how there was an initial jump in percentage proficient on the state assessment in 2003, when data teams began operating at the school. However, proficiency rates were consistently above 90% beginning in 2007, when full implementation of RTI in mathematics began.

HIGH-QUALITY TIER 1 INSTRUCTION

Less-than-adequate classroom instruction often leads to large numbers of students needing remedial instruction, placing a continual burden on a school or district's limited resources. *If a substantial number of students continually requires remediation, schools are generally not able to provide the intensity of intervention instruction needed by students who have fallen behind.* The goal of having 80% or more of all students making adequate progress reinforces a general education orientation when one is implementing RTI. Although it is not necessary for schools to wait until 80% of their students are at benchmark, it will be difficult to sustain the implementation of RTI if general classroom instruction is not of sufficient quality to ensure the success of a substantial majority of students.

High-quality instruction depends on teacher skill, knowledge, and motivation. The first, and often the most difficult, challenge when one is first introducing RTI lies in teacher resistance to what really requires a paradigm shift in how we look at student achievement levels and assessing responsibility for the results. Response to intervention requires a belief that *all* children can learn regardless of the demographics of their background or the degree of their learning problems. When student achievement is low, blame can no longer be placed on the child.

"An effective accountability system must answer at least four common-sense questions: one about individual student achievement, a second about school performance, a third about ways to help students learn, and a fourth about determining educational effectiveness" (Reeves, 2000, p. 26). We must look not only at student achievement data but also at teacher delivery of effective instruction, what schools do for our nonproficient students, and the overall performance of our schools.

The use of evidence-based curricula and instructional practices can help to ensure that a large percentage of students make adequate progress, allowing schools to devote more substantial resources to those students making less-than-adequate progress. However advantageous it may be, the practice of using evidence-based curricula and instructional practices may present education leaders with a variety of challenges that include limited resources, resistance, and lack of professional support.

Limited Resources

In any particular classroom, children are likely to respond very differently at times to the instruction being provided. To ensure the greatest success for the most children, it is advantageous to identify children who are struggling and falling behind before they reach the point where there is little hope of them keeping pace with the general education curriculum. For these students it is important to apply some of the knowledge that we have gained in the area of reading when we are expanding the implementation of RTI to include mathematics. In reading, students making less-than-adequate progress in the core curriculum require supplemental instruction.

The provision of these additional minutes of supplemental instruction often presents a substantial scheduling dilemma for building-level administrators that requires both creativity and leadership to solve. Because of the limited number of minutes available during the school day, adding supplementary minutes of instruction often results in a reduction in the minutes available for other activities that may be highly valued by both staff and parents. We provide an example of such scheduling later in the chapter (see Figures 12.5, 12.6, and 12.7). In addition, teachers need time to discuss student progress toward the objectives and changes in instruction for students failing to make adequate progress. Finding the time for such collaboration is particularly challenging when one considers that the implementation of RTI implies the provision of supplemental instruction as well. Both activities—teacher collaboration and supplemental instruction—are likely to require changes to school schedules.

Ocean View is currently using part-time (four days a week, six hours a day) retired teachers for most Tier 3 intervention groups funded with American Recovery and Reinvestment Act (PL 111-5; stimulus money) and Title I funds. Resource and administrative personnel can also be scheduled for portions of each day to provide intervention support if hiring part-time personnel is not an option. Because the stimulus money will be gone next year, the funding challenge continues. Tier 3 intervention can be provided without buying any new materials, but intervention instruction cannot happen without an instructor.

Resistance to Change

Teachers do not always welcome a change that puts a spotlight on the academic levels of their students when they know that it will reflect their instruction. Too often, they cannot let go of the belief that socioeconomics, ethnic origins, or learning problems predict academic achievement. Sometimes teachers have grown comfortable with teaching a certain way and resist changing even when their students are not demonstrating success. Faced with teacher resistance, the school principal must make some hard choices if RTI is to be fully implemented. The principal must be bold enough to develop a list of nonnegotiables that teachers are directed to follow, provide extensive professional development, closely monitor implementation, and employ consequences for noncompliance.

At Ocean View, the math nonnegotiables are the following:

- Students receive 60 minutes of direct math instruction every day.
- Teachers provide step-by-step modeling of problem solving.
- Students must *always* show their work by traditionally working out the problem; drawing pictures, tallies, or number lines; or using an alternate problem-solving structure (we teach multiple methods for solving problems). (This is an example of our power strategy, "Justify your answer.")
- Students complete daily math review (district required): five teacher-created review problems that students complete at the beginning of the math period that are based on assessment-identified areas of concern.
- Administrators conduct ongoing formal and informal observations, monitoring lesson plans and instruction to ensure that teachers are following the master schedule and implementing the instructional power strategies in the school.

Providing Adequate Ongoing Support

Typically, professional development is necessary to effectively implement evidence-based instructional strategies that support high rates of student engagement and student success. There is a wealth of information to suggest that the provision of information alone is seldom enough to support changes in teaching practice. Without adequate implementation fidelity, simply providing teachers with information regarding effective teaching practices is likely to have little impact on student performance. One approach to this problem is the development of professional learning communities. Another approach is to provide math coaches to support ongoing use of effective teaching practices.

ONGOING ASSESSMENT AND TIERED INSTRUCTION

Through use of multiple assessment measures, schools implementing RTI identify those students most at risk of academic failure and attempt to provide supplemental instruction that will subsequently allow those students to participate successfully in the regular education curriculum. Thus, a student identified as at risk or performing less than adequately on a math assessment measure would receive supplemental instruction while continuing to participate in core grade-level math instruction in his or her general education classroom.

The key point here is that the instruction that students are provided is proportional to the student's progress through the curriculum. It is not adequate to simply assess and place. An instructional delivery system, whether it be in reading or in math, needs to be closely linked to the ongoing progress of the student through the curriculum. For this to take place, it is necessary to provide tiers of instruction that can increase the intensity of instruction by providing more time for instruction; providing instruction in smaller groups; and/or providing more explicit, highly structured instruction specifically designed to address student deficits. To ensure that such increases in the intensity of instruction have the desired effect, it is necessary to add an additional essential component of RTI—ongoing assessment.

Formative and summative data collection is a fundamental aspect of RTI. These assessments allow schools to

1. Identify students at risk for academic failure before the point at which they are no longer capable of functioning in the regular education setting
2. Evaluate the effectiveness of instruction being provided in both regular education and intervention settings

This is a critical point, in that the role of assessment is not simply to evaluate students, but also to evaluate the instruction that is being provided to those students.

Although the notion that supplemental instruction will be provided to students not making adequate progress is not novel, the provision of such instruction in conjunction with the use of screening measures to identify students at risk represents a substantial change in educational practice. At this point there is likely to be considerable variability in the manner in which schools and districts implement RTI assessment systems in mathematics. This is quite appropriate given the fact that our understanding of measures of the trajectory of skill development in mathematics is much less developed than the measures that have been developed in the area of early reading.

When implementing RTI, districts or schools typically administer benchmark assessments three or four times a year and use the results to stratify students according to degree of risk. In accordance with the public health model, students are generally placed in one of three groups: students meeting benchmark (those likely to perform adequately on high-stakes assessments and generally able to benefit from regular classroom instruction), students falling below benchmark who are likely to need additional support to keep pace with the regular classroom and perform adequately on the next high-stakes assessment (some risk), and students falling significantly below benchmark who are unlikely to perform adequately on the next high-stakes assessment without considerable intervention (high risk).

Although these quarterly measures typically correlate well with high-stakes assessments, they often do not generate sufficient specific information regarding instructional needs. To determine exactly what sort of additional instruction these students need, it is often necessary to conduct additional diagnostic assessments, which should be closely related to established instructional objectives. Many districts utilize mastery assessments to determine student progress and to monitor the effectiveness of the instruction.

Recently, Marshall (2009) identified a number of problems with mastery assessments including poor alignment with standards, external scoring, long turn-around times, lack of adequate follow-up, and failure to provide adequate rationale for the use of these assessments in the first place. In addition, there is often lack of clarity regarding the distinction between more immediate or, as Marshall has referred to them, "in the moment" (mastery) assessments and

other less-frequently administered assessments. These less-frequently administered assessments, including curriculum-based measures, administered quarterly can provide valuable information regarding student progress, but they are less
likely to provide information that can be used to shape day-to-day instruction.

LEARNING OBJECTIVES

During the course of the past decade there have been a number of initiatives
to identify common core standards in major academic areas (e.g., the Common
Core State Standards Initiative at http://www.corestandards.org/the-standards).
In addition, many states and school districts have invested a great deal of time
and energy specifying desired learning outcomes. Unfortunately those desired
outcomes have not always been made available to teachers in a manner that
supports instruction clearly aligned with those outcomes. This is a critical point
because, for one to implement RTI successfully, there must be a close alignment
between agreed-upon outcomes, assessments that measure progress toward
those outcomes, and interventions designed to address the needs of students
who fail to respond to instruction. This is particularly important in the area of
mathematics because of the complex and multifaceted nature of objectives that
characterize the math curriculum. Clearly identified performance outcomes,
whether they are identified as focal points or power standards, are a critical
component of RTI implementation. They provide a clear description of the
understandings and specific skills that students must develop as they progress
through the mathematics curriculum.

Given the almost continuous variation in instructional content in math, a
number of states and districts have developed a variety of assessments that can
be utilized throughout the school year to continuously evaluate student
progress. At Ocean View, math objectives for each grade level are determined by
the state of Virginia. At the district level, these objectives are divided into four
grading quarters and then grouped at the building level into power standards
each month. The chart in Figure 12.1 provides an example of these power standards for each month of the fifth-grade school year.

Consider the month of December. All students receive Tier I core instruction
in the power standards, fractions, and statistics. At the end of the month, all students are given a 10-question assessment on these standards. Each monthly
assessment, which the school uses to collect data for progress monitoring, is
directly aligned to the power standards for each month. The December assessment appears in Figure 12.2.

Information from these assessments can then be used to determine which
students are making adequate progress toward mastery of the agreed-upon
objectives and which students need supplemental instruction to continue to
make progress in the general education curriculum.

Of greater importance than the specific features of the Ocean View implementation are the principles at play in the development of the model. Teachers
are provided very clear instructional objectives. These objectives and the

Aligning Instruction to the Standards

District Standards

Grade 5—Monthly Math Assessments 2009–2010

September: Decimal place value (to the thousandths)
- Rounding/comparing/ordering decimals
- Relationship between fractions and decimals

October: Multiplication/division (3D × 2D/4D ÷ 2D)
- Multiplication and division of whole numbers
- Equivalent expressions in equations (including variables)
- Real-life situations where area and perimeter are used

November: Measurement/concepts of fractions and decimals
- Equivalent fractions and equivalent fractions/decimals
- Determine the appropriate unit of measurement (linear, weight, mass)

December: Fractions/statistics
- Add/subtract fractions with like/unlike denominators
- Mean, median, mode of data sets

January: Probability/concept on a variable
- Tree diagrams; represent probability of a single event with fractions/decimals
- Write word problems to match open sentences
- Concept of a variable in an expression or open sentence

February: Graphs/decimals, circles
- Multiplication and division of decimals
- Graphs: stem/leaf, bar, line, picture
- Identify and describe parts of a circle

March: Geometry
- Identification of shapes/geometric solids
- Measure and classify angles and triangles
- Area of right triangles
- Reflections, rotations, translations

April: Problem solving/measurement
- Length, mass, weight, liquid volume, temperature
- Elapsed time
- Solve whole number problems

May: Patterns
- Repeating, growing, numeric

Ocean View Elementary Grade 5 Roadmap

Grade 5 2nd Quarter	Week 1	Week 2	Week 3
Communication skills	5.4A Context clues, (4.5 main idea) R5.4A/E Root words (word study) 5.6C Locate, support information W5.8A.B Planning, organizing W5.8E Vary sentence structure	R5.6D Course and effect R5.8C Use charts, graphs, maps R5.8NF Use print direction R5.48/E Prefixes/ suffixes (word study) W5.8 A,B Planning, organizing W5.8 E Vary sentence structure	5.5A Compare/contrast R5.8C Use charts, graphs, maps W5.9A,D Plural possessives Apostrophes (word study) W5.8 I Elaborations W5.8F Revise writing for clarity
Math	5.2A Create equivalent fractions, use anchors 0.1/2.1, to classify fractions 5.2 B Classify numbers as prime or composite (calendar math) 5.2C Compare and order fractions using various models and the symbols <, >, =	5.11A Determine/use appropriate use of linear measurement 5.11C Determine/use appropriate unit of measure for weight/ mass 5.11D Liquid volume 5.11 E Solve problems involving length, weight/mass,and temperature	5.11A Determine/use appropriate use of linear measurement 5.11C Determine/use appropriate unit of measure for weight/ mass 5.11 D Liquid volume 5.11 E Solve problems involving length, weight/ mass, and temperature
Science/social studies	SC 5.7 A rock cycle VS 5A,B,C Revolution	SC 5.7 A Rock cycle VS5 Revolution assessment	SC 5.7 B Fossils VS6A, B, C New nation

Figure 12.1. Aligning instruction to the standards: Ocean View Elementary School.

Grade 5—Monthly Math Assessments 2009–2010

September: Decimal place value (to the thousandths)
- Rounding/comparing/ordering decimals
- Relationship between fractions and decimals

October: Multiplication/division (3D (2D/4D + 2D)
- Multiplication and division of whole numbers
- Equivalent expressions in equations (including variables)
- Real-life situations where area and perimeter are used

November: Measurement/concepts of fractions and decimals
- Equivalent fractions and equivalent fractions/decimals
- Determine the appropriate unit of measurement (linear, weight, mass)

December: Fractions/statistics
- Add/subtract fractions with like/unlike denominators
- Mean, median, mode of data sets

January: Probability Concept on a Variable
- Tree diagrams; represent probability of a single event with fractions/decimals
- Write word problems to match open sentences
- Concept of a variable in an expression or open sentence

February: Graphs/decimals, circles
- Multiplication and division of decimals
- Graphs: stem/leaf, bar, line, picture
- Identify and describe parts of a circle

March: Geometry
- Identification of shapes/geometric solids
- Measure and classify angles and triangles
- Area of right triangles
- Reflections, rotations, translations

April: Problem solving/measurement
- Length, mass, weight, liquid volume, temperature
- Elapsed time
- Solve whole number problems

May: Patterns
- Repeating, growing, numeric

Grade 5 December Monthly Problem-Solving Assessment   Form A

Name _____ Date _____

Directions: Circle the correct answer. Show your work.

1. A radio station manager kept track of the number of times a popular song was requested each day:

Number of Requests

Sunday	15
Monday	35
Tuesday	38
Wednesday	44
Thursday	38
Friday	39
Saturday	40

What is the **median** number of times the song was requested?

A   29

B   38

C   38.5

D   44

2. What is the **mode** of this data?

3, 1, 3, 1, 1, 2, 3, 3, 1, 3, 1, 3

F   1

G   2

H   3

J   4

3. The chart below shows the ages of the employee at Pizza Chef.

Ages of Employees

18	23	31	34	17
21	20	23	27	35

How can you find the **mean** (average) of the ages?

A   Divide 249 by 5

B   Subtract 17 from 35

C   Find the middle age when the ages are put in order from least to greatest.

D   Divide 249 by 10

4. What is the **mean** (average) number of nonfiction books checked out?

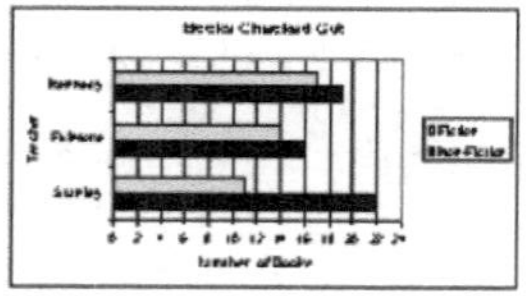

F   14

G   19

H   22

J   57

Figure 12.2. December monthly assessment, Grade 5 math, Ocean View Elementary School.

common assessments that accompany them make it clear that the goal is for all students to achieve clearly specified competencies. Progress monitoring is closely yoked to the curriculum content that is being delivered.

Figure 12.3 depicts the organizational structure utilized at Ocean View to support the data team process. Note that the principal and assistant principal work closely with the Lead Team. Also, both vertical and horizontal teams are heavily data driven and are overseen by members of the Lead Team.

Note that the row of all the grade levels represents the vertical team (even though it appears horizontal in the depiction) and within each box are multiple classroom teachers representing the horizontal level. The Lead Team, which includes the principal, the vertical team leaders, and a special education member, responds both to the classroom and/or grade level (horizontal) and across grade levels at the building level (vertical). Grade-level teams discuss their data each week, identifying struggling students and successful instructional strategies and providing support to each other. The grade-level representative for each vertical team then takes grade-level findings to the vertical teams (meeting every other week) who look for schoolwide patterns and develop intervention strategies. Then the vertical team leaders bring their team's findings to the Lead Team (first

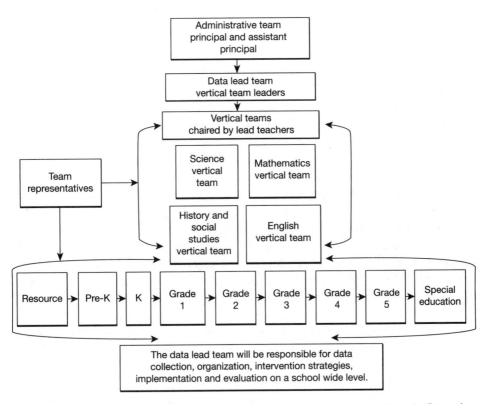

Figure 12.3. Data-driven organization: Ocean View Elementary School. (From Rose, A., Peery, A., Pitchford, B., Doubek, B., Kamm, C., Allison, E. et al. [2010]. *Data teams: The big picture – Looking at data teams through a collaborative lens* [p. 120]. Denver, CO: Lead and Learn Press; reprinted by permission.)

Friday of each month) where decisions about who will receive Tier 2 and Tier 3 interventions will be determined and resources (human, material, and time) allocated. Finally, the grade-level teams meet with the Lead Team the following week to finalize placement in tier interventions, adjust and resolve scheduling conflicts, and determine teacher support. (The data not only let us know what students need support, but they also let us know what teachers need additional support.)

Initially, teachers needed training on how to conduct these data team meetings efficiently and effectively, and they regularly scheduled time to meet and collaborate regarding the use of newly available data. Without training and time for data analysis and collaboration, this new and potentially rich source of information may not be adequately utilized.

OCEAN VIEW EXAMPLE

In this section, we provide an extensive example of how the assessments at Ocean View are utilized to drive instructional intervention identification, planning, and monitoring.

We administer our *universal (benchmark) assessments* (STAR Reading and Math, Renaissance Learning) in Grades 3–5 and PALS (Phonological Awareness Literacy Screening, Curry School of Education, University of Virginia) in Grades K through 2 the first week of school and again in January and May. We use our classroom weekly assessments and our school monthly power standard assessments (Form A) in all subjects along with our district's quarterly content area assessments to monitor student progress (*progress monitoring*). We also use Form B monthly assessments to assess the effectiveness of our interventions, which change both weekly and monthly depending on student performance on our assessments. STAR takes about 10 minutes, is computer-based, and an entire class can be done together in our computer lab. PALS is much more time consuming. We use parts of it for first grade and all of it for kindergarten, but not until October. It is useful for sorting students. Our weekly and monthly assessments are 10–12 questions, and it is hoped that they are completed in 30–60 minutes.

We create our own weekly and monthly assessments. The district creates the quarterly assessments, which average 60 or so questions and are very long—1 to 2 hours or more. The district provides a computer-based program for scoring quarterly and monthly assessments, which not only scores the assessments for us, but also produces numerous reports disaggregating our data.

Monthly progress monitoring assessments are administered to all students following instruction in monthly power standards (see Figure 12.2). Grade-level horizontal and content vertical data teams meet to analyze student data, identify nonproficient students, and develop intervention strategies. The Lead Data Team looks at class data results to identify which teachers were successful in teaching the standards and can share their strategies. Then the team looks at which teachers were less successful and in need of additional support. See Figure 12.4, in which the arrow is pointing to the standard for December, fractions and statistics.

DATA ANALYSIS

Grade Level Data

2009–2010 Grade 5—Monthly Math Assessments

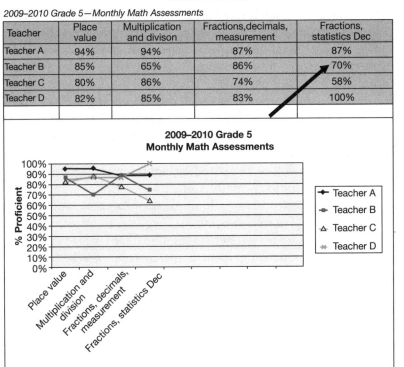

Teacher	Place value	Multiplication and divison	Fractions,decimals, measurement	Fractions, statistics Dec
Teacher A	94%	94%	87%	87%
Teacher B	85%	65%	86%	70%
Teacher C	80%	86%	74%	58%
Teacher D	82%	85%	83%	100%

2009–2010 Grade 5
Monthly Math Assessments

Figure 12.4. Data analysis of grade-level data: Ocean View Elementary School. (From Rose et al. [2010]. *Data Teams: The Big Picture—Looking at Data Teams through a Collaborative Lens.* Englewood, CO: Lead+Learn Press, p. 127; adapted by permission.) *Key:* Dec, December.

In Figure 12.4, we see that Teachers A and D are on track and can share successful strategies with teammates. However, Teachers B and C are struggling in specific areas—the data reveal uneven student success in both classes. The math resource teacher needs to meet with these teachers to provide strategies for intervention for this month's standards, as well as begin to meet with both teachers before instruction in new standards. The math resource teacher must provide training and strategies before they teach any more standards and monitor their instruction before assessment to ensure that the instruction they are delivering is appropriate and effective.

Next, the data must be used to identify students in need of intervention and to determine whether Tier 2 (small group) or Tier 3 (intense one-to-one) is needed. Often, it is not the single assessment for 1 month, but a pattern of nonproficiency over a number of months (progress monitoring) that distinguishes the need for Tier 3 over Tier 2 support. The team will, for example, identify nonproficient fifth graders on the math power standard in fractions and statistics by looking at their scores on the fractions and statistics assessment. Once again, student assessment scores are juxtaposed with standards to show how closely they are aligned.

Looking at assessment scores will help to identify which students are nonproficient on this power standard, but exactly what is their problem? To determine this, we must dig deeper into the data and look at each question. It is pointless to waste time providing additional instruction where it is not needed. Intervention support must be sharply focused. This can be done by administering a diagnostic assessment to reveal exactly which subskills need to become the focus for intervention. For example, a 10-question assessment is aligned to the standard fractions and statistics, but each question is aligned to a specific subskill (e.g., median, mode, mean, fraction word problems). By creating a table that denotes each question or subskill at the top, and filling in the students who answered incorrectly underneath, the team can create a list of students who had trouble with each subskill of the standard. Intervention groups are pulled by question to more sharply focus instruction.

Once we know exactly what each of our nonproficient students needs, we can plan intervention. We should point out here that this process is only useful if we create the possibility for teachers to respond differently to students who are not making progress. One component is the creation of schedules that create

SOL intervention program schedule Grade 5 January 13–February 26			
9:15–10:00	10:10–10:30	10:30–12:20	1:20–3:00
Resource	Whole group English/social studies	English guided reading	Teacher A/Teacher B: Math, 1:20; Science, 2:20 Teacher C/Teacher D: Science, 1:20; Math, 2:00

Tier 2 math intervention
 	
Pull-out skill groups for math intervention based on assessment data
 	
Math coach: M–F
 	
Tier 3
 	
Multiple choice writing intervention
 	
Below 60
 	
Reading specialist: Instructional interventionist 1 M–W, F
	Tier 1 whole-group instruction	**Tier 2 writing intervention**
		
		Small skill-group instruction in the classroom based on assessment data—alternate direct writing and multiple choice
		
		Instructional interventionist 1: Teacher D
		
		Instructional Interventionist 2: Teacher C
		
		Instructional interventionist 3: Teacher A
		
		Reading specialist: Teacher B
			Tier 2 math intervention*
			
			Small skill group instruction in the classroom based on assessment data
			
			Math coach Instructional interventionist 4 (2/2)
			
			M/T
			   1:20–Teacher A 1:20–Teacher C
			W/Th
			   2:10–Teacher D 2:10–Teacher B
			
			Tier 3 Math interventionist: Tier 3 intervention: intensive-needs students

Figure 12.5. SOL (Virginia Standards of Learning Tests) intervention program schedule, Grade 5, January 13 – February 26: Ocean View Elementary School.

Math push-in intervention Thirty-minute sessions daily						
Tier 1		Tier 2		Tier 3		
Extension		Intervention		Intensive support		
Classroom teacher 1	Classroom teacher 2	Classroom teacher 3	Classroom teacher 4	Math specialist	Intervention teacher	SOL teacher
20–28 students	20–28 students	8–10 students	8–10 students	2–4 students	2–4 students	2–4 students
Seven Kagan groups	Seven Kagan groups	Specific skill needs group	Specific skill needs group	Intensive needs group	Intensive needs group	Intensive needs group
Cooperative group learning activities, problem-solving, and projects	Cooperative group learning activities, problem-solving, and projects	Data-identified focused skill instruction	Data-identified focused skill instruction	Data-identified focused skill instruction	Data-identified focused skill instruction	Data-identified focused skill instruc-tion

Data analysis ➡ Grouping ➡ Instruction ➡ Monitoring
Regroup monthly based on progress monitoring

Figure 12.6.   Math push-in intervention, 30-minute sessions daily: Ocean View Elementary School. (*Key:* SOL, Virginia Standards of Learning Tests; Kagan, Kagan Cooperative Learning Structures.)

options for the provision of supplemental instruction when students have failed to master specific skills. Figures 12.5 and 12.6 show examples of scheduling tiered interventions without interrupting core instruction.

In Figure 12.5, we see Ocean View has designated four instructional blocks, with the second block (10:10 a.m.–10:30 a.m.) devoted to Tier 1 whole-group instruction. Fifth-grade students who receive Tier 2 math intervention are pulled out of class in the first block (9:15 a.m.–10:00 a.m.), and Tier 2 and 3 math interventions occur in class among small skills groups in the fourth block (1:20 p.m.–3:00 p.m.), 4 days a week. Students receive Tier 2 writing interventions in class among small cooperative groups during part of the daily guided reading block (10:30 a.m.–12:20 p.m.).

Once intervention is complete, students are reassessed with a parallel form of the assessment to determine the student's mastery, the effectiveness of the interventions, and the need for further intervention. If we do not reassess, how can we know whether what we are doing is working? This process of assessment–intervention–assessment helps to ensure that students continue to make progress in the general education curriculum. We emphasize this repeatedly because available evidence suggests that once students are exited from the general education curriculum and placed in alternative core programs, their rate of progress does not improve and they are seldom able to rejoin the mainstream curriculum successfully.

Once we have reassessed, we look at the new data at the student level to determine mastery and at the grade level to determine effectiveness of the intervention. This is best done by simply entering students' posttest scores beside their pretest scores (on the parallel test of equal difficulty) and looking for increases in student proficiency.

Tier 3 students are monitored separately, with weekly reports throughout the intervention month. Figure 12.7 is an example of one weekly Tier 3 monitoring report.

Finally, postassessment data are reviewed to determine the overall effectiveness of our intervention program. Student proficiency percentage before and after intervention are shown in Figure 12.8, in which the black line represents preintervention and the gray line represents postintervention proficiency percentages. Note that in each of the 4 months tracked, proficiency percentages increased to above 90% after nonproficient students received tiered intervention.

By tracking individual student, individual class, and grade-level proficiency rates before and after intervention, Ocean View data teams can determine

Tier 3 intervention log						
Subject: Math Month: January Week of: January 2, 2010						
Time	Student name	Form A score	Form B score	Focus skills	Activity week 1	Comments
1:40–2:00 Teacher B	Artesian Joel	30 50	70 80	Mean: Week 1 Fractions – Word problems Weeks 2 and 3	Day 1 Redo monthly; compare and discuss.	Both boys are struggling; need more concrete examples.
2:00–2:20 Teacher C	Isaiah Renardo	40 40	100 80	Mean: Week 1 Fractions – Word problems Weeks 2 and 3	Days 2–3 SOL coach: Lessons on determining mean	Isaiah really grasps the concept: retest. Renardo continues to struggle: needs more time.
2:20–2:40 Teacher D	Markisha Linda	40 40	100 70	Mean: Week 1 Fractions – Word problems Weeks 2 and 3	Day 4 Use same data from Days 1 and 2 to compare mean, median, and mode.	Markisha is ready to retest. Linda needs another week.

Figure 12.7. Tier 3 intervention log (Ocean View Elementary School).

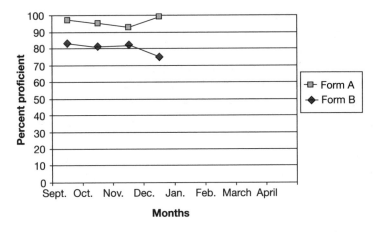

Figure 12.8. 2009–2010 Grade 5 monthly math assessments: Percentage proficient on Forms A and B, Ocean View Elementary School. (From Rose et al. [2010]. *Data Teams: The Big Picture—Looking at Data Teams through a Collaborative Lens.* Englewood, CO: Lead+Learn Press, p. 128; adapted by permission.)

which students, teachers, and grade levels need additional support. In addition, and equally important, we know exactly how well our intervention program is working. For fifth-grade math, these data tell us our program is effective.

CONCLUSION

Although there is a dearth of research regarding organizational challenges to the implementation of RTI, we have identified several challenges that merit the attention of schools and districts attempting to implement RTI in mathematics:

1. *Professional development* to support teaming, data utilization, and enhanced instruction. This needs to start *before* implementing RTI, especially the initial training in data-driven decision making, data teams, and RTI (the concepts of teacher accountability and tiered intervention that are in addition to, rather than instead of, classroom instruction) and needs to be ongoing *forever*, coaching.

2. *Strategies to address potential teacher resistance* both to the change in perspective and the magnitude of changes needed to successfully implement RTI. We suggest teaming professional development with nonnegotiables and monitoring for program fidelity.

3. *Selecting assessments:* Attention must be paid to obtaining and/or developing robust measures for universal screening and progress monitoring.

4. *Developing vertical and horizontal data teams* to analyze and respond to the data being collected as part of the RTI process. It is very important that time allocated for data team meetings is used wisely to analyze data and develop goals and strategies. Teachers must receive training and be given time to work with the data and their data teams.

5. *Identifying research-based instructional strategies:* Once determined, these must become nonnegotiable in all classrooms. We have three at Ocean View that we call "The Three": Compare and Contrast (taken from Marzano, Pickering, and Pollock's [2001] similarities and differences—*Classroom Instruction that Works*), Focus on Content Vocabulary (Marzano, 2004, *Building Background Knowledge for Academic Achievement*), and "Justify your answer" (really modeling by both the teacher and students). Each school must, of course, determine its own.

6. *Organizational changes,* for example, changes in scheduling at the building level to allow for both interventions and teacher collaboration. Also, flexibility in the schedules of resource teachers to allow their participation in tiered intervention is a critical component for staffing.

7. *Acquiring and using evidence-based instructional materials:* Care must be taken to choose materials wisely, especially with the growing number of prepackaged "RTI" programs on the market. Everyone in educational publishing is now selling RTI products of questionable value (and they all have "research" to back up their products). Limited funds are often better spent on professional development and coaching in quality instruction.

We end this chapter with a list of resources Ocean View teachers found helpful for overcoming the organizational challenges faced in implementing RTI at Ocean View Elementary School. This list is not comprehensive; instead, we hope it provides readers with a place to start when taking on similar challenges. Ocean View's story can be found in *Data Teams: The Big Picture—Looking at Data Teams Through a Collaborative Lens* (Rose et al., 2010, Chapter 7) and a full description of the RTI math intervention program at Ocean View can be found on the RTI Action Network web site at http://www.rtinetwork.org/rti-blog/entry/1/38.

REFERENCES

Marshall, K. (2009). Measuring results: A how-to plan for widening the gap. *Phi Delta Kappan, 90*(9), 650–655.

Marzano, R.J. (2004). *Building background knowledge for academic achievement.* Alexandria, VA: Association for Supervision and Curriculum Development.

Marzano, R., Pickering, D., & Pollock, J. (2001). *Classroom instruction that works.* Alexandria, VA: Association for Supervision and Curriculum Development.

Reeves, D.B. (2000). *Accountability in action: A blueprint for learning organizations* (2nd ed.). Denver, CO: Advanced Learning Centers.

Rose, A., Peery, A., Pitchford, B., Doubek, B., Kamm, C., Allison, E. et al. (2010). *Data teams: The big picture—Looking at data teams through a collaborative lens.* Denver, CO: Lead and Learn Press.

SUGGESTED RESOURCES

Carnine, L., & Silverstein, J. (2010, April). *Powerful procedures for team meetings: The vehicle for refining RTI data-driven decisions.* Presented at the Idaho State Department of Education RTI Conference: The Shape of Innovation, Boise, Idaho. Proceedings retrieved from http://www.sde.idaho.gov/site/rti/rticonf.htm

Fielding, L., Kerr, N., & Rosier, P. (2007). *Annual growth for all students: Catch-up growth for those who are behind.* Kennewick, WA: The New Foundation Press.

Gersten, R., Beckmann, S., Clarke, B., Foegen, A., Marsh, L., Star, J.R., & Witzel, B. (2009). *Assisting students struggling with mathematics: Response to intervention (RtI) for elementary and middle schools* (NCEE 2009-4060). Washington, DC: National Center for Education Evaluation and Regional Assistance, Institute of Education Sciences, U.S. Department of Education. Retrieved from http://ies.ed.gov/ncee/wwc/publications/practiceguides/

National Center on Response to Intervention: http://www.rti4success.org/

Marzano, R., Norfold, J., Paynter, D., Pickering, D., & Gaddy, B. (2001). *A handbook for classroom instruction that works.* Alexandria, VA: Association for Supervision and Curriculum Development.

Marzano, R.J. (2004). *Building background knowledge for academic achievement: Research on what works in schools.* Alexandria, VA: Association for Supervision and Curriculum Development.

Peery, A. (2011). *The data teams experience: A guide for effective meetings.* Denver, CO: Lead and Learn Press.

Reeves, D.B. (2010). *Transforming professional development into student results.* Alexandria, VA: Association for Supervision and Curriculum Development.

RTI Action Network: http://www.rtinetwork.org/

Schmoker, M. (2011). *Focus: Elevating the essentials to radically improve student learning.* Alexandria, VA: Association for Supervision and Curriculum Development.

Stein, M., Kinder, D., Silbert, J., & Carnine D.W. (2006). *Designing effective mathematics instruction: A direct instruction approach* (4th ed.). Upper Saddle River, NJ: Prentice Hall.

Index

Tables and figures are indicated by t and f, respectively.